Meaningful Learning Using Technology

WHAT EDUCATORS NEED TO KNOW AND DO

EDITED BY

Elizabeth A. Ashburn

Robert E. Floden

TEACHERS COLLEGE PRESS

Teachers College
Columbia University
New York and London

Published by Teachers College Press, 1234 Amsterdam Avenue, New York, NY 10027

The chapters in this volume were developed with funding from the U.S. Department of Education (Grant Award Nos. R303A990109 and R303A990109-01A) to Battle Creek–area school districts in partnership with Michigan State University College of Education. The content does not necessarily represent the policy of the Department, and endorsement by the federal government should not be assumed.

Library of Congress Cataloging-in-Publication Data

Meaningful learning using technology : what educators need to know and do / edited by
  Elizabeth A. Ashburn, Robert E. Floden.
     p. cm. — (The TEC series)
   Includes bibliographical references and index.
   ISBN-13: 978-0-8077-4684-4 (pbk. : alk. paper)
   ISBN-10: 0-8077-4684-3 (pbk. : alk. paper)
   1. Educational technology.   2. Learning.   I. Ashburn, Elizabeth Alexander.
  II. Floden, Robert E.   III. Series.

   LB1028.3.M412 2006
   371.33—dc22

                                                                          2005046648

ISBN-13:   ISBN-10:
978-0-8077-4684-4 (paper)   0-8077-4684-3 (paper)

Printed on acid-free paper

Manufactured in the United States of America

13 12 11 10 09 08 07 06   8 7 6 5 4 3 2 1

This book is dedicated to all the educators in Battle Creek, Michigan, who have joined the adventure of teaching for meaningful learning using technology.

Contents

Contents

INTRODUCTION

It's TIME: Technology Integrated into Meaningful Learning Experiences

Elizabeth A. Ashburn

In May 2002, a group of 100 Michigan educators gathered for a day of conversation with one another and national researchers about the knowledge and skills needed to teach for meaningful learning using technology (MLT). Researchers were invited to address two questions in their symposium presentations:

1. The *teacher learning content* question: What do teachers need to know, believe, and be able to do in order to teach for meaningful learning using technology?
2. The *teacher learning context* question: What do district leaders need to know, believe, and do to support teaching for meaningful learning using technology?

Responses to these two teacher learning questions lie at the intersection of knowledge about (a) teacher learning and professional development, in content knowledge, content-specific pedagogy, and technology; (b) student learning for enduring understanding; and (c) the integration of technology into curriculum and the management of technology in instruction. Although bodies of work exist within each of these arenas (e.g., Resnick & Klopfer, 1989; Sandholtz, Ringstaff, & Dwyer, 1997; Wilson & Berne, 1999), there is little research-based knowledge that integrates them to speak to these questions directly. This volume, based on the researchers' papers presented at the 2002 symposium, attempts to address this gap.

The two questions considered in these chapters emerged from the work of Project TIME, a $5.7 million 5-year Technology Innovation Challenge Grant from the U.S. Department of Education. This grant was awarded in 1999 to Michigan's Battle Creek–area public school districts and private schools, with Michigan State University's College of Education as a partner. The symposium was funded through an additional award from the U.S. Department of Education.

Project TIME's goals focus on three areas:

- *Meaningful student learning.* Goal: To increase students' abilities to understand complex ideas and learn challenging content using technology.
- *Technology integration.* Goal: To integrate technology into teaching for students' deeper understanding of complex ideas and skills in working with challenging content and problems.
- *Teacher learning.* Goal: To expand teachers' understandings, beliefs, and skills in teaching for meaningful learning using technology.

Project TIME's approach to professional development for meaningful learning using technology addresses each of these three areas. Grounded in research and in standards for effective professional development, the principles guiding the approach include:

1. Linking professional development to school and district goals for student learning and performance.
2. Anchoring professional development in continual and strategic inquiry into student learning.
3. Creating and sustaining a culture of inquiry for professional learning.
4. Including teachers in leadership roles.
5. Organizing professional learning around constructing and teaching curriculum units with lessons based in state content standards and characterized by attributes of meaningful learning using technology (MLT) that are research-based.
6. Developing the knowledge and skills in specific technologies that support meaningful learning related to the subject disciplines.

The central task that organizes the professional development is the design and implementation of curriculum units with lessons that conform to the widely used "understanding by design" framework of Wiggins and McTighe (1998) and integrate technology that supports meaningful learning. Under the leadership of the Michigan State University team, two curriculum units in social studies were developed that model the MLT attributes (see chapter 6 for further description). Teachers who piloted these units were also provided with related professional learning opportunities. In addition, MLT professional development was offered to all the project's social studies teachers in grades 6 through 12.

As these learning experiences were designed and implemented, the project's professional development planners realized the need to examine underlying assumptions about what teachers needed to know and be able to do to teach for meaningful learning and to use technology to support this kind of teaching. Teaching for meaningful learning was broadly defined by the project as creating systematic and intentional opportunities for students to achieve deep and enduring understanding of complex ideas, and skill in addressing complex content that is both central to the discipline and relevant to their lives. What teachers need to know and be able to do to use technology to teach in this way is not readily apparent.

Moreover, the project planners also saw the need to consider assumptions about what district leaders needed to know and do to support this kind of teaching and learning. Early in the project, for example, numerous courses were offered in basic technology skills that were taken by a minority of teachers, based on their interests. Other professional development in the project focused on designing units of instruction that reflect meaningful learning attributes. How to both select and integrate technology tools and resources into units of instruction in ways that add value to student learning became an increasingly apparent problem, the solution to which requires deep knowledge of the content and also knowledge and skill in technologies that support learning for enduring understanding. How to locate and develop the expertise to coach teachers in doing this became a critical question for district curriculum and instructional leaders, since the aim of the project was to systematically make teaching for meaningful learning using technology the way of doing business. Formulating and living with these two questions, then, became essential to the continuing reflection about improving the effectiveness of the project's professional development design and practices.

RESPONSES TO THE TWO ESSENTIAL QUESTIONS

The chapters that follow the introduction to this volume address the two teacher learning questions from various perspectives. Several are broad and synthetic, while others focus more tightly on specific disciplines—science and social studies—and on technology itself.

In chapter 1, Elizabeth A. Ashburn sets the stage by describing six attributes of meaningful learning using technology that Project TIME adopted to guide both curriculum unit development and professional learning. She also discusses some implications of these attributes for what teachers need to know and be able to do. Although these attributes are drawn from the work in Project TIME, they have a generality that makes them useful for framing a broad discussion of the two questions.

Martha Stone Wiske in chapter 2 provides a comprehensive response to the questions, discussing the nature of meaningful learning and its significance, as well as the significance of MLT. She describes five key areas in which technology can support meaningful learning and which she and her colleagues have labeled the Teaching for Understanding (TfU) framework: generative curriculum topics, learning goals that focus on student understanding, performances of student understanding, ongoing assessment of student learning, and content that is difficult to learn. In order to teach for meaningful learning using technology, Wiske argues, teachers must engage in an extended process of developing knowledge and skills in areas of curriculum, pedagogy, assessment, and the culture of learning, as well as about technology. She describes what teachers need to know and be able to do in each of these areas. Finally, Wiske points to a variety of contexts in which school leaders can support and promote MLT. Beyond the obvious technical and human resource issues, she describes the kind of support needed in organizational structures as well as in the cultural and political dimensions. The chapter concludes with an outline of resources that can supplement face-to-face professional development for learning how to teach for MLT, including descriptions of such projects at Harvard's Graduate School of Education.

In chapter 3, Marcia C. Linn responds to the two questions by relating findings from her research at the University of California, Berkeley, linking student learning with teaching strategies and professional development in middle school science. Six teachers in one school implemented Web-based Science Environment (WISE) projects, which are based on research in learning and instruction that promote knowledge integration and have been refined over 20 years of classroom trials. Over a 2-year period, these teachers were guided by a retired teacher mentor. The mentor followed the same "scaffolded knowledge integration framework" for teacher learning that was used in the design of WISE projects, with the goal for teachers to integrate inquiry teaching into their practices. A vivid description is provided both of what teachers needed to learn in order to implement inquiry-based teaching using technology and of the role of the mentor in supporting their learning by making the process of inquiry teaching visible. Linn concludes the chapter with important lessons for those who want to teach for meaningful learning, both with and without technology.

In chapter 4, Nancy Butler Songer responds primarily to the professional development question by describing a university–urban district partnership for teacher learning that addresses the challenges faced in teaching for MLT. The partnership's research-based professional development model sees curriculum as the agent of change; instructional units are collaboratively developed based on research about how students learn, and teachers implement and refine the lessons and teaching practices based on student learning data. The environment created by this model, as she describes it, engages teachers, administrators, and researchers in dialogue and shared understandings about inquiry-focused curricula and the appropriate use of technological innovations to achieve the learning goals. The research from her study of MLT in science in one urban middle school during this 3-year partnership has generated lessons that she discusses: (a) the importance of using curricula that foster student inquiry and integrate technologies in ways that promote deep understanding and discipline-specific reasoning; (b) the transformation of technology resources into tools that are powerful for inquiry-based learning related to curriculum standards; (c) the need for valid and reliable evidence that technology has added value for students learning important concepts and achieving deep understanding; and (d) the need for a broad-based set of exemplars of MLT in the classroom to share with professional development communities.

Addressing MLT in social studies, Robert B. Bain frames chapter 5 around three questions. He sets the context with his first question, which addresses how history teaching is typically conducted and portrayed. After describing the stereotypical classroom recitation of historical facts and the growing use of primary source-based lessons, he then asks what there is beyond primary sources and driving questions that makes history meaningful. The bulk of the chapter is a response to this question. He argues that in order to teach for meaningful learning in history or any of the social studies disciplines, teachers need to understand and use the intellectual processes and organizational logic that give pattern and meaning to the disciplinary "stuff"—the substance, content, and events of the discipline. He labels these as "second-record concepts," which he identifies in history as periodization, change, causation, consequence, evidence, significance, accounts, and historical perspective-taking. These concepts, he explains in some depth, can help teachers think about how students understand history and social studies and therefore how effective learning environments can be designed. Bain's final question is how discipline-specific thinking tools can support meaningful learning in history. He uses instances from his own teaching to respond to this question, including an explication of one Web-based scaffolding tool from his world history class. He concludes that educators' development of knowledge and skill in using second-record concepts supported by technology thinking tools is no small task, and that professional development is needed that is coherent, strategic, and long-term.

In chapter 6, Elizabeth A. Ashburn, Mark Baildon, James Damico, and Shannan McNair use the metaphor of mapping to address the question of what teachers need to know and be able to do to teach for MLT in social studies. Using one of Project TIME's model curriculum units (Mexico and Migration) as an example, they offer a framework and set of tools to help teachers "map" the learning terrain, which consists of big ideas, content, and methods of the discipline. In a case study, they follow a sixth-grade teacher as he uses the tools to navigate the learning terrain with his students, including details of the challenges he manages. The authors conclude that the complexities of using a disciplined inquiry process within a curricular infrastructure to provide a sense of direction for instruction requires time, risk-taking, reflection, and a community of supportive colleagues.

Chapters 7 and 8 emphasize the nature of technology knowledge and skill needed to teach for MLT. Within the context of a large number of technology literacy standards for teachers, Raven S. McCrory argues for bounding the technology knowledge base by instructional needs directly focused on meaningful student learning. Based on data from classroom observations, she claims that this focused approach to a knowledge base is sufficient as well as manageable. Two broad instructional needs inform the boundaries of the knowledge base—the need to identify and develop technologies into tools for meaningful learning and the need to have a portfolio of technology tools that engage students in meaningful learning. In order to teach effectively with technology, she argues, teachers need to know (a) what technology offers in general to support teaching for meaningful learning, (b) what effective use of technology looks like in practice, and (c) the what and the how of technologies that support meaningful learning in the content and contexts in which they teach. She concludes with implications for school district leaders of this knowledge base necessary for meaningful learning using technology: the provision of time, access, and support, and the expectations important for developing this kind of expertise.

Yong Zhao, Kenneth A. Frank, and Nicole C. Ellefson make an argument consistent with McCrory's view of teachers' technology knowledge base. The knowledge of technology that is important includes (a) the inherent functions of the technology and how they relate to the pedagogical problems in specific contexts; (b) the various conditions that enable the use of a particular technology, such as prior knowledge; and (c) how to negotiate relationships related to using technology in contexts that often have the potential for disturbing well-established patterns of interaction. In addition, the authors claim that two beliefs are important to teaching for MLT: that the benefits of the technology are worth the perceived costs, and that changing pedagogical practices is necessary and important for using technology effectively for meaningful learning. The chapter builds on findings from a survey intended to characterize the relationship between the characteristics of professional development and teachers' use of computers. They describe survey responses from elementary teachers in four districts, suggesting a relationship between teachers' greater use of computers and professional development that (a) promotes experimentation with district-supported software; (b) focuses on student learning; (c) supports teachers' accessing the expertise of other teachers; and (d) is provided locally. The chapter concludes with recommendations for school districts for supporting professional development for MLT in two key areas: organizing groups for teacher learning and building a support infrastructure.

In the final chapter, Robert Floden and John Bell bring their perspectives to a synthesis of this volume that includes not only substantial scholarship in this arena, but also their deep involvement in Project TIME. They add a third question to the initial two: How can teachers; learn what they need to know and do to teach for meaningful learning using technology? This question is addressed along with the original two in an elaboration of six recurrent themes related to knowledge and skills needed to teach for MLT: (1) deep, flexible subject matter knowledge; (2) organizing group inquiries; (3) assessment of meaningful learning; (4) skill with a small set of technological tools; (5) collaboration; and (6) working beyond school walls. They conclude with additional questions that must be addressed if teaching for MLT is to become a widespread reality.

CHAPTER 1

Attributes of Meaningful Learning Using Technology (MLT)

Elizabeth A. Ashburn

Discussions of the design of professional development for teaching for meaningful learning using technology (MLT) must begin with a clear description of what is meant by "MLT." For the symposium that led to this volume, the planners used the analysis of MLT developed by Project TIME, the U.S. Department of Education Technology Innovation Challenge Grant described in the Introduction. Broadly speaking, the Project TIME team defined "meaningful learning experiences" as systematic and intentionally created opportunities to achieve (a) deep and enduring understanding of complex ideas, and (b) skill in working with complex problems and content that are both central to the discipline and relevant to students' lives. Those involved in Project TIME developed greater understanding of MLT as a result of thinking together about what this big idea means and reflecting on experiences of enacting this idea in various contexts. To aid in thinking about the responses to the teacher learning content and context questions outlined in the Introduction and addressed in the remainder of this volume, this chapter draws on Project TIME's work to give a detailed description of teaching for meaningful learning using technology. It also describes the knowledge and skills that teachers appear to need most if they are to be successful in teaching for MLT.

Answers to the questions about what teachers need to know to successfully teach for meaningful learning using technology will vary depending on how MLT is conceptualized. Although the authors in this volume do not completely agree on what constitutes teaching for MLT, they drafted their chapters with knowledge of Project TIME's MLT attributes framework. It is worth beginning this volume, therefore, with a description of this framework and concrete examples from the project's attempts to foster teaching for MLT. This should provide some practical grounding to be considered in reading the later chapters, along with the ideas offered about what teachers need to know based on these attempts to teach for MLT. These ideas are a valuable and perhaps provocative point of comparison to the analyses to follow, which draw on varying domains of theory and practice in developing their positions on what teachers need to know and be able to do, and how school district leaders might help them to achieve these understandings and skills.

To organize thinking more specifically about what MLT means, the project team developed an "MLT attributes framework." This framework is an adaptation of five research-based attributes of meaningful learning described in the work of Jonassen, Peck, and Wilson (1999). A sixth attribute was added and labeled "content centrality," to make explicit that subject matter content must be at the heart of all classroom learning that is meaningful and that the use of technology must support learning grounded in content standards. With this addition, meaningful learning is defined in the framework as learning characterized by:

1. *Intentionality*: Using clearly articulated learning goals to guide the design of learning tasks and assessment of learning progress.
2. *Content centrality*: Aligning learning goals and tasks with the big ideas, essential questions, and methods of inquiry that are central to the discipline.
3. *Authentic work*: Constructing multifaceted learning tasks that represent the challenges, problems, and thinking skills required outside the classroom.
4. *Active inquiry*: Using a disciplined inquiry process for learning that builds on students' own questions and develops habits of mind that foster high levels of thinking.
5. *Construction of mental models*: Embedding the articulation of cognitive models of content within the learning tasks.
6. *Collaborative work*: Designing learning tasks so that students working together adds value to achieving the learning outcomes.

All six attributes are interdependent, as Jonassen et al. (1999) suggest, and the use of technology is expected to support these attributes.

In order for teachers to understand these attributes and develop related skills, Project TIME developed curriculum units that provide a model for using the attributes in teaching and learning. The units, which contain substantial guidance for teachers, are located in a comprehensive password-protected interactive Web-based application titled MLToolbox. An outline of the units is provided in the site map for mltoolbox. org (see Appendix A). Originally there was only one unit on Mexico and Migration; this has subsequently been divided into two units. The one titled "Inquiry: A Way of Knowing Differently" is designed to precede the Mexico and Migration Unit, as well as to serve as a model for inquiry-based learning tasks in other content areas. Each lesson page in the units is accessible by students. The lesson page contains learning tasks that may link to Word files, images, other Web sites, or tools within the MLToolbox. It also contains focus questions for the lesson and a link to key vocabulary. The tools within MLToolbox have been designed to support collaborative inquiry-based learning, both within the model units and in others developed by teachers. They are described in Appendix B.

The following descriptions of these attributes focus on what teachers and students do in a classroom that fosters meaningful learning and how technology might be used toward these ends. Examples of these attributes from classroom observation data collected informally as well as in the case studies of MLT teachers by the Project TIME project evaluator are included in these descriptions. Ideas about what teachers need to know are also presented as each attribute is discussed.

INTENTIONALITY

One defining aspect of meaningful learning is that it is intentional. Project TIME defined "intentionality" as having clearly articulated goals for learning that guide the work of both teachers and students. For learning to be. meaningful, all classroom activity should be directed toward achieving specific learning outcomes. Both teachers and students see themselves as learners, holding responsibility for specifying their own learning goals and how to make progress toward them. Teachers are learning about what students know and are able to do, as well as raising questions about what more they themselves want to know related to both the content and how they teach it. Teachers frame the content for student learning both by determining the standards-based learning outcomes to be addressed in curriculum units and by designing learning tasks that move students toward those outcomes. Within that framework, students may have choices about what and how they learn, including opportunities to ask their own questions about what they want to know and to use these questions to guide their learning tasks. Students think and talk about what they know and don't know and why, how they have learned what they know, and what else they need to know and how they will learn it. They track their own progress toward achieving their learning goals, through self-assessments and rubrics, as well as other forms of feedback.

The implications of this attribute for what teachers need to know and do are multiple. First, they need to be skillful in planning for instruction by initially defining student learning outcomes that are related both to the curriculum standards and to the particular content of the unit of instruction. Second, teachers must be able to (a) design learning experiences that move students toward accomplishing those outcomes, (b) develop ways of assessing each student's progress toward those outcomes, and then (c) reflect on necessary revisions in instructional strategies based on the evidence of outcomes. And finally, teachers need to be able to foster students' thinking and skill along all these dimensions of intentionality.

These are such challenging, comprehensive, and labor-intensive competencies that it seems unlikely they can be achieved without a technology infrastructure that makes possible both efficient management and the collaboration necessary for continual development of professional judgment. Project TIME's model MLT curriculum units provide examples of how technology can be integrated into instruction in ways that support these intentional learning activities. In the project, a Web-based application was developed for teachers to construct their own MLT curriculum units and lessons; this software is formatted with clear specifications for learning goals and their relationship to state curriculum standards, learning tasks, and learning assessments. Components of the unitCreator/lessonBuilder are listed in Appendix A. The two Web-based model MLT curriculum units were constructed so that each lesson launch page specifies questions that guide students' learning in that lesson. For example, in the lesson on forming a community of inquiry, the focus questions are: What is a community of inquiry? How does it support the inquiry process? The learning tasks include students asking and responding to their own questions and examining the significance of those questions for guiding their own learning. Students use criteria to continually reflect on whether a particular question is worth pursuing and whether a data source is relevant and credible.

The technology tools within the unit compel this kind of reflection and pursuit of information to inform students' thinking about these questions. With the teacher's guidance, students make decisions about which questions to address and how to proceed with the investigation. Continual assessment is made more manageable by the Web-based infrastructure of the units, which guides teachers in gathering and reflecting on evidence of student learning. The iJournal tool, for example, provides a way for teachers to quickly access each student's thinking and to provided immediate feedback.

Data from the project's external evaluation conducted by SPEC Associates (2003) suggest that other teacher knowledge and skills are also
needed to craft instruction for intentional learning. Knowing how to balance students' own learning goals within those defined by the curriculum
unit is a critical skill. According to the evaluation report, one MLT teacher
reflected on the tension between allowing students to develop their own
questions and ensuring that specific content is learned:

> How far do you go with letting students do what they want? . . . You want
> to see them excited, engaged in what they are doing [which is what occurs
> when they pick their own questions]. On the other hand, you have certain
> things you want them to learn. Weighing one against the other can be tricky.
> (SPEC Associates, 2003, pp. 24–25)

Observations of how teachers constructed this balance during instruction
suggest also that skill is needed in refocusing from the control of students'
task completion to the coaching of students' thinking about their learning. The following sixth-grade teacher's story provides one instance of how
this coaching can occur:

> I said to them [the students] today, "It *is* a big question, but that doesn't mean
> it is etched in stone. If you come across a road block we can look at the ques-
> tion again and change it to fit our needs." So they are okay with that. We
> settled on the overarching question, "Can the United States control the num-
> ber of immigrants coming into the country?" And then from there we can
> take some of these other questions that they chose [and connect them]. This
> is the main question. So this process takes some time. But it was actually
> their idea. We had criteria for a good question, and they decided that well,
> this or that question doesn't fit the criteria. I said, "You guys are in charge.
> It is your story." Eventually, they settled on these questions. (SPEC Associ-
> ates, 2003, p. 24)

Structuring students' ownership of the investigative questions and then
using criteria with students to reframe and refine those questions throughout the inquiry process is a coaching skill needed for balancing student
engagement with achieving the desired learning outcomes.

Finally, teachers must have skill in coaching students to take responsibility for their own learning. One teacher described this transition as
"rough" for students:

> . . . It is something that goes against, for the most part, how they think learn-
> ing occurs. For some kids, this is cool. They get to talk and think, and this
> benefits them, and for others, it is kind of a struggle. They still need me to

do it for them—[to tell them exactly,] "This is the information you need to know." (SPEC Associates, 2003, p. 53)

The project evaluator reported that all four case study teachers indicated that "they encountered the challenge of empowering students to see themselves as capable of constructing rather than receiving knowledge and understanding" (SPEC Associates, 2003, p. 129).

At its core, the attribute of intentionality is about making explicit the desired learning outcomes and the learning processes to achieve those outcomes, and about engaging students' thinking in this visible articulation.

CONTENT CENTRALITY

Teaching content that is central to the discipline and also relevant to students' lives is a second fundamental attribute for designing meaningful learning experiences. This attribute calls for students to be challenged by the big ideas, essential questions, and methods of inquiry that are central to the discipline. (See chapter 6 for further discussion of big ideas and disciplinary methods of inquiry applied to a particular instructional unit in social studies.) Big ideas, along with curriculum standards, guide the selection of specific content for instruction, and they are the "connective tissue" for the content that students learn. As connective tissue, big ideas enable students to relate classroom learning to their lives outside school, to connect what they are learning to what they already know, and to apply their learning in other contexts (Bransford, Brown, & Cocking, 2000).

The Project TIME model MLT curriculum units provide an illustration of the content centrality attribute. For these units, three big ideas were used as connective tissue. In the Inquiry Unit, the big idea is: Knowledge is subject to change and interpretation. Two more were added in the Mexico and Migration Unit: Space becomes place (i.e. , people transform physical settings into social settings), and culture as a human creation. These big ideas informed selection of particular social studies content and the generation of "essential questions" to focus and guide student learning throughout the unit lessons. (See Wiggins & McTighe, 1998, for elaboration on the nature and importance of essential questions.)

One of Project TIME's teachers described essential questions as "broadly-based," with a "lot of layers." The students, he stated,

> Investigate those layers and kind of peel them away. And . . . each new layer is going to give them a different level of understanding. And if you start with kind of a broad question, not too broad but it focuses on a particular area,

and then you try to think of some questions to go with that [in particular lessons] and then as they begin to find information about these other questions, then they are going to learn more information. It makes them want to dig deeper, as opposed to "I want to finish this lesson, this chapter, and do my worksheets and then go home." I think it [meaningful learning] encourages kids to dig deeper. (SPEC Associates, 2003, p. 22)

The enduring understandings desired as learning outcomes for students, the essential questions used to guide learning throughout the unit, and assessments of student learning are also tied to these big ideas. For the big idea that knowledge is subject to change and interpretation, for example, there are two enduring understandings:

1. Understand that knowledge changes as a result of inquiry, and
2. Understand that experience, background, and information shape perspective.

The related essential questions used in the unit are: Why does knowledge change? And why do people have different understandings about the same data and information? Rubrics for evaluating student learning include descriptions about how students show that they recognize that knowledge is subject to change and interpretation (for an example, see Appendix C).

Technology tools are selected because they add value to learning about complex ideas and difficult subject matter. They foster kinds of learning that could not be efficiently managed or even possible without such tools. Pursuing investigations related to the essential questions and using the methods of inquiry in the social studies disciplines might entail the use of surveys, for example. The project's model unit makes this easily manageable with the use of an online survey tool that efficiently engages students in the process of data collection, aggregation, and interpretation.

The content centrality attribute implies that teachers need to understand their content in a deep and flexible way in order to be able to craft big ideas with related essential questions and disciplinary methods and use them in ways that foster students' learning for enduring understanding. Illustrations of contexts in which this need occurs are provided by the sixth-grade teachers who were teaching the MLT model curriculum unit on Mexico and Migration. (See chapter 6 for further description of the use of big ideas in this unit). They were reported as making the big ideas visible to students

by frequently "naming" them. . . . The teachers were heard to point out how students' remarks provided an example of the big idea, and how connections made in discussion can be interpreted through the lens of a big idea.

> This strategy of making the big ideas visible and of frequently cueing students to the applicability of the big ideas modeled for students how naming a situation as "space becomes place" or an account of history "as story" can open students' learning about these situations and accounts to richer understanding and interpretation. (SPEC Associates, 2003, p. 42)

Naming a big idea may appear simple on the surface, but as the project evaluator noted, it is often the act of naming in context that becomes significant for students' understanding; the naming process gives meaning and thus reality to concepts, relationships, feelings, and other social phenomena.

Another key competency suggested by this attribute is balancing instruction for learning specific information with teaching for understanding of big ideas and complex issues. One of the ninth-grade teachers, who was not teaching the model unit, was described as engaging in

> an ongoing balancing act . . . to have students learn facts on the one hand (e.g., what indicators are used to measure countries' quality of life, and what is the difference between bilateral and multilateral foreign aid), and to organize, analyze, evaluate, and construct understandings on the other. . . . In a review of the assignments and graded assessment activities throughout the unit, one teacher talked about finding the right balance between students' acquisition of facts and their construction of content understandings. . . . She said "When you go away from those more concrete [facts] . . . when you move away from that, things seem loosey goosey. [You keep asking] is this rigorous? How do you make it rigorous?" (SPEC Associates, 2003, p. 51)

This balancing act between acquiring facts and developing understanding is made more complex in a context where students do authentic work.

AUTHENTIC WORK

The nature of the work that students are assigned or encouraged to do is important to understand, if the work is to be meaningful for student learning (Schlechty, 2002). In an MLT classroom, students engage in authentic work. They work with multifaceted challenges and problems encountered outside the classroom, doing tasks that require higher-order thinking skills and involve complex solutions of varying quality. They also do the work of historians, for example (or authors or scientists), including making sense of historical artifacts and connecting past events to real-world issues and current problems.

Lessons designed for authentic work require students to frame questions meaningful to them and to connect their personal experiences with the content to be learned. Students often use actual documents, such as photographs and news articles, that provide multiple perspectives on issues and raise questions that are real for students. Students think about information—its relevance and credibility—and they categorize, analyze, and synthesize it for communicating their understandings and solutions to specific audiences. For example, the MLT model unit on Mexico and Migration provides opportunities for students to encounter dissonance between what they believe to be the case and what they find through inquiry to be the case. The project evaluator observed that students were highly engaged in puzzling questions about why many individuals and families would illegally cross the border when the possibility of negative consequences was so great. Students are also confronted in this unit with the dissonance between what they take for granted in everyday life, such as having plentiful running water, and the circumstances of many families in Mexico, who deal with scarce and contaminated water.

Another aspect of authentic work in this unit is that students do the kind of work social scientists and historians do, thinking about claims and evidence, the relevance and credibility of the evidence and arguments, and the uncertainty and perplexity that are part of the real issues of life. The model unit introduces students to the reality that no single information source provides a one-and-only correct or true explanation of historical or social phenomena. The sixth-grade teachers were observed by the project evaluator to discuss with students how individuals' perspectives impact the claims that authors and researchers make about the world. One of the teachers described an instance of this; her students reported that they had found a "great" Web site on the causes of the Civil War. She reported saying to them, after discovering that the Web site was based in Georgia:

> I said, "Okay, stop one minute here. How do you think that this Web site is going to be biased?" . . . So it's also teaching the kids that there are different biases, and it's a big concept sometimes for them to learn. (SPEC Associates, 2003, p. 33)

Questions are foregrounded in authentic work. Teachers were frequently observed to approach subject matter by posing their own wonderings to students, most of which were open-ended questions without clear-cut answers. Teachers also encouraged students to develop their own questions related to the subject matter and what they were learning about it. When students asked questions of the teachers, they often responded by framing the question for other students in the class to address.

The project evaluator observed that the model unit teachers frequently asked questions encouraging students to think about how the subject matter related to students' personal experiences or to the experiences of people close to students. One teacher expressed a great deal of enthusiasm about the fact that students were relating material to their personal lives. She suggested that learning that is "meaningful" has to be meaningful to students' lives, not so far removed from their personal experiences that it is abstract. She noted: "It's real life to them. Meaningful learning has got to be real life. They have to make that connection through something that is real" (SPEC Associates, 2003, p. 32). Connecting new content to students' lived experience helps them both to grasp its relevance and also to have a basis for meaningful connection to the content.

To create a context for authentic work, teachers need to understand the value added to learning of connecting students' lived experience to the content (e. g., Renzulli, Gentry, & Reis, 2004). They also need to coach students in making the transition from rote memorization of textbook information to authentic work in the classroom, since the different expectations may cause some frustration. As Project TIME teachers reported, some students occasionally disengaged when they experienced a disconnect between MLT instruction and the kind of instruction they expected, such as reading the textbook chapter and writing answers to the chapter questions. When students realized that there is no single source for a right answer to an investigative question, for example, teachers described some becoming confused and overwhelmed by having to take responsibility for constructing explanations or answers based on analysis of different sources of information.

Teachers also need to be able to design learning tasks and performance assessments that make this work "real" for students, and to do this in such a way that learning goals within the curriculum standards are met. Beyond the design of learning opportunities and assessments, they also need skill in making connections between the content and students' own experiences as opportunities arise within the course of instruction. In addition, teachers need to understand the knowledge work of the discipline in order to craft more authentic work for students in the classroom; for example, when teachers understand who creates history knowledge and how it is created, they are able to make explicit for students how the inquiry process in their classroom work is connected to the "real" work of historians. Finally, teachers need skill in selecting and managing the technologies and the resources available through technology that bring authenticity to the work of student learning. Having Internet access to multiple primary source documents is an obvious example. Also, students may easily perceive schoolwork to be more authentic with the daily use of wireless laptops for learning; as one Project TIME eighth-grade student observed, "Having a laptop makes me feel important. It's like having my own office."

ACTIVE INQUIRY

Students conducting their own inquiries can deepen the authenticity of their work. Learning through a process of active inquiry compels students to become deeply engaged in challenging content as they (a) collaboratively develop their own investigative questions; (b) acquire, evaluate, manipulate, and analyze information addressing those questions; and (c) use higher order thinking skills to make interpretations and claims supported by evidence and reasoning. As McTighe, Seif, and Wiggins claim, "Students can only find and make meaning when they are asked to inquire, think at high levels, and solve problems" (2004, p. 27).

The project's model unit illustrates the role of active inquiry in teaching for meaningful learning in social studies. Students develop familiarity with a four-step inquiry process:

1. Explore and develop the investigative question.
2. Gather and evaluate information.
3. Analyze and interpret the information.
4. Communicate your new understanding.

These steps are easily viewed by students from the subnavigation bar on each lesson page; they are pictured graphically in a circle to show that the "final" step leads to more exploration and questions. Students use this process in the unit to learn standards-based content on Mexico, migration, and implications of migration for immigrants and resident populations. As the project evaluator observed, "Students were not simply taught an abstract, sequential series of steps ascribed to the inquiry process. Rather the unit led students (and sometimes was led by students) through a substantive inquiry process about a real world subject matter" (SPEC Associates, 2003, p. 18). The inquiry process as it is used in the unit goes beyond typical research assignments by intentionally establishing a classroom culture of inquiry, building on students' own questions, and using real-world content and tools of the discipline. In one lesson, for example, students discuss what it means to work in a community of inquiry and then use a structured process to interview one another about questions they have about Mexico and migration. This approach contributes to developing habits of mind that support inquiry, specified as outcomes of the unit as follows: observing carefully; asking questions and identifying problems;

being open to new ideas and perspectives; taking a critical stance; looking for connections and relationships; expressing ideas and opinions; supporting ideas with evidence; and acting on decisions based on evidence.

Including active inquiry as an attribute of meaningful learning has implications for what teachers need to know and be able to do. (Later chapters in this volume also speak to teacher knowledge related to inquiry learning.) Teachers first need to know, for example, how to embed inquiry into units and learning tasks; doing this requires skills in developing and sustaining a culture of inquiry in the classroom, as well as in pacing the learning tasks within the boundaries of the standards-based content and the boundlessness of the inquiry process.

Second, teachers need skills in using students' questions as an instructional strategy to teach standards-based content related to big ideas. Students' ownership of the questions significantly influences their engagement in the inquiry process and related learning tasks. How to manage the use of their questions for instruction within a standards-based curriculum unit with prespecified learning goals is an important skill. In social studies, for example, skills in guiding students' access to and use of Web-based resources is key to managing their inquiries both efficiently and effectively. In Project TIME's model units, students generate their own questions through a guided process over several lessons; the process includes developing and using criteria for good investigative questions. Guidance for teachers in the unit includes information about doing this.

The importance of student ownership of the questions for inquiry is illustrated in the following description of how one sixth-grade teacher used student questions in the Mexico and Migration model unit:

> After several lessons and considerable substantive discussion, one class decided they wanted to pursue the question, "Did the U.S. steal the Southwest from Mexico?", while another class asked, "How can Mexican workers gain enough control to get U.S. corporations to pay them more?" The teacher believed these were noteworthy questions because they encouraged thinking beyond the level of recall and required students to investigate a range of information and perspectives. These class questions were then broken down into sub-questions for student groups to investigate. As students located information [from Web resources, using wireless laptops] to help them answer their questions, the teacher focused on how students might make decisions about information they would include in their buckets [a component of the MLToolbox Inquiry Station that was designed for storing information gathered by students]. He offered examples of information gleaned from various web sites and modeled ways of analyzing and evaluating the information by considering the credibility, accuracy, sufficiency, and significance of the data sources. (SPEC Associates, 2003, p. 27)

Using students' questions effectively for student learning presents multiple challenges for instruction, particularly when students begin to grasp both the possibility and complexity of "questions within questions," as one eighth-grade student described the process. Encouraging students to work with emerging questions that deepen their grasp of the content while maintaining a strategic focus on the curriculum standards requires teachers' continuous reflection and decision-making, particularly in relation to desired and actual student learning outcomes.

Third, teachers need skill in modeling use of the inquiry process and related habits of mind, as well as in coaching these kinds of habits of mind in students' thinking. As a ninth-grade teacher noted, students

> just want to know the answer so they can write it down there. They don't want to think about the answer and they don't ever want to think that maybe the answer is within themselves. They think that there is some pure answer out there. (SPEC Associates, 2003, p. 63)

To deal with changing this habit of mind, this teacher asked students to make daily journal entries on puzzling questions. He followed up with class discussion on the multiple interpretations in their responses and the importance of perspective and context in interpretation. He described one aspect of how his instruction differs as a result of his participation in the project:

> Not to answer so many questions for the kids all of the time . . . it's really easy when someone is asking you for the answer just to give it so they'll quit . . . Now I will say things like "I really think you need to read a little bit more and think a little bit more and . . . you're going to get it." Or I'll answer a question with a question, instead of an answer. (SPEC Associates, 2003, p. 64)

Fourth, teachers need skill in recognizing and making explicit key habits of mind and aspects of the inquiry process. Middle school students do not typically see themselves as investigators or researchers, for example, and data from interviews with Project TIME students indicated that sixth-graders "had difficulty articulating their activities in inquiry language" (SPEC Associates, 2003, p. 19). Teachers' articulation of the process guides a conscious transfer of students' learning and skill in inquiry to other contexts. Project TIME sixth-grade teachers demonstrated this practice with statements to students such as "You are researching the questions you formed" and posing questions such as "What else do you need to know to answer your question?" In addition, teachers tied students' responses to the inquiry process. For example, a student contributed information from a source outside those defined by the learning task, and the teacher re-marked, "So you are bringing in something [information] from the out-side?", articulating for the class that a new data source had been added.

Finally, teachers need skills in using technology tools that support and help manage the inquiry process as both a learning strategy and an instruc-tional tool. Project TIME Web-based software was designed around the four-step inquiry process described above. Facilitating active inquiry across multiple classes using students' own questions is a highly complex task. Skillful selection and use of technology, as well as resources made acces-sible through technology, can make doing active inquiry both feasible and effective in ways that would not be possible without these tools. Selection of appropriate technology tools is also important for students to construct representations of what they understand as a result of their inquiries.

MENTAL MODEL CONSTRUCTION

The process of learning is the construction of mental models of the con-tent. Mental models consist of internal images, assumptions, and stories about how the world works. These invisible maps determine what we see and how we make sense of the world—whether they are simple generaliz-ations or complex interactions—and shape how we take action; they may be flawed and are always incomplete. The task in teaching for meaningful learning is to make them visible in some form in order to examine and modify them to be more complete and accurate.

Creating representations of mental models helps learners to see and test their own understandings of how the world works; to construct knowl-edge they are unaware that they have; to see diverse perspectives; to iden-tify, analyze, and interpret differences and relative merits among mental models; and to articulate thinking about complex subjects (e.g., Bransford et al., 2000, p. 215; Senge et al., 2000, pp. 254ff). As Jonassen et al. (1999) state, "Ever more complex models will enable them [students] to reason more consistently and productively about the phenomena they are ob-serving" (p. 9). Constructing mental models may include, on one end of the spectrum, mapping concepts, big ideas, metaphors, problems, webs of connection, book chapters, or the meanings of words. At the other end, a mental representation of understanding may include historical narratives and other written forms of interpretive accounts, PowerPoint presenta-tions with speaker notes providing specifics of explanation or argument, simulations, and imagined scenarios.

In the MLT classroom, technology is used to demonstrate and to scaffold the development of mental models. A graphic organizer software

(Inspiration), for example, is suggested for use in Project TIME's MLT model units in order to map connections among students' questions and to construct larger questions worthy of investigation with related subquestions. The MLToolbox Inquiry Station, developed by the project to support inquiry activities, scaffolds the development of students' constructions and presentations of their understandings that result from investigating complex questions using diverse sources of Web-based information.

Teachers' understanding of how learning occurs, including aspects of cognitive and neurological research that support the construction of mental models, is important. Understanding, for example, that learning produces changes in the brain and that knowledge consists of "networks of neurons," that emotion chemicals can strengthen the responsiveness of neuron networks, and that mistakes can help identify gaps in students' networks suggests ways that designing opportunities for mapping mental models can make learning more meaningful for students (e.g., Zull, 2002, 2004). Teachers also need to understand that students arrive in their classrooms with prior knowledge and complex understandings about the world, which are often inconsistent and incorrect, and that these preexisting mental representations must be taken into account in order for learning to be meaningful. Designing learning tasks that provide opportunities for students to construct a variety of mental models in multiple areas of subject matter content is a skill teachers need to have, along with skills in identifying gaps in students' mental models of their understanding and in coaching and scaffolding the reconstruction of the flaws and inconsistencies. The use of technological tools to support the construction and reflection on mental models can be very useful, when teachers have the skills to select and use them in ways that support the learning goals rather than for merely "production" purposes.

COLLABORATIVE WORK

Doing collaborative work is the final defining aspect of meaningful learning in the MLT framework. Small groups of students work collaboratively on common tasks to achieve their learning goals. They have content-focused conversations with their peers to share information, explain their ideas, examine multiple perspectives, and negotiate common meanings, and they think together and help one another in posing and investigating questions, solving problems, and creating products together.

To design and implement collaborative work tasks for students that foster meaningful learning, teachers need to understand the theory that undergirds this approach (see, for example, Brown & Campione, 1998; Johnson & Johnson, 1998; Windschitl, 2002). They need to be able to design tasks that both challenge students to develop their individual potential and that also "create a synergistic learning experience where the sum is greater than any of its parts" (Schniedewind & Davidson, 2000, p. 24). Teachers also need to know how to develop students' skills and motivation to function effectively in collaborative work groups, and how to assess student learning from group products that are responses to open-ended questions. In addition, they need to know how their role differs in this context from that in teacher-centered instruction, and to what they need to pay attention in modeling and coaching students in order to move learning forward in groups. Finally, teachers need to know how specific technology tools can add value to learning in small groups, and how to manage the use of technology by student groups.

In the Project TIME model units, collaborative learning tasks predominate. The unit on inquiry focuses in early lessons on building a community of learners, developing norms for a collaborative classroom culture, and roles students might take in the group learning process. The small group tasks often build on individual work. For example, a photo analysis task first requires independent work for students in generating their own questions. Next they work with a partner to discuss their questions, and then refine them further in a small group and finally within a whole-class conversation. Throughout this process, students use a set of criteria developed by the class with the teacher's coaching to determine which questions have value for further investigation.

Since the MLT model units were designed to teach highly challenging content and thinking skills to middle school students, the small group work is seen as particularly advantageous for making thinking visible and creating peer support to encourage the risk-taking required in doing this. Working individually first, a student's initial observations and questions are not influenced by classmates. Next, sharing with a partner provides safety for practice in thinking out loud. As the conversation group increases in size, additional ideas and data are raised for consideration, and students learn to see alternative views and to explain their own perspectives.

Project TIME's MLToolbox was designed to support collaborative learning. The iJournal, for example, makes individual and small group thinking quickly visible to the entire class by projecting student responses to questions. Students who are reticent to voice ideas and opinions are able to enter the conversation through the written text from everyone that is projected for the whole class to read. In some cases, anonymity may be important for encouraging conversation; the teacher can choose whether to attach student names to their responses.

Observations by both the teachers and the project evaluator indicate that students gain confidence in sharing their thinking through the use of this technology. As they hear different perspectives within their small group conversations and then see multiple responses simultaneously in the projected texts, "students get that it is alright to critique one another's ideas in an impersonal manner," according to the project evaluator (SPEC—J. Farley, personal communication, July 22, 2004). Students moved

> toward the overarching norm that acquiring understanding is the goal, not being shown to be right or wrong. It's this "we're all in this together" mode of working in groups that is just crucial to the conduct of inquiry. . . . And unlike the fears of some of the teachers that the kids will learn that "anything goes," they in fact were learning to actively engage in sense making that is initially tested by counter arguments and alternative interpretations within the context of their small learning group, before being tested in the broader context of the whole class. (J. Farley, personal communication, July 2004)

The MLToolbox Source Explorer also promotes collaborative learning. It guides students to efficiently analyze and interpret information on a Web site, either individually, in a small group, or with the whole class. Similar to the use of iJournal, students' projected responses encourage discussions in which students explain and challenge the evidence found to support their claims.

Working collaboratively often engaged students deeply in the MLT model unit learning tasks and stimulated student thinking. As one teacher reported: "I see this interaction between the students. It's really amazing, their faces are right on the computer, and they say 'Wow! Look at this! Can we use this?'" Students tend to be more engaged in the activity as the group's specific learning goal begins to take shape, according to the case study teachers. One teacher stated: "There is a lot of compromising [to reach consensus about the group investigation] . . . it's tough to teach some students to give and take. There's been a lot of arguments but it comes with working in these group situations." Another teacher described one instance of what she has observed among her groups:

> Each table of students was having a different conversation . . . Each had its own slant on the question they were working on. And even different part-ners had different information that they were working on at the time. . . . They would show each other information from different Websites. That's a lot different than reading lesson three in textbook chapter 16 and having the do-gooders raise their hand and answer the question while others let them do their thinking for them. Now everyone is thinking. I think that's a real positive. (SPEC Associates, 2003, p. 30)

Teachers also reported that students who had more skill and knowledge about computers and the Internet were typically willing to help other students, which teachers saw as beneficial to everyone. One teacher noted that as a result of her students being more fully engaged, she found that her "lower learners" and the shyer students were more inclined to contribute to the conversation in the small work groups. The project evaluator confirmed that using technology in a collaborative context provided opportunities for students to find both new strengths and also reasons to be excited about learning; she reflected,

> With the technology available and classmates who are increasingly open to different forms of evidence and connections, these middle school students were able to explore their own ideas and thinking abilities—not a typical classroom occurrence. (J. Farley, personal communication, July 2004)

Teaching and learning in collaborative work groups is highly challenging. The use of technology in this context increases the challenge significantly. The project's case study teachers reported experimenting to find effective strategies for grouping students to get the best results and expressed a need for learning more about grouping students. The challenge here goes beyond the class grouping questions, however, to designing and managing collaborative tasks using technology in ways that lead to the desired learning outcomes.

CONCLUSION

In order to teach for meaningful learning using technology (MLT), teachers must understand what makes learning experiences meaningful, know how to construct and implement these kinds of learning tasks and to assess students' progress on them, and have skill in using technology in ways that support this kind of teaching and learning. Project TIME has used six attributes to define meaningful learning experiences: intentionality, centrality of content, authentic work, active inquiry, construction of mental models, and collaborative work. These have been described in this chapter within the context of teachers' implementation of Project TIME's curriculum units designed to model the attributes. The demands for understandings and skills inherent in the descriptions of these attributes would challenge even the most competent of teachers. These demands suggest that in order for teaching for MLT to occur, professional learning should be closely aligned with these characteristics.

CHAPTER 2

Teaching for Meaningful Learning with New Technologies

MARTHA STONE WISKE

New educational technologies and teaching for meaningful learning can be synergistic innovations, each enhancing the other, if they are thoughtfully planned and supported. Accomplishing these changes constitutes a complex, multifaceted, and major transformation of traditional school practices. It requires sustained professional development for teachers. It also requires coordination of other human resource, technical, structural, cultural, and political changes on the part of school leaders at the building and district levels. This chapter describes online resources and professional development activities that can help teachers and school leaders work together on teaching for meaningful learning with new technologies.

WHY MEANINGFUL LEARNING?

Over the past several decades a growing body of research on teaching and learning emphasizes that learners must actively construct their own understandings rather than simply absorb what others tell them (Bransford et al., 2000). Unless students connect new learning to what they already understand, believe, and know how to do, they are likely neither to remember the new information nor be able to apply it in new contexts. Existing conceptions are often firmly entrenched and must be consciously reconsidered and modified. Otherwise, prior conceptions tend to reassert themselves and block comprehension of contradictory models or expla-

Meaningful Learning Using Technology, edited by Elizabeth A. Ashburn and Robert E. Floden. Copyright © 2006 by Teachers College, Columbia University. All rights reserved. Prior to photocopying items for classroom use, please contact the Copyright Clearance Center, Customer Service, 222 Rosewood Dr., Danvers, MA 01923, USA, tel. (978) 750-8400, www.copyright.com.

nations, like a spring that assumes its original shape after having been stretched.

Active construction of understanding needs to encompass learning not only about new content or knowledge, but also about methods of inquiry, purposes of learning and knowledge, and modes of effective expression (Boix-Mansilla & Gardner, 1998). In a world that is complex and rapidly changing, effective citizens must be able to think for themselves and make thoughtful decisions about when and how to use their knowledge. They must learn how to generate new knowledge and cultivate habits of mind that support continual learning, reflection, and responsible action.

Traditional forms of instruction, in which learners attempt to recall and recite the knowledge generated by others, are inadequate to foster meaningful learning. Furthermore, such pedagogical practices are not conducive to cultivating the kind of learners needed to protect and guide a rapidly changing and diverse global community. Instead, we must help students construct understanding that includes the capacity and dispositions to develop and apply knowledge creatively, flexibly, and appropriately in a range of situations.

WHY MEANINGFUL LEARNING WITH TECHNOLOGY?

At the same time that research on cognition and pedagogy emphasized constructivist approaches, rapid developments in new technologies generated pressure to integrate computers and related tools into schools. Initially, technological enthusiasts argued that schools should purchase computers so that students would have opportunities to learn how to use these new tools and be prepared to use them in the workplaces of tomorrow. This line of reasoning led many schools to invest heavily in hardware, to hire "computer teachers," and to substitute "computer classes" for other special classes such as art, music, and physical education. This approach is a recent response to an enduring claim about schooling, namely that it must prepare the workforce of the future. But the approach is misguided in at least two ways.

First, learning about technology *per se*, separate from the contexts in which the tools are fruitfully applied, is limiting. Learning the functionality and menu of a word processing program is tedious and hard to remember when taught in isolation. When the features are introduced as ways of accomplishing necessary tasks in the writing process, they are easier to learn and recall. Furthermore, both the applications and the limitations of the new tool become apparent in the course of attempting to use it to do real work (Blacker, 1993). Developing facility with new technologies is more effectively accomplished through meaningful learning.

Second, new technologies can enhance meaningful learning in ways that are not possible with traditional educational tools. New technologies support interaction, dynamic displays, multiple and linked representations, interactive models and simulations, networked communication, hyperlinked text, multimedia, and the storage and retrieval of multiply categorized information. In these and other ways, new technologies offer means of tailoring instruction, engaging a wider range of intelligences, connecting schools with the real world, and supporting collaborative learning. These possibilities are the subject of a later section of this chapter. Here it is enough to argue that meaningful learning with technology is desirable both because it supports better understanding of technology and because it can promote more meaningful learning of all kinds of subjects.

WHAT IS MEANINGFUL LEARNING?

Project TIME has generated extensive descriptions of the attributes of meaningful learning and of the ways new technologies can support such learning (see chapter 1). They emphasize the qualities of content centrality, authenticity, intentionality, active inquiry, construction, expression, and cooperation. My own thinking about meaningful learning is consistent with these ideas but also includes a focus on the role of assessment in support of learning. My efforts to promote meaningful teaching and learning with new technologies are structured by a framework developed through a multiyear collaborative action research project conducted at the Harvard Graduate School of Education. Researchers at Harvard worked with schoolteachers to clarify the elements of effective teaching for understanding. This group defined understanding in ways that are similar to Project TIME's conception of meaningful learning, that is, understanding is a capacity to think with what you know and apply it flexibly in a range of appropriate situations (Perkins, 1998). The conception of understanding as a performance capacity, not just a mental product, is central. Ultimately this project developed a framework that maps out ways of answering core questions about teaching:

1. What topics are worth teaching for understanding?
2. What do we want students to understand?
3. How can we help students develop and demonstrate understanding?
4. How do we use assessment to promote and document understanding?

The project addressed these questions by conducting case studies of effective practice and analyzing them in relation to theories of teaching and learning. The resulting Teaching for Understanding (TfU) framework is structured around four elements (Blythe, 1998; Wiske, 1998). The framework recommends:

1. Organize curriculum around *generative topics* that are central to the subject matter, related to students' experience and teachers' passions, and approachable through multiple entry points. Generative topics have a bottomless quality in that they merit continued inquiry rather than being topics one learns by absorbing information.

2. Define and publish explicit *understanding goals* focused on important knowledge, methods, purposes, and forms of expression. These statements about what students will learn focus on understanding, that is, a capacity to extend and apply knowledge rather than simply the ability to repeat information or rehearse routine skills. Clarify overarching goals and purposes for a course and then be sure that more specific goals for a lesson or project clearly relate to the long-term goals. Connect the teaching of basic skills and information, as well as more complex curriculum standards, to understanding goals. In other words, clarify the application of basic skills to meaningful learning.

3. Engage learners in a rich and varied set of *performances of understanding* that develop and demonstrate understanding. When understanding is conceived as a performance capacity, it follows that understanding is developed from engaging in performances that require students to think with what they know and to apply new knowledge in flexible and creative ways. Design a sequence of learning activities that ramp up from what students already know, through guided inquiry, to culminating performances of understanding.

4. Conduct *ongoing assessment* of student products and performances on the basis of public criteria that are related to understanding goals and provide frequent feedback to help students improve their work. Involve learners in using the assessment criteria to conduct self- and peer assessments.

· All the attributes of Project TIME's conception of meaningful learning are consistent with the Teaching for Understanding framework. Authenticity is a quality of generative curriculum. Intentionality can be seen as an aspect of reflective understanding. Active inquiry and construction are aspects of performances of understanding, which may include inquiry, communication, and expression of learning. Cooperation and collaboration can be fruitfully incorporated into the design of performances of understanding and are directly encouraged as part of ongoing assessment processes.

HOW CAN TECHNOLOGY SUPPORT
MEANINGFUL LEARNING?

Thinking about meaningful learning in terms of the Teaching for Understanding framework helps to provide a structure for clarifying educational goals, designing learning activities, and orchestrating assessments that not only document learning but also inform both teachers and students about ways of improving their work. The elements of the framework also suggest specific points of leverage where new technologies may contribute significantly to teaching and learning for understanding. Technologies such as computer software, graphing calculators, multimedia, and networked telecommunication systems can help us better fulfill the criteria for each element of the TfU framework.

Technology That Supports Generative Curriculum Topics

Using current data from online sources—for example, the Bureau of Labor Statistics and the National Space Administration—can make curriculum more generative by connecting schoolwork to matters of widespread concern in the world. Interactive multimedia can allow students to approach a topic from more entry points than traditional static textbooks permit. Helping students present their work to an authentic audience via the World Wide Web can make schoolwork more relevant and interesting to students.

Technology That Supports Understanding Goals

Graphing calculators that instantly relate the graphical and symbolic representations of mathematical expressions can help make understanding goals more accessible to students. Simulations that make abstract concepts, such as friction, visible and manipulable can help students comprehend the nature and application of key ideas. Numerous online educational projects, such as I*EARN, engage students and their teachers in collaborative inquiry and social action initiatives that help students develop a deeper appreciation for their own and other cultures.

Technology That Supports Performances of Understanding

Software for creating multimedia presentations can enrich performances of understanding by enabling students to work together on creating products and to combine multiple forms of expression in conveying their ideas. E-mail, which seems to be a cross between spoken and written language, may help students ramp up their reading and writing skills. Students can use generic tools such as spreadsheets, databases, word processors, and programming languages to help them analyze and present their own ideas in ways resembling the work of practicing mathematicians, scientists, historians, and writers. Producing ideas, not just consuming them, is fundamental to understanding.

Technology That Supports Ongoing Assessment

Finally, computer tools facilitate cycles of ongoing assessment in many ways. They capture student work in forms that make the process of analysis and revision much easier than it is with traditional static tools. The Web allows students and teachers to post their work in places where they can get feedback from a wider range of critics, including authentic audiences who really care about learning from the students' work. Online threaded discussion forums and other forms of telecommunication may support reflection and analysis by requiring participants to communicate in text and enabling them to compare their work with peers' products.

Additional specific suggestions about Web sites and software that can enhance each element of Teaching for Understanding may be found in a PowerPoint presentation called "Teaching for Understanding with New Technologies" filed under special reports in the Library of the Education with New Technologies (ENT) (Corr, 2001).

Targets of Difficulty as Bases for Choosing to Use Technology

Faced with all these possible ways of enriching learning with new technologies, educators may wonder, "How do I decide when and how to make use of new technologies?" One approach is to ask where new technologies might supply the greatest educational leverage. The Educational Technology Center (Perkins, Schwartz, et al., 1995) coined the term "target of difficulty" to characterize an educational topic that is central to the subject matter, perennially difficult to teach and learn, and potentially amenable to the distinctive advantages that a new technology can provide. An example in science is heat and temperature. Understanding these concepts and their relationships is central to understanding energy and its transfer. Heat and temperature are difficult to understand for many reasons, including the fact that the two terms tend to be used interchangeably in everyday English. Computer software programs can help learners distinguish between heat and temperature by allowing students to interact with dynamic conceptual models of molecules excited by the addition of heat. A target of difficulty in mathematics is ratios or functions, which learners can understand more easily with software or graphing calculators that illustrate the correlations between graphical and symbolic representations of these mathematical constructs.

Thinking first about targets of difficulty focuses attention on the improvement of learning and frames technology as a means to that goal, rather than an end in itself. Maintaining this focus helps to avoid adding technology to a lesson simply to enhance students' motivation or to generate a more snazzy result. Certainly, interactive and multimedia technologies may engage and motivate students in valuable ways, but they are expensive to purchase, maintain, and use. Teachers and students benefit most when they use complex technologies to enhance understanding of subjects that are *really* important and *really* difficult to teach with less complex technologies.

WHAT DO TEACHERS NEED IN ORDER TO PROMOTE MEANINGFUL LEARNING WITH TECHNOLOGY?

Promoting meaningful learning with new technologies is daunting because, for most teachers, it requires a significant reconsideration of several dimensions of their practice. It may entail changing the organization and sequencing of curriculum into topics or projects that are more generative and meaningful for students. It may also involve a significant redesign of pedagogy, including learning activities, patterns of interaction among members of a class, and homework assignments. If curriculum and pedagogy shift significantly, new forms of assessment may also be needed. All of these changes relate to efforts to foster meaningful learning, regardless of whether one uses new technologies or not. So these educational changes must be addressed in *addition* to the development of knowledge and expertise with the technology. Let's consider each of these dimensions individually and then think about how they must be woven together to promote meaningful learning with technology.

Curriculum

In order to plan meaningful curriculum, teachers need to understand their subject matter deeply and flexibly. If we conceive of meaningful learning as understanding, then we hope that students will not only learn facts and formulas, but will also come to understand core concepts; disciplined ways of evaluating evidence and formulating reasoned arguments; purposes for studying and thinking about science, history, literature, or mathematics and the situations in which such forms of thinking are appropriate or misapplied; and alternative modes of expressing ideas including proper syntax, forms, and rhetoric depending on the audience and context. Mapping the subject matter in rich and varied ways is necessary if teachers are to formulate curriculum that is meaningful and generative for their students and to guide students through the domain in a range of ways, not just the path taken by the text. Unfortunately, many teachers have not had opportunities to study in depth the subjects they teach. Indeed, they may have little experience with the subject beyond what they studied in elementary and secondary school. In those cases, teachers tend to rely on a textbook and regard its content, structure, and sequence as equivalent to the subject.

Pedagogy

As Shulman (1987) writes, transforming one's own understanding into forms that help students requires more than knowledge of the subject matter. It requires understanding of the learners, including their prior knowledge, misconceptions, and interests. "Pedagogical content knowledge" is the phrase Shulman uses to designate understanding of subject matter in forms that can be effectively presented to students. In addition, teachers who want to engage students in constructing their own meaningful understanding must do more than simply provide clear presentations. Teachers must design learning activities and assignments that actively engage students in inquiry, thinking, constructing, and expressing their knowledge. In many cases, students can learn more from working with other students than by laboring in isolation. Thus teachers may need to devise new forms of participation and interaction that involve students in collaboration and communication with one another.

Allowing students more autonomy in investigating subject matter may contribute to more meaningful learning, but it can create a managerial nightmare for teachers. Lampert (1995) offers a memorable metaphor to capture the quality of this challenge. A teacher-guided lesson, she asserts, is somewhat like a guided tour in which all the students sit on the same bus while the teacher points out the sights as they ride around town. She compares lessons that include more student-centered inquiry to letting students get off the bus and giving them motorcycles to zoom around the environs independently. Oh, and the students all left their cameras on the bus, so tracking their progress is complicated! Providing students with a balance of guidance and autonomy and organizing ways for learners to capture and present their thinking are all part of the challenge when teachers shift from transmitting their knowledge to helping students construct meaningful understanding.

Assessment

Assessment of meaningful learning may require forms of evaluation that go beyond the usual quizzes, multiple-choice tests, and short-answer writing assignments. The Teaching for Understanding project discovered that assessments of a wide range of performances of understanding were possible by defining clear understanding goals and devising assessment rubrics with criteria directly related to those goals. Oral debates, multimedia presentations, and artistic performances could all be assessed as performances of understanding so long as the work was guided and analyzed in relation to assessment criteria derived from understanding goals. When students understood the assessment criteria or rubrics early in the process of their work, they were able to use them as performance guides throughout the process of drafting, critiquing, and revising their work. In this way, assessment became a supportive part of the learning process, rather than simply a means whereby the teacher decided at the end of the learning cycle whether students had succeeded or failed.

This kind of ongoing assessment is significantly different from what occurs in many classrooms. First, the focus of assessment shifts from students' acquisition of information and basic skills to their synthesis and application of knowledge and skills in coherent, thoughtful performances. Second, assessment becomes a shared responsibility in which many members of a learning community participate, including the students themselves. Students are asked to take on some intellectual authority and responsibility by using criteria to examine their own work and perhaps their fellow learners' work. In this way students come to understand the criteria for high-quality work, alternative approaches to meeting those criteria, and their own progress in relation to those criteria. Third, because assessment is done frequently, it can contribute to improving both teaching and learning. By checking to see what students do and do not understand at several stages in the learning process, teachers may discover how they must tailor their interventions to connect with their learners' evolving understanding. Similarly, by providing students with information about their progress and suggestions for revising their work, ongoing assessment helps students work toward meeting high standards.

Culture of Learning

For many teachers, making these kinds of changes in curriculum, pedagogy, and assessment would constitute fundamental challenges to classroom culture. They contradict commonly held beliefs and accustomed behaviors in traditional schools. In order to develop meaningful learning, students may need to revise their beliefs about the nature of knowledge, the process of learning, and their part in a collaborative learning community.

Researchers in the Teaching for Understanding project analyzed students' perceptions about understanding and how it is developed. They discovered that students in middle and high school see a major difference between learning in school and outside school (Unger & Wilson, 1998). Whereas students readily appreciate that learning on their sports team or on the job or at home requires active thought and practice, they may believe that learning at school is simply a matter of absorbing right answers and remembering them correctly. These findings take on special significance when considered in light of Dweck's research on children's views of learning. Dweck (1986) distinguished between students who think learning is a matter of getting right versus wrong answers—what she called *entity learners*—and students who believe that learning is a gradual process that progresses through thinking and practice—*incremental learners.* She found that students with a more incremental view of learning tended to persevere and ultimately succeed with challenging work more often than entity learners.

Through interviewing students about their ideas regarding learning, Unger and his colleagues discovered that in schools, more than in other settings, students tend to view themselves as entity learners who see knowledge as something one either gets or does not get. If this discourages them from tackling and sticking with challenging or ambiguous problems, students may need to reconsider their beliefs in order to stay involved in meaningful learning.

Another important aspect of the culture of meaningful learning concerns roles and responsibilities. In traditional classrooms, teachers and textbooks are authorities on knowledge. They are the source of right answers, and teachers are empowered to judge the correctness of student work. The concepts of meaningful learning and understanding discussed in this chapter imply attributing some authority to students. Students have some part to play in defining what is interesting and, through their inquiry, may extend or challenge the teacher's conception of what is important and true. Furthermore, the Teaching for Understanding framework implies that students must accept greater responsibility for generating learning. Students must actively construct their understanding. In addition, they have an important role to play in assessing the quality of their own work and in providing considered assessments and feedback to peers.

A classroom dedicated to meaningful learning and understanding is one in which all the participants share responsibility and authority for both teaching and learning (Wiske, 1994). Even if the teacher is a leader owing to greater experience and more extensive study of the subject, students participate as knowledge makers. Acknowledging the depth and complexity of these changes in beliefs and values is important if teachers are going to be given sufficient opportunities and time to cultivate what is often a deep transformation in the culture of learning.

Technical Training and Expertise

Teachers need technical training and support if they are to integrate new technologies into these kinds of meaningful learning experiences. Of course they need opportunities to learn about educational technologies and their possibilities, including examples of curriculum and models of practice that take effective advantage of new technologies. They need to gain fluency in the technical aspects of the technology itself—the menu structure and program functions, for example—so that they understand the potential applications of the technology. Then teachers need to relate this understanding to their own context, including their curriculum priorities, their students' needs, their own pedagogical preferences, and the technical and structural realities of their settings.

Meeting Teachers' Evolving Interests and Needs

This description of the many dimensions of meaningful learning with technology makes clear that teachers must engage in an extended process of learning. Researchers who have studied the process of transforming practice through the integration of new technologies recognize that teachers may want different kinds of assistance and support, depending upon their own goals and concerns. Sandholtz et al. (1997) studied teachers involved in a multiyear effort to integrate technology and perceived a progression of stages in teachers' concerns and needs:

> *Entry*: exposure to images of possibilities
> *Adoption*: technical training, assistance, and support

Adaptation: time for curriculum design, classroom observations, and pedagogical practice with on-site coaching and support

Appropriation: collaborative curriculum development, collegial exchange, and feedback

Invention: opportunities to conduct research, be a mentor for other teachers, and collaborate with other innovators

These researchers and others who have studied technology integration in classrooms (Means, Penuel, & Padilla, 2001) recommend that teachers receive support that is tailored to their particular concerns and needs. Focusing on technical details is of little interest to teachers who are not yet convinced that technology has much to offer or who will not have immediate access to the equipment they are being trained to use. Similarly, teachers who have developed considerable fluency with technology-enhanced lessons may appreciate opportunities to share their expertise and collaborate on design research studies.

Programs like Project TIME clearly recognize the importance of providing a range of kinds of learning and support for teachers over time. This initiative wisely addresses support for changing curriculum and pedagogy, as well as educational technology, and for generating systemic support over time. Teachers need opportunities for cycles of learning about new approaches; developing strategies they can apply in their own classrooms; trying out new practices, preferably with coaching and feedback; assessing results; and revising their practices in light of these analyses.

HOW CAN SCHOOL LEADERS PROMOTE MEANINGFUL LEARNING WITH TECHNOLOGY?

Few teachers working in isolation will achieve all the kinds of changes that meaningful learning with new technologies requires. Those individual teachers who are highly motivated and persistent may acquire technical knowledge and resources and learn how to integrate them in their classrooms. Such teachers may discover that they need to learn new ways of understanding their subject matter, to define new ways of designing lessons, to orchestrate new ways for students to interact in their classrooms, and to define appropriate new ways of assessing students' progress. A few pioneer teachers may be able to accomplish these changes without support from their school administration, but they will be rare and they will probably be exhausted.

To achieve meaningful learning with new technologies on a wide scale, support for changing the craft of teaching must be combined with creating conducive organizational contexts in schools. In analyzing the relationship between professional development and school reform, Little (2001, pp. 41–42) recommends coordinated attention to "individual, collective, and organizational capacity for reform," including development of a pervasive "culture of inquiry." School leaders at the building and district level must work together with teachers to build conducive contexts and organizational capacity to support innovative teachers.

Bolman and Deal (1991) analyze four dimensions of organizations that leaders must address: human resources, structural, cultural-symbolic, and political. In addition, school leaders who aim to scale up meaningful learning with technology must deal with technical issues. Change in each of these five dimensions must be driven by clear educational goals and policies, coherently aligned and focused on meaningful learning. Let's take a closer look at what school leaders can do to coordinate each of these facets of school change.

Technical Issues

The technical dimension is often the most visible and the one that many parents, business leaders, and politicians support most strongly. As a result, many school leaders interested in integrating technology into their programs focus almost entirely on acquiring machines and networks. School systems invest significant amounts of time and money in selecting and installing hardware, often without paying much attention to the educational agenda they ultimately hope to promote. As Cuban (2001) documents in *Oversold and Underused*, technology disconnected from educational planning rarely generates much impact on teaching or learning. Certainly technical resources are necessary, including well-maintained hardware, conveniently distributed to support effective use of the equipment for teaching and learning. Educational software is also important. Many schools find that general application software (such as word processors, spreadsheets, database managers, and presentation software), along with easy access to Internet connections, is more broadly valuable than subject-specific software programs. To serve meaningful learning, however, decisions about selecting and distributing technology must be guided by a clear educational agenda. And let us not forget the more traditional technologies of schools—textbooks, tests, and other instructional materials. If meaningful learning is the goal, these tools as well as the new technologies must be selected to support that goal.

Human Resources

Building human resources includes helping teachers develop the knowledge, skills, and beliefs to alter their craft. Hiring a few technology specialists who take students out of their regular classes for special lessons with computers is not enough. Schools working toward using their technology to support meaningful learning may hire technology integration specialists who work with regular classroom teachers. They help teachers plan curriculum, select and acquire the necessary resources, and devise feasible ways of allowing members of a class to work effectively with the available technology. These specialists can also work with a teacher as she or he tries out a new lesson, helping to answer questions, overcome technical difficulties, and provide assistance. If technology specialists begin by working with eager teachers, effective examples of technology-enhanced curriculum gain acclaim, and many of the teachers who were initially skeptical about technology may become interested.

Structural Dimensions

Organizational structures include roles, relationships, schedules, and both formal and informal groupings that determine how people interact. As we have already seen in the case of technology specialists, integrating technology for meaningful learning may require defining some new roles. School leaders may also need to create formal or informal task forces at both the district and the building level to coordinate planning and technical support around technologies. Effective use of technology in schools may also require altering schedules, for example, to provide longer class periods for some inquiry-based lessons and time for teachers and students to work on interdisciplinary, cross-subject projects.

Cultural-Symbolic Dimensions

The symbolic and cultural dimensions of organizations are often overlooked as important aspects of planned change. Symbols, rituals, and norms define and celebrate values. They are means by which members of an organization express meaning, affirm their own sense of belonging, and honor the importance of their communal ties. Introducing new technologies may be an important symbolic act that ratifies a school system's identity as modern, committed to high quality, and innovative. Interactive technologies may also challenge traditional norms and values by luring students out of their seats and into excited conversations and by replacing familiar assignments with new forms of expression such as multimedia products and presentations. School leaders must be attentive to these cultural dimensions of technological change. When the principal or superintendent uses e-mail, makes a presentation with new technologies, or celebrates the launch of a new Web site, the symbolic ramifications can be significant.

Political Dimensions

A fifth dimension of organizational change is political—the management of power, authority, responsibility, and commitment from various stakeholders. Teaching for Understanding, as we have already discussed, depends upon distributed allocation of intellectual authority and responsibility among teachers and students. They must all be willing to negotiate meaning and to debate truth on the basis of evidence and principles. This kind of intellectual community cannot thrive in an autocratic organizational environment. If school leaders want teachers to promote meaningful learning with their students, the leaders must foster policies that engage all members of the school organization in meaningful learning. Of course, classrooms, schools, and all organizations need leadership, and leaders must sometimes make unilateral decisions. Unlike heavy-handed, top-down management, collaborative leadership (Perkins, 2003) is more conducive to the kind of innovation, inquiry, and risk-taking that meaningful learning with new technologies requires of teachers and students.

Case studies of school organizations that have promoted meaningful learning with new technologies reveal that tending to these multiple facets of change, with a steady focus on the educational agenda, must be sustained over a period of years (Means et al., 2001). Stable leadership, networked across levels of a school system and focused on a common vision and not swayed by fickle fads, is necessary to accomplish what is ultimately a transformation of traditional schooling.

ONLINE RESOURCES THAT HELP TEACHERS DEVELOP MEANINGFUL LEARNING WITH TECHNOLOGY

Traditional forms of professional development rarely provide the kind of cyclical, sustained, collaborative experiences called for in the previous sections. One-shot or short-term workshops are the norm, often offered at a time and place disconnected from the teacher's usual setting and focused on a topic that is not tailored to the teacher's particular needs and interests. Teachers rarely have opportunities to try out new practices with assistance and feedback from an experienced coach and from colleagues engaged in similar inquiry. The pedagogy of professional development activities frequently contradicts the educational principles that its providers espouse. Adults can learn a lot from the "hidden curriculum" when effective teaching is modeled in their own learning experiences, but this opportunity is lost in many workshops provided for teachers.

Efforts to provide effective professional development with cycles of support and sustained access to resources are often foiled by basic bottlenecks caused by time and distance. Schedules are difficult to synchronize, people with adequate expertise are few and far between, travel is expensive, and time is limited. Appropriate resources and information may be inaccessible or so plentiful that they are overwhelming. New technologies, especially the Internet and the World Wide Web, hold significant potential for supporting teachers in learning how to foster meaningful learning with new technologies.

Online resources and activities can supplement face-to-face meetings and overcome some of the usual barriers to effective professional development. Multimedia tools can provide images of effective practice to complement more abstract descriptions. With hypertext links, multiple annotations can be attached to exemplary models. Thus, teachers and researchers can emphasize important qualities, indicate alternative choices, and share the thinking behind chosen interventions. Interactive tools provide guidance and scaffolding that support principled practice with prompts and suggestions that users can evoke or suppress according to their needs. The Internet is a vast, searchable archive of resources including interactive, multimedia, hyperlinked materials. Search engines help users navigate this limitless library to find what they need. Telecommunication technologies also provide means for teachers to communicate with experts, coaches, and like-minded colleagues to help them form communities of practice. Because the Internet captures and stores messages, teachers can participate in such dialogue asynchronously, freeing them to participate in professional development exchanges at times that are convenient. The Web also provides a way for teachers to publish and share their work with a much wider audience and more quickly than they could through traditional print publication channels.

Yet research shows that simply providing access to new technologies is unlikely to transform educational practice (Cuban, 1986, 2001). Putnam and Borko (2000) point out that, just as existing norms and practices of teachers' discourse communities constrain face-to-face professional development, they will shape and limit teachers' electronic interactions. Effective professional development must combine the use of Web-based resources with activities that motivate, focus, support, and sustain teachers' participation.

ONLINE PROFESSIONAL DEVELOPMENT BASED ON TEACHING FOR UNDERSTANDING

Several projects based at the Harvard Graduate School of Education are developing and studying ways of using the Internet to support professional development. The Education with New Technologies (ENT) Web site (Harvard Graduate School of Education, n.d.) is an online learning environment designed to help educators interested in Teaching for Understanding with new technologies. It includes a range of resources, interactive tools, multimedia pictures of practice, and electronic forums. These components are provided within the context of a village metaphor with a meeting hall, a gallery with online examples of technology-enhanced lessons or curriculum projects, a library of resources that users can search and add to, a workshop, and an online learning center. More than 4,000 registrants have enrolled in the site and a related site known as Active Learning Practices for Schools (ALPS; Harvard Graduate School of Education, 1998) since they were launched in 1998. During the following 2 years, registrants created nearly 2,500 curriculum designs with online curriculum development tools. The electronic forums support dialogue and exchange among educators who are interested in the research frameworks presented through these Web sites. Nevertheless, many educators have noted that online resources alone are not enough to help them develop a deep understanding of the educational models that ENT and ALPS present.

Desire to provide more sustained and intensive assistance led to the development of online professional development. A new initiative at the Harvard Graduate School of Education called WIDE World (President and Fellows of Harvard College, 2005) offers online courses that use the resources of the ENT and ALPS Web sites. WIDE World (Wide-scale Interactive Development for Educators) offers modules or courses that take place over a 6-to-12-week period. Learners in the courses are formed into study groups of 8 to 12 learners. An experienced coach works with each study group, fostering collaboration and interaction among them and providing individual feedback and support to the learners. These online courses provide additional guidance, timebound structure, interpersonal coaching, and sustained interaction with a team of educators to supplement the resources of the ENT and ALPS Web sites.

Currently, two courses offered through WIDE World focus on helping educators learn how to promote meaningful learning with technology. One is called "Webtools in the Classroom." It gives participants direct experience with a range of Internet-based environments that can enhance meaningful learning and supports them in designing a lesson that integrates one of these tools.

A second WIDE World online course titled "Teaching to Standards with New Technology" helps participants understand how to design curriculum that incorporates new technologies to enhance students' understanding of key learning standards. It both models and teaches about the Teaching for Understanding framework. Participants learn about the framework through experience as well as from analyzing curriculum examples and reading about the framework elements. They also learn how to discover and select educational technologies that can enhance one or more elements of Teaching for Understanding.

As the title implies, Teaching to Standards with New Technology is organized around a generative topic that is important and meaningful to teachers. The course design explicitly reflects the elements of the Teaching for Understanding framework. Overarching understanding goals for the course as a whole are introduced at the beginning, and each session is clearly organized around more specific understanding goals. The assignments that learners complete every session include performances of understanding linked to goals. For example, participants read about the criteria for understanding goals and then review curriculum standards in their subject matter. Then they post a message on the threaded discussion area of the online course about an example from their own standards that meets the criteria for an understanding goal. Working either individually or with other learners in the online course, participants gradually work through a process of designing a lesson around the elements of the Teaching for Understanding framework and incorporate new technology to enhance one or more of these elements.

For this curriculum development, the course participants use an interactive online tool housed in the workshop of the Education with New Technologies village. This Collaborative Curriculum Design Tool (CCDT) provides an online workspace where users can plan each element of the Teaching for Understanding framework: topic, goals, learning performances, and assessments. The tool offers various forms of support and assistance that users can call up if they wish, such as examples, prompts, and criteria for each element. The tool also links to curriculum standards in various subject matters and educational organizations, as well as to online resources for selecting new technologies. In addition, the CCDT includes a built-in threaded message board and a means of adding other members to one's design team. In this way, fellow learners and the coach can record and catalogue their questions, feedback, and suggestions about the emerging curriculum design.

Participants in WIDE World courses praise the advantages of learning from and with other experienced and reflective colleagues through online communication. Although some of them wish for direct contact, many of them note the conveniences of online learning: working in their own setting according to their own schedule; seeing the work and comments of many different teachers; receiving regular feedback and suggestions from a coach; being able to revisit and revise a curriculum design over time as their ideas evolve. Learners in WIDE World courses also emphasize the value of experiencing the kind of pedagogy that they are learning to enact. They appreciate that the process of learning through collaboration, reflection, feedback, and revision may be more educational and important than the product. They value engagement in a community of professionals who share their interests and a common language for designing and analyzing practice. They recognize the benefits of online technologies for promoting collaboration, reflection, and progressive refinement of educational design.

A long-term aim of this course and the WIDE World initiative is to develop a sustainable reflective community of practice linking educational practitioners and researchers in mutually beneficial dialogue. Such dialogues, sustained over time and extended across levels of educational systems, will be necessary in order to support change on the multiple dimensions that meaningful learning with new technologies require.

CONCLUSIONS

Meaningful learning with new technologies is a process that requires continuing learning for teachers as well as their students. Principles of effective learning apply to all learners, including teachers. Professional development should model the attributes of meaningful learning, both because it will promote better learning and so that teachers can learn from analyzing their own experience.

Learning to teach for meaningful learning with new technologies is a process that requires attention to multiple dimensions of practice: curriculum, pedagogy, assessment, technology, and the culture of learning. Helping teachers learn how to address and connect all these dimensions of practice must involve cycles of learning/practice/feedback and reflection.

Networked technologies can provide resources, tools, and interactive support that both model and promote meaningful learning with new technologies. Such supports can help to overcome the barriers of time and distance that often impede effective professional development. On-site support is an important supplement to online learning, however. Local coaches, collegial study groups, and supportive administrative structures can augment online training and resources.

Professional development is only one dimension of organizational change that must be addressed in order to achieve significant educational improvement. School leaders must also integrate technical, structural, symbolic, and political supports if teachers and students are to take full educational advantage of the potential that new technologies offer.

CHAPTER 3

WISE Teachers:
Using Technology and Inquiry
for Science Instruction

Marcia C. Linn

To better understand what teachers need to know to implement meaningful learning using technology in their classrooms, this chapter reports
on the experiences of middle school science teachers as they incorporate
Web-based Inquiry Science Environment (WISE) projects into their curriculum. WISE projects offer one way to support teaching for meaningful
learning using technology. In WISE, inquiry instruction involves engaging students in the intentional process of diagnosing problems, critiquing
experiments, distinguishing alternatives, planning investigations, researching conjectures, searching for information, constructing models, debating
with peers, and forming coherent arguments. Most curriculum frameworks
and standards for science emphasize this form of meaningful learning, yet
national and international surveys show that only about 10% of science
courses engage students in this form of intellectual work (Alberts, 2001;
Becker, 1999).

The science teachers featured in this chapter used one to six WISE
inquiry projects annually during the 2 years of the study. The conditions
for implementing WISE at their middle school were exemplary. A mentor
provided both technical and pedagogical support. On balance, the teachers who participated in this study were typical and included every teacher
of science at the middle school.

WISE AND MEANINGFUL LEARNING

Project TIME describes meaningful learning as achieving deep understanding of complex ideas that are relevant to students' lives (Battle Creek Area Educators' Task Force, 2002). This view resonates with the views of meaningful learning put forth by Jonassen et al. (1999) and by Wiske (1998). The WISE project has a similar goal of promoting knowledge integration reflected in a cohesive, robust understanding of complex science.

The WISE research program investigates ways to achieve this form of understanding. Linn and Hsi (2000) summarized 15 years of research on inquiry learning in the scaffolded knowledge integration framework and associated principles. Linn, Davis, and Bell (2004) extended this framework, added a perspective on the learner, and described more specific principles, based on a broad range of research programs. Linn (in press; Linn & Eylon, in press) summarizes the knowledge integration perspective and synthesizes the findings in design patterns.

The scaffolded knowledge integration framework characterizes aspects of instruction that promote integrated understanding. Students typically come to science class with a repertoire of ideas about scientific phenomena. Instruction helps students add new ideas to their mix of views and then organize these ideas into a coherent whole. Students add ideas easily as the result of instruction but may retain a repertoire of ideas that would appear contradictory to others. And new ideas may remain fragile and fragmented, ultimately becoming ignored rather than integrated (D. Clark, 2000; D. Clark & Linn, 2003). To make the process of adding ideas and sorting them out more effective, the framework emphasizes four general purposes: make science accessible, make thinking visible, help students learn from others, and promote lifelong learning.

Making science accessible means designing topics that connect to student concerns and specific examples that, when added to the mix of student ideas, catalyze understanding of scientific concepts. Too often, curriculum materials are decreed by standard-setting groups or textbook authors without research to demonstrate whether they benefit students. Research (Linn & Eylon, in press) illustrates how decisions about how to represent scientific concepts, such as depicting chemicals as being composed of single molecules, promote nonnormative student ideas. When confronted with illustrations of single molecules, students often assume that each molecule has color, viscosity, or a boiling point. Even when materials are tested with students, designers often simplify vocabulary rather than altering instruction to promote knowledge integration. Vocabulary simplification may actually reduce the impact of written material (e.g., Kintsch, 1998) rather than promote knowledge integration.

Making thinking visible means creating curriculum materials that illustrate scientific ideas with models, simulations, or verbal accounts of reasoning. Teachers can make thinking visible when they work out problems, explain wrong paths, or distinguish among alternatives. Research shows that some simulations, animations, or explanations add ideas that students can integrate, but many do not (Lewis, 1996). Designing instruction that makes thinking visible requires trial and refinement. Curriculum designs and teachers can ask students to make their thinking visible on assessments, in discussions, and in project reports. This student work can guide improvement of materials.

Helping students learn from others means enabling students to develop norms for scientific arguments by explaining ideas to others, critiquing one another's ideas, and discussing how alternatives might fit together. For example, in class and online discussions, students hear the ideas of others and defend their own views (Linn & Hsi, 2000). Methods such as the jigsaw guide students to specialize in one topic and tell others what they have learned (Aronson, 1978; A. L. Brown & Campione, 1994; Clarke, 1994). By participating in collaborative forums, students can learn new ideas and also develop criteria for sorting out their ideas.

Promoting lifelong learning means enabling students to monitor the cohesiveness of their ideas and their progress in understanding. When students are prompted to reflect, they analyze their progress (Chi, deLeeuw, et al., 1994). Projects enable students to practice lifelong learning skills such as critiquing evidence, debating arguments, or designing solutions to personally relevant projects. Teachers and learning environments can guide this process and encourage students to warrant their ideas with evidence, form arguments, and critique arguments of others.

Instruction designed following these principles has the potential of fostering meaningful learning. The WISE technology helps designers follow these principles by supporting curriculum design patterns based on the principles (Linn, Clark, & Slotta, 2003).

WISE PROJECTS AND TECHNOLOGY

The WISE technology enables partnerships to create projects that incorporate recent research on learning and instruction to promote knowledge integration (Bransford, Brown, & Cocking, 2000; Brown & Campione, 1994; Champagne, Klopfer, & Anderson, 1980; Cognition and Technology Group at Vanderbilt [CTGV], 1997; diSessa, 2000; Driver, 1985; Glaser, 1976; Linn & Hsi, 2000; Scardamalia & Bereiter, 1992; R. T. White, 1988; B. Y. White & Fredricksen, 1998). WISE instructional materials also benefit from 20 years of trial and refinement investigations in science classrooms (see Linn et al., 2004; Linn & Hsi, 2000; Slotta & Linn, 2000). WISE inquiry projects guide students in varied activities such as debating the causes of declining amphibian populations, critiquing Web-based evidence concerning insulation and conduction, building models of stream ecology, synthesizing evidence concerning the worldwide threat of malaria, and comparing Wisconsin "fast" plants to typical garden plants. Projects qualify for the WISE library after extensive testing and refinement.

The WISE interface (see Figure 3.1) enables students to follow promising inquiry patterns such as reviewing evidence, writing reflection notes, and constructing arguments using the inquiry map. Students respond to prompts in "notes" boxes and can receive hints from the Panda icon to guide their investigations. A variety of additional features such as discussion tools, modeling tools, data analysis tools, and other supports for science investigations appear in WISE projects (see http://wise.berkeley.edu).

FIGURE 3.1. WISE Interface (http://wise.berkeley.edu)

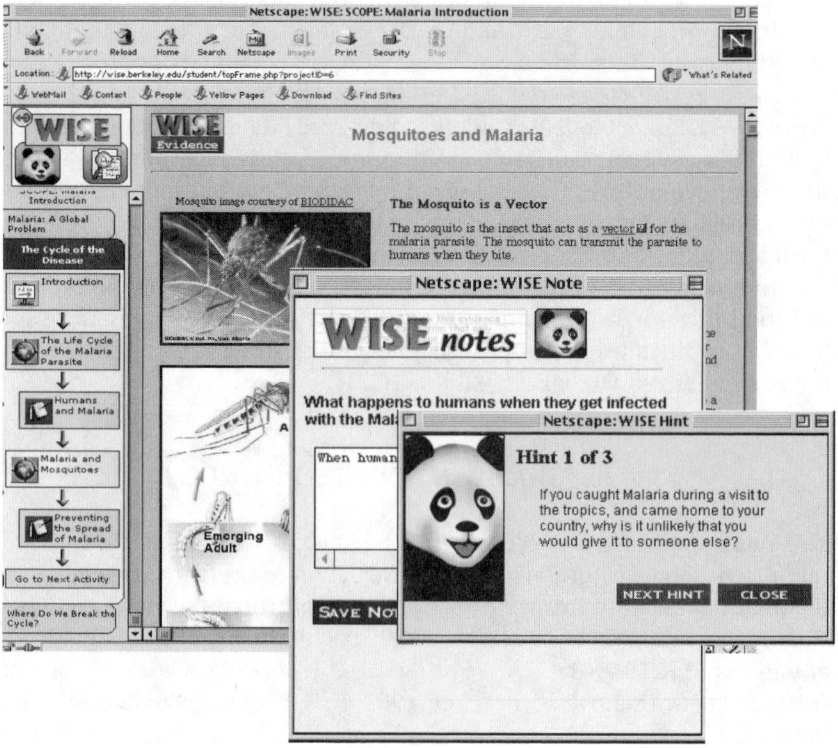

The WISE interface enables teachers to interact with individuals in small groups, while the technology keeps the class on task. Furthermore, teachers can customize WISE projects easily by modifying prompts and discussion topics. With more effort, teachers can change the patterns of investigation or the materials that students review.

METHODS

This research is one aspect of a larger study that links achievement of students, teaching strategies, and professional development (Linn et al., 2004). This chapter reports on the impressions of the teachers during the 1st and 2nd year of WISE instruction.

Participants

This research took place in a middle school serving a middle-class population in a California metropolitan area that includes immigrants from Asia, Eastern Europe, and Mexico. Students study earth science in sixth grade, life science in seventh grade, and physical science in eighth grade. Each teacher had 6 classes of about 30 students.

The six teachers had varied experience. Two teachers were new to the school when the study began. Two teachers were at the beginning of their teaching careers, and four had a reasonable amount of experience. All the teachers believed that students should engage in inquiry as defined by the WISE project. They all felt that their students already had inquiry opportunities in their classes, either in laboratory or other research activities, and saw WISE as strengthening this emphasis. All of the teachers considered themselves novice technology users. Four could use technology for productivity tasks such as e-mail or word processing. Two were uncomfortable using e-mail when the study began.

Interviews

Interviews were conducted after the 1st and 2nd year of teaching by WISE project staff. They were recorded and transcribed.

In this analysis, only comments on technology and teaching practices are examined. Interpretation of these interviews draws on extensive observations by the researchers in the classrooms of all six teachers (see Slotta, 2004). The interpretation also reflects informal discussions with the teachers and among members of the WISE research project, including the mentor.

WISE Instruction

In the 1st year, all the teachers agreed to use the same WISE project to introduce inquiry in their classrooms. This project, called Life on Mars, could be completed in 2 days and required the inquiry teaching techniques of introducing a challenging question, evaluating conflicting evidence, and constructing an argument. Each teacher worked with the mentor to implement this project. The mentor typically taught the project during the 1st class and then remained in the classroom while the teacher taught the project to the remaining five classes. The mentor helped the teacher register each student in WISE so that student work could be stored online. In addition, the mentor answered questions posed by the teacher and modeled ways to troubleshoot any computer problems.

Each teacher selected one or more projects to teach later in the year from the WISE project library. Together, they established a schedule for using the computer lab throughout the school year. In the 2nd project year, this sequence was replicated.

The students studying each WISE project participated in pretests, posttests, and measures of beliefs about science. They made progress in learning the science content, critiquing scientific evidence, and constructing arguments (Linn et al., 2004). Furthermore, between the 1st year and the 2nd year of their use of WISE projects, these teachers became more adept at teaching, and their increased skill was reflected in more sophisticated progress on the part of their students (Slotta, 2004). Both the students and the teachers had additional experience with WISE by the 2nd time projects were taught in the seventh and eighth grade, since students in those grades had participated in WISE projects in prior years.

Mentored Professional Development

Tracking the trajectories of these teachers over 2 years reveals both the strengths of mentored professional development and the paths followed by individuals responding to inquiry and technology. The teachers participating in this study had extraordinary respect for the mentor. The mentor had recently retired from the school and was respected for developing effective, technology-enhanced instructional practices. He enthusiastically encouraged the middle school teachers to incorporate WISE into their instructional programs.

Each teacher interacted with the mentor somewhat differently, but in all cases the mentor was present on the 1st day when WISE was used and available at any time teachers wanted to use WISE projects during the 1st year of the study. In the 2nd year the mentor was available on demand and assisted when new projects were introduced. In addition, members of the WISE partnership visited classrooms at the school and worked with teachers who had agreed to pilot-test new WISE projects.

For each project run, the mentor met with the teacher before the enactment to establish goals for the project and the evidence the teacher would use to determine whether the goals were met. The mentor then observed the instruction, making videotapes if the students and teacher consented. After instruction, the teacher and the mentor examined the evidence for success, determined how well the goals had been met, and customized the curriculum on the basis of evidence.

The WISE-mentored professional development program follows the same scaffolded knowledge integration framework that guided the design of WISE projects (see Table 3.1). This model has been tested in several investigations (Sisk-Hilton, 2002; Williams & Linn, 2002).

To make inquiry teaching accessible in mentored professional development, the mentor encourages the teacher to review the WISE projects, select one compatible with her or his instructional program, and predict how the students would respond. The teacher then works through the program and constructs an argument. To make new inquiry teaching strategies visible, the mentor teaches the first inquiry project to one of the six classes. In addition, the mentoring process illustrates inquiry teaching by engaging teachers in predicting and observing student learning. To help teachers learn from others, the mentor encourages group members to discuss their views with one another, observe one another, and consult one another when they encounter difficulties. To promote the lifelong process of continuous improvement of inquiry teaching, the mentor scaffolds evidence-based project customization.

The WISE project library met teacher needs unevenly. The sixth-grade teachers had developed a curriculum on water quality and merged their activities with the WISE water quality project. The sixth-grade and eighth-grade teachers adopted the WISE earthquake project. The WISE projects on declining amphibians and malaria met the needs of the seventh-grade teachers. Because science standards were changing in California at that time, some of the teachers were modifying the topics in their courses and seeking materials consistent with the new state framework. The How Far Does Light Go? and malaria activities appeared relevant when the study began but less relevant after standards had changed. All of the teachers found some WISE projects that looked relevant to their curriculum, but the teachers varied with regard to the match they perceived between their instructional program and available WISE projects.

WISE professional development aimed to scaffold integration of inquiry teaching practices. Often programs expect professionals to incorporate new

TABLE 3.1. Scaffolded Knowledge Integration Framework and WISE
    Curriculum Design Patterns

Scaffolded Knowledge Integration (SKI)	Curriculum Design Pattern
Make Science Accessible	Engage students in investigating a personally relevant, complex question by reviewing evidence and using hints.
Make Thinking Visible	Illustrate complex thinking using representations, models, simulations, and first-person narratives. Prompt students to produce and question the ideas so they can connect them to their own ideas.
Learn from Others	Guide students in generating their own ideas and criticizing the ideas of others in online discussions.
Promote Lifelong Learning	Encourage students to revisit their ideas, look for connections, construct arguments, and reflect on their progress. Connect projects to other science topics so learners can identify common themes.

practices rapidly on the basis of new recommendations. In contrast, most clinical programs acknowledge that new practices emerge slowly, and only with extensive interaction and monitoring by a trained professional. The WISE professional development program recognizes the pace of knowledge integration and provides a mentor to help teachers realize their own potential and take advantage of what WISE offers.

TRAJECTORIES OF TEACHERS

At the initial meeting to introduce technology and inquiry to the teachers, the mentor and the research group were prepared for many questions about whether technology could enhance learning. The teachers raised questions about access to computers at home, about the potential for students to access inappropriate Internet sites, and about how technical problems would be resolved. The teachers endorsed inquiry teaching; most adopted a wait-and-see attitude about the impact of technology.

Technology and Inquiry Teaching

Of the six teachers, one was skeptical and five were neutral about the role of technology. The skeptical teacher believed that technology had little place in the science classroom, arguing that anything the computer could do could be done without the computer, either as well, or possibly better. This view arises regularly in news accounts of technology and education and deserves serious consideration.

The teachers worried about the reliability of the computer technology. Although this school had a technology coordinator, the coordinator was rarely available and did not have expertise with networking. The WISE project reassured the teachers that technical assistance would be available at any time it was needed during the 1st project year. At the same time, the research team recognized that technical support remained a serious issue.

Year 1 Role of Technology. During the 1st year, the WISE technology operated erratically because of networking problems in the school district. It took the technology experts from the WISE project and those from the district several months to figure out the problem. Eventually the mentor teacher, by conducting experiments at the school, discovered a fault in the school wiring and fixed the problem. By this time all of the teachers were relatively frustrated by the technology glitches, and the skeptical teacher had concluded that technology was not ready for school use.

At the same time, all the teachers developed strategies for coping with network breakdowns. They became skilled in continuing an activity off line and finding alternative mechanisms for exploring the topic of the WISE project. The fear of facing a classroom of students who were unable to access the network was alleviated by dealing with the unfortunate problems faced during the first year. Nevertheless, the middle school science curriculum includes far more topics than can be taught, and any lost instructional time seriously frustrates teachers (Linn & Hsi, 2000).

When asked about the value of technology, the skeptic said that the students "probably gained some computer skills" and went on to explain, "I don't think there was any material that couldn't have been covered conventionally." When asked to elaborate, the skeptic said, "We used those temperature probes for the hot and cold—the black and white cups. I mean, I've done that lab before, and the kids learn exactly the same thing, which is what they kind of know going into it, anyway. But we didn't need the computer there, you just need a thermometer to put in each cup."

This response surprised the mentor, who had found substantial advantages for real-time data collection over student-collected data (Linn & Hsi, 2000; Linn, Layman, & Nachmias, 1987; Tinker, 1996). The mentor asked the teacher whether there were any benefits of having the computer do the graphing. The teacher responded, "I think they get more out of graphing it themselves. The computer didn't do more because they weren't quite sure what was happening, and they were gabbing with their friends while they were collecting the data and graphing." The skeptic identified several problems with any inquiry project, including keeping students focused on the task and ensuring that students can interpret the material presented. This skeptic accurately reported that while the computer was assisting in the graphing, the students were not necessarily paying attention.

The mentor made his experience with this technology visible. He said that when students encounter inquiry learning for the first time, they often need scaffolds to learn how to guide their own learning. For inquiry using real-time data collection, research shows the benefit of asking students to make predictions and reconcile the predictions with their observations (e.g., Linn & Hsi, 2000). When students make predictions and then look for confirmation, they pay more attention to the data collection. Furthermore, although the WISE activity supported this pattern of interaction, the students needed more guidance to follow the pattern. The skeptic expected the WISE software to provide all the guidance.

Most of the teachers held a pragmatic attitude toward the computers. When asked about the role of technology during the 1st year of the project, they pointed out the difficulties with the network, remarked that some of their students had gained computer competence, and turned to discussing their role in the computer lab. One teacher, remarking on the technology, said, "Most of these kids are computer literate in terms of knowing how to turn it on and knowing how to play with it. I don't think a lot of them have really used it as a tool for learning or for getting new concepts." This teacher said that the students used computers primarily as typewriters, to chat with their friends, or to play computer games. When the students came into the classroom, the teacher said, they were not worried or scared of using computers, but instead their attitude was, "We get to play with a computer." The pragmatic teachers saw their role as facilitating a view of the computer as learning partner. They noted that the software succeeded in guiding the students and gave teachers options for new roles during science instruction.

A number of teachers, when probed, commented on their own expertise with technology, noting that they had learned about technology by using the WISE software. Most had developed strategies for unfreezing computers, dealing with forgotten passwords, and helping students keep track of where they were in the project. The teachers barely considered these developing skills worth mentioning. When they did mention their own developing expertise, they tied it to their professional goals, remarking that they were using technology for other parts of their work, such as communicating with peers or finding out about educational conferences, in addition to helping their students with WISE technology.

Year 2 Role of Technology. During the 2nd project year, all the teachers again used at least one WISE project, and the technology operated smoothly. The mentor and teacher refined WISE activities to meet the classroom needs. New projects were created to align with the curriculum and the new standards. At the end of the 2nd year, teachers had remarkably little to say about technology.

The skeptical teacher was the least participatory and the most critical of technology. In the interviews at the end of the 2nd year, the skeptical teacher had two main insights. First, the teacher remarked, "The kids seem to be more focused on working with the material because it was delivered through a medium that they are attracted to at their stage of development, which is the computer." In addition, the teacher noted, "Other benefits are working together in small groups, being able to collaborate, and to help each other." The skeptic also, however, complained that in the WISE lab, because students work in pairs, there are more groups to monitor than in the classroom, where typically groups of four conduct projects.

The skeptic remained convinced that the material could also be presented without technology, but remarked, "There still is good material in the WISE project, and it was good for them to see that material presented in another way." In addition, the skeptical teacher was able to recognize that WISE projects fit with the standards for science education, while at the same time complaining that the WISE projects currently available were not well aligned with the new content standards. The skeptic volunteered to create a project that would more closely align with the new standards.

The skepticism of this teacher contributed to the whole-school effort at developing a perspective on technology and education. By responding to these skeptical but legitimate concerns, the whole group of teachers developed arguments to support their own views of technology in science instruction that drew on evidence from their classrooms. Just as classroom science projects benefit from multiple perspectives, so did the school benefit from conflicting and diverse perspectives on the potential of technology to improve science learning. After 2 years, the skeptic remained skeptical, but reflected more about the experience with WISE projects.

By the 2nd year, the pragmatic teachers no longer distinguished the technology from the WISE projects, and when asked about the impact of WISE technology, they spoke primarily about their changing roles in the science classroom as a result of the guidance available in the WISE technology. These changing roles are discussed below in the context of science inquiry. Overall, both individually and collectively, the skeptical and pragmatic responses to technology at this middle school led to a developing view of technology as integral to effective inquiry instruction.

In summary, the trajectories of the six teachers, in integrating their understanding of technology and education, follow a similar path. Teachers come with some apprehensions and reluctance concerning the technical requirements of using computers in classrooms. In all cases, these apprehensions dissipate as experience grows. Since all the teachers used the same WISE project for all six of their classes and also taught two or more WISE projects during the course of each year, most of them had used technology with more than 1,000 students and for at least ten weeks by the end of the second year. As one teacher remarked, "I've grown . . . I felt like I'd been doing it forever, because it seems like it's been part of my life," and went on to explain, "I've learned every time that I've done it. I've added new skills and gotten more familiar with the information, so that has been helpful."

Conclusions for the Role of Technology. Over the 2 years, the teachers reported spending more and more time considering roles for technology and becoming technologically competent. The WISE project has motivated a deliberate effort on the part of these teachers to become technology savvy. All the teachers found ways to use more and more features of the technology, including modeling, e-mail, and online assessment. Indeed, by the end of the 2nd year, the teachers' biggest complaint was about personal access to computing away from school.

Another indicator of the teachers' growing sophistication with technology concerns their requests for enhancements to WISE. Each year the teachers asked for more sophisticated tools. Initially, the teachers requested the ability to send notes back to students on their work. More recently, the teachers asked for online grading options, and more than half have developed the capability of sending group as well as personalized messages to their students. The middle school teachers have become full partners in the WISE research program, both as authors of curriculum materials and as contributors to the design of WISE technology.

The expectation that teachers will gain sophistication in using technology permeates the school culture. Not every school would have a similar perspective. This perspective is a credit to the mentor, who introduced all the teachers to the technology and regularly revisited the school to provide guidance and continuity.

This implementation was atypical in some ways. Most schools have considerable difficulty implementing technology because of technical support issues. At this school the research group took primary responsibility for technical support during the 1st year and worked closely with the school and the teachers to ensure at least minimal technical support for the following years. Technical support remains a serious issue. All the teachers worry that as the research group becomes less involved in the day-to-day activities of the school, the technical issues will take more time and cause more difficulties. The teachers vary in their ideas about how these problems might be addressed. Some believe that adept students might be used as teaching assistants to provide straightforward technical support, while the districtwide technical coordinator could be used for more serious problems. Others worry that the program itself will wither unless better technical support solutions are found.

Many schools worry about the "digital divide" and access to technology. This school, in part because all students used the WISE projects, had less concern. In addition, students in this school often have computer access at home and can also access computers before and after school and at the community center. The important equity issues in computer access are less central here but remain of concern to the WISE project, and indeed to the teachers at this school, who wonder whether other schools can replicate their experience.

Classroom Interactions and Inquiry Teaching

WISE inquiry projects guide students through patterns of activities, as shown in the inquiry map; provide opportunities for students to reflect on their progress, as shown in the notes window; and even provide hints to students concerning how their projects might be conducted (see Figure 3.1). Other features of WISE also guide students in inquiry activities. These features change the interactions between students and their teachers and can potentially free teachers to provide more detailed and comprehensive tutoring to students as they encounter difficulties.

The WISE-mentored professional development process modeled and encouraged teachers to develop strategies for dealing with the new responsibilities. The mentor teacher modeled the process of introducing a WISE project, and all of the teachers attempted to emulate this model. The mentor introduced specific inquiry teaching strategies. The mentor also provided specific guidance and clues about how to help students succeed in WISE projects.

The mentor recounted his own inquiry teaching trajectory. He suggested that teachers pay attention to the specific problems and concerns each group of students face. He said that when he started talking to students individually in his classroom, he was amazed to discover how many of them retained nonnormative ideas after instruction.

The mentor introduced inquiry teaching strategies such as helping teachers decide when to address the whole class. The mentor pointed out that if three or more pairs ask a similar question, the teacher should intervene. He recommended interrupting the class, asking a group to explain the dilemma, and discussing the problem with everyone rather than answering the same question again and again for each of the 15 or 16 pairs of students.

Another inquiry strategy involved looking for subtle issues in understanding the science. The mentor encouraged teachers to provide students with specific suggestions and feedback on their progress. The mentor modeled this process of providing specific rather than general feedback, pointing out that encouraging statements, such as "That's great," while motivating, may actually deter students from further intellectual work. Instead, the mentor recommended specific questions and comments. The mentor advocated what WISE calls "pivotal cases" to stimulate thinking (Linn, 2005). For example, the mentor explained that a piece of evidence showing how night goggles work helped students sort out their ideas about light propagation because it contrasted with their usual experience of less visual activity at night.

The mentor also illustrated a specific inquiry strategy for answering students' questions. Often, according to the mentor, answering a question with a question was more successful than simply answering the question. For example, if students ask the teacher to explain a piece of evidence about the role of pesticides in frog blindness, the teacher might respond by (a) asking students which aspect of the evidence connects to the overall question about frog deformities, (b) asking students whether they believe the results of the Web page reporting this finding, or (c) suggesting that the students identify words on the page that they do not understand. Teachers, according to the mentor, might also encourage students to consult their partner, and possibly the group sitting next to them, when questions confuse them. The mentor teacher modeled all of these processes when introducing inquiry teaching.

Year 1 Inquiry Teaching. During the 1st WISE year, the mentor teacher introduced the 2-day Life on Mars activity for each teacher. He modeled the process of registering students in WISE, helping students navigate through the software, and encouraging students to interpret evidence. He also repeated this modeling for each new project. All the teachers commented on the advantage of this approach. For example, one teacher remarked, "He was always there to lend a hand or fix the problem. He would just basically always be there. That was good, because that's what we needed. In the first year it's always nice to have that backup. This year . . . it's like we're growing up and getting on our feet more."

During the 1st year, teaching strategies for WISE projects varied considerably. Some teachers closely emulated the mentor and gradually instituted a few changes. Other teachers relied primarily on the strategies they employed for classroom science laboratories, modifying their approach as they tested it in the WISE environment. Some teachers, and most of the teachers some of the time, experimented with the new strategies and analyzed the impact of their approaches on student progress and behavior.

One teacher carefully followed the mentor and intensively tutored each student group before trying new techniques. During the 1st year, this careful teacher reported, "I first tried to touch bases with every single group, like, walk around and listen to the conversation, and react to their responses, which I usually don't do." This teacher could spend 2 or 3 minutes with a single group, leaving the rest of the class to pursue projects following the WISE inquiry map (see Slotta, 2004). WISE supported this strategy for classroom interaction by guiding the remaining students effectively. The careful teacher worried about neglecting groups that could not be visited during each class. This teacher spent time helping students make connections and remarked, "I'm hoping they see the interaction of all the different sciences, you know—within one subject they were studying, like, malaria—it's not just cells, but the whole interaction of the people, the insects, the life cycle." This teacher, who saw the role of the instructor as one of asking questions so that the big picture would emerge, guided students to get the big picture. The careful teacher was "questioning what they wrote down—what did they mean—things like that" to ensure that students made valid connections.

The teachers who initially viewed teaching WISE projects as similar to teaching science experiments in the classroom developed a more nuanced view over time. During the 1st year, one teacher said that most of the time "I was just moving around, monitoring the students' progressing if they needed help, if they were going in the right direction, if they were visiting all the different areas that they needed to, and checking to see if they were working cooperatively." After a while the teacher realized the need to "take a look at the responses to questions and problems." This teacher became aware of the need to "clarify some of what they were working on—what they were trying to answer," and remarked that during the first use of WISE projects, connecting them to other aspects of the curriculum was difficult. But the 2nd year these connections were made more explicitly. This teacher gained insight into the projects during the 1st year and could monitor more complex activities in the 2nd year.

The skeptical teacher saw running a computer lab as very similar to running any kind of science lab, saying, "You just float around putting out fires, basically." The teacher expected a great deal of the technology and the projects, saying, "The way the questions were worded didn't really lead the students to come up with a response of their own. I mean, I even looked at the questions and shrugged my shoulders and said, 'Just put something down.'" This teacher left much of the teaching to the WISE technology. Other teachers saw their role as augmenting the technology.

One teacher, who also saw parallels between teaching science experiments and teaching WISE projects, picked up on the mentor's recommendation to interrupt the class when students started to have the same problems, saying during the interview, "When you start getting questions from groups that are kind of similar, you stop and you make sure that everyone goes to that place so you can explain what they need to do." This teacher described working in the WISE lab as focusing students on evidence and argument. The teacher remarked, "The key is just using evidence and information to really develop solutions." This teacher felt that the WISE projects resonated with the goals for science that arose in the laboratory as well. However, the teacher remarked that the WISE activities went further than typical laboratory activities, saying, "Being able to give all the kids the same kind of information and then have them make predictions about stuff—they've never had to do that before. Half of them still don't really understand analysis, prediction, and the relationship between the two." Summarizing the WISE experience, this teacher remarked, "My management skills just improved immensely."

Several teachers viewed the WISE classroom as requiring new teaching strategies and offering new opportunities for teaching. One teacher was enthused about the chance to "really hear the learning process." This teacher said that when looking at what students wrote and listening to their discussions, "it felt almost like eavesdropping, and it was very nice, because it's a very different dynamic than standing in front of the room teaching. . . . When I'm in front of the class I'm an authority figure . . . when I'm moving around the classroom in the computer lab, it feels . . . much more egalitarian." This teacher argued that the depth of learning changed because students were required to support statements with evidence and build more cohesive arguments. The teacher also remarked that when students had to resolve their differences of opinion, they frequently became frustrated, and this frustration motivated new teaching tactics on the part of the inquiry instructor. The teacher explained that "This was really my first introduction into 'don't give them the answer, let them grapple with it.'" The teacher noted that this was the first time that students were using data to resolve their disputes but also recognizing that there were times when the data could not inform the discussion. The teacher concluded, "I think one of the big struggles that we all have—I mean, as adults or as kids—is that there can be more than one answer to a question."

Another teacher also gained new insights into teaching using the WISE materials. This teacher started with the notion that the role of the instructor was "just wandering around to make sure that they were focused." After some time, the teacher recognized that helping the students become focused meant looking closely at their work and identifying mechanisms for increasing focus. For example, this teacher remarked, "They weren't getting the big in-depth thing, so you had to stop and redirect them and say why it is important." This teacher, who also experimented with explaining things and having the students read the material and discuss it with their partners, reflected, "I think they understood it better reading it versus listening to me drone on." This teacher observed that students were distressed when assigned to support a point of view they felt was wrong. The teacher explained to the class that supporting a view they disagreed with could increase understanding and summarized, "They were able to express themselves in the paper because they could choose any side," but having defended a position they didn't agree with resulted in more coherent and stronger arguments when they chose their own position.

These observations and experiments conducted by the teachers in the classroom reveal an unanticipated benefit to inquiry teaching with technology. Since these teachers repeat a lesson for five or six classes, they could experiment with inquiry procedures and quickly test their assumptions. As a result, they could identify practices that made sense for them. The teachers were helped by the mentor to create experiments that contributed to successful inquiry. Instilling in teachers the belief that practices can be tested and refined in the course of a single day of teaching adds a useful dimension to professional development. In the 2nd project year, most of the teachers were able to select WISE activities that matched well with their curriculum and continued to hone their skills in delivering inquiry instruction.

Year 2 Inquiry Teaching. During the 1st project year, virtually all the teachers complained of exhaustion after teaching with WISE, pointing out that not only did they have to concentrate on new subject matter, but they also had to institute new teaching practices. One teacher remarked, "Teaching in the lab is very intensive. You're in motion all the time, you're engaged all the time, and there's not a moment of down time." The teacher went on to explain, "I'm listening to conversations here, I'm paying attention to an activity there, while I'm trying to focus on this student here, and it's exhausting." By the 2nd year, most of the teachers had found ways to reduce the exhaustion while maintaining their personal contributions. When the teachers were interviewed after their 2nd year of instruction, many repeated varying their practice and trying new strategies.

The careful teacher had added a portfolio requirement to the science course and found that many students picked their WISE projects for the portfolio. The teacher observed, "They felt like real scientists looking at evidence out there. They felt the connection between what we do in school and what's currently happening in the world." This teacher also remarked that students were developing analytical skills and that in the 2nd year they seemed more adept at analyzing information than they had in the 1st year, possibly because they were now using WISE for a 2nd year, having studied other WISE projects the year before. This teacher, in the 2nd year, focused more on helping students connect ideas, saying, "It's difficult to show the whole picture" when using a textbook, but "this is the perfect vehicle."

The careful teacher also reported a new tactic for interacting with students, one that surprised the WISE research group but that the teacher found very promising. The teacher said, "Last year . . . I had them all print out their finals so I could take my time grading them. This year, I decided to do something different. I decided to use the online comments." As a result, the teacher sat at the back of the room typing comments while the students were working. Observers found this frustrating, assuming that the teacher was not engaged with the students. The teacher felt differently. First, the teacher reported that, having taught the project before, it was possible to ask more informative and specific questions online. Furthermore, the teacher reported, "I like making comments to the kids on the computer, and they can also come up to me as they're working." "When I review their work," this teacher commented, "some kids, when I read their final notes, I ask where did you get this? And those are usually the ones that I didn't get to, because I didn't have enough time." This careful teacher depends heavily on the WISE software to guide students and has experimented with efficient ways to communicate to the students about their progress. The careful teacher moved from emulating the model of the mentor to experimenting with new practices.

Those who viewed teaching with WISE as like teaching with science experiments reached new insights during their 2nd year. One teacher

remarked that using WISE enabled students to develop better communication skills because they had to write down their own answers and pay
close attention to conflicting evidence. The teacher remarked, "They picked
up writing skills. They realized that the way they were reading and interpreting the question wasn't necessarily on target, and they also learned
from the first time around that if there was anything that wasn't understood, they have to communicate more openly with their partner and with
me." This teacher, whose role in the classroom had changed dramatically
since the 1st year, remarked, "The first time around I was closely monitoring what was going on, and then I had the tendency to go 'hands off' and
let them do their own thing. After reading the first results of the first project
that they did, I realized that I needed to be more involved and to monitor
more closely what was going on, and take a sampling of the answers that
each group was coming up with." This teacher also realized the need to work
on writing skills and help students become more adept at communicating
their ideas. The teacher reported that spending more time analyzing the
project helped with instruction, saying, "The first time around I hadn't gotten into the project myself, and read through it." In the 2nd year, "I was
able to prepare them going into the project by giving them a little more
background on what they were going to be doing and seeing." This teacher
also reported integrating the WISE material more closely into the curriculum, remarking, "I just made a reference to the malaria project this morn-
ing, because now we're studying anthropoids." This teacher continued to
follow the mentor's model for classroom interactions but also experimented
with varied approaches; studying the project more carefully had dramatically improved both the WISE experience and student learning outcomes.

The skeptical teacher saw little difference between WISE and other
laboratory teaching, but mentioned the advantage of understanding the
tasks more deeply and of connecting the WISE project to other topics. The
skeptical teacher said, "We had that power crisis. We talked about
the power crisis in my room and we looked at what devices use power
and how PG&E (Pacific Gas & Electric) was raising the rate. That integrates
what they're dealing with when they're home with their parents" with
the science activities in WISE.

The teachers who viewed WISE inquiry teaching as requiring new
strategies gained even more insights during the 2nd year. One teacher
experimented with spreading a WISE activity across the whole year and
adding insights at each revisiting of the topic. This teacher reported, "I think
the more opportunities we have to take the kids out as they're doing some
of these units, the more sense it will make."

Another teacher who described WISE as requiring new teaching
strategies commented, "I think what I learned in WISE I also do in the

classroom now, which is stop giving the kids the answer." This teacher enthused, "I don't teach a particular subject, I teach kids to learn. I think that WISE has made me much, much, much, much better at that."

During the 2nd year, all of the teachers reported a deeper understanding of their students' ideas. One teacher remarked, "I get to sit down and talk one-on-one with a group of kids, and I can really figure out where they are, how much they're getting of the information. I see a lot of growth in some kids, specifically, in this term, and some kids who weren't really into school." Another teacher remarked, "You can go there and kneel down between them and get to know the kids better. It became much more of a personal relationship between me and the kids. I was able to clean up some misconceptions they had at the same time, by pointing them back where to go." Another teacher remarked, "I was a little dismayed when the kids were working on the earthquakes and the plate tectonics at how little they retained from the earthquake unit. When I really sat down and thought about it, I realized that most of the children had not been born in 1989. They haven't experienced a big earthquake yet, so they have general information about it, but they just don't have the experience of the earthquakes."

All the teachers also commented on the importance of balancing their work with individual students and their work with the group. They all credited the mentor teacher with modeling this process. One teacher commented, "Here's how you can tell that the problem needs to be addressed room wide rather than individual—Oh, look, four people have come up with the same question! We need to stop and talk."

The WISE projects also motivated teachers to recognize areas for personal growth. One teacher commented on the difficulty of deciding when to interrupt and when not to interrupt the class and how to arrange the flow of activities. The teacher reflected, "I have to work on that, and that's something that I have to do. It's not a problem with WISE, I have to change the approach for the kids." Another teacher remarked, "It takes about two years to refine where you want it to go. I'll probably refine it even more next year."

All of the teachers, when asked how to prepare to use WISE projects effectively, stressed the importance of carefully working through the WISE project and really understanding what was in it, so that when students had questions the teacher would know what they might or might not have read or done to reach that insight. All the teachers also stressed that these projects require an iterative process of refinement in order to work well. The teachers applied the same approach to their own practice, noting that they, too, followed an interactive process. For the lessons, teachers refined their practice from class to class. For a topic, teachers refined their practice from year to year. They reported substantial increases in their expertise and effectiveness from year 1 to year 2, and each expected to continue along this trajectory in the future.

These insights from the teachers are consistent with results for student learning. Slotta (2004) reports that although two of the teachers who taught the same malaria unit used distinctly different practices, they both saw improved student outcomes in the 2nd year of teaching. One teacher interacted intensively with each group, whereas the other monitored progress by circulating around the room. On the project posttest, student performance was similar for these teachers. On the embedded project notes, the students of the intensive teacher were more successful. In the 2nd year, students in both classes were more successful—reflecting additional experience with WISE for both teachers and students. Consistent with teaching practices, the students of the intensive teacher continued to write more coherent project notes than the students of the monitoring teacher.

These teachers illustrate the complexity and challenge of implementing new practices. They have succeeded both individually and as a community. They support one another and benefit when students who studied WISE in prior years enroll in their classes.

CONCLUSIONS

The trajectories of all the science teachers in one school as they use technology-enhanced inquiry science demonstrate the impact of mentored professional development on teaching for inquiry. They showcase the challenges of inquiry teaching and illustrate techniques for promoting meaningful learning.

Mentored Professional Development

The mentor provided a compelling model of inquiry teaching. Most teachers made every effort to emulate each aspect of the mentor's performance. Several of the teachers went so far as to note the specific questions and approaches used by the mentor and to copy them directly when they taught the same project. Many invited the mentor to come back into their class to observe and help when they started on new projects. These teachers asked the mentor for specific recommendations and guidance and often began with questions supplied by the mentor when interacting with students. The mentor succeeded in making the process of inquiry teaching visible by emphasizing inquiry teaching strategies.

First, the mentor sought to encourage teachers to listen closely to students and provide the kinds of guidance that enable students to keep working on their arguments and to construct more integrated and compelling accounts of scientific phenomena. Many professional development programs report difficulty encouraging teachers to listen to students (e.g., Putnam & Borko, 2000). The mentor teacher introduced a pivotal case that enabled teachers to become better listeners in their classrooms. The mentor told the teachers that they needed to listen to what each group of students was saying in order to identify problems that two or more groups were facing so they could interrupt the class to provide this information to all sixteen groups. During the interviews, every single teacher mentioned the importance of listening to the students so that they could communicate important information to all the groups when appropriate.

Second, the mentor instilled the practice of communicating information by asking students questions rather than simply telling the class an answer. This process of encouraging teachers to listen carefully to students in order to formulate a question rather than to provide an answer redirects attention toward the process of constructing an argument and away from the potentially unproductive cycle of question-answer-question-answer that frequently permeates inquiry classrooms. Furthermore, by answering questions with questions, teachers communicate to students that they believe the students can find answers to their problems when directed toward important aspects of the situation.

Third, the mentor motivated teachers to develop expertise in the discipline of the project and monitor student progress to be sure that the students were getting the main ideas. All the teachers reported a desire to gain a deeper understanding of the topic and the project their students were undertaking in order to be more effective. The teachers spent time reviewing the materials their students were studying and developing questions they could ask their students to stimulate thinking. A number of teachers identified specific difficulties that students faced and sought ways to customize or modify activities based on their analysis of student problems. For example, one teacher, using the earthquake project, noted that students had difficulty determining the building materials used in their homes, the school, and in public places. As a result, the teacher modified the instructions to help students recognize wood and stucco buildings and distinguish them from buildings constructed with reinforced concrete or stone.

In summary, the mentor teacher made inquiry teaching strategies visible. The mentor also promoted autonomy by encouraging teachers to learn more about WISE project topics. The teachers reacted uniquely to these insights and pivotal cases, but in all cases the instruction from the mentor resonated with the teachers and motivated a deeper exploration of inquiry instruction.

Teacher Trajectories

The professional development model, as well as the WISE projects, supported unique trajectories for the participating teachers. The teachers incorporated technology and inquiry into their practice somewhat differently. Overall, the skeptical teacher was the least involved. Two enthusiastic teachers taught the most projects, and all teachers made use of the opportunity to teach inquiry using technology.

Each of the six teachers found it stimulating to listen to students and respond to their concerns as they interacted with science content. The skeptical teacher tended to complain about the software and the activities, noting that students became confused and had questions that were not answered by the WISE projects. The pragmatic teachers also noted that students became confused, and they saw this as a chance to guide students to sort out the conundrums and complexities of the science introduced in the projects.

All the teachers recognized eventually that they had an important role to play in helping students make sense of complex WISE projects. By the 2nd year every teacher acknowledged the difficulties of supporting students in complex projects, but also recognized the advantages of the software in guiding students through inquiry activities and the importance of studying the activities in order to be an effective supporter of student work.

Teaching for Meaningful Learning

This study of science teachers implementing inquiry teaching has several important lessons for those interested in teaching for meaningful learning. First, WISE inquiry teaching is a form of meaningful learning in which students conduct projects on complex science topics. As teachers using WISE have demonstrated, these projects enable students to develop linked and connected understanding of science that fits the definition of meaningful learning.

Second, the WISE learning environment scaffolds students so their teachers can interact with small groups and monitor classroom progress. WISE includes several technological supports that can contribute to meaningful learning. The WISE inquiry map models the process of scientific investigation; when students perform multiple WISE projects, they learn both how to investigate scientific topics and how the techniques for investigation vary across different disciplines (Slotta & Linn, 2000). WISE prompts for reflection guide students to monitor their progress and look for gaps in their understanding (E. A. Davis, 1998, 2004). WISE modeling and simulation tools provide opportunities to compare theories about phenomena such as water quality or the rock cycle with experimentally collected data (Baumgartner, 2004; Kali, Bos, Linn, Underwood, & Hewitt, 2002). WISE graphing and visualization tools help students learn how to represent data and interpret the representations of others (Williams & Linn, 2002). WISE discussion tools enable students to make conjectures and critique the ideas of others. WISE argument construction tools enable students to visualize their ideas and understand the nature of scientific thinking (Bell, 1998; Bell & Linn, 2002).

Third, teachers using WISE have multiple sources of information about the way their students think and can use these insights to improve their own teaching. By looking at the ideas students generate in WISE projects, teachers get a minute-by-minute sense of how students generate and reconsider their ideas. In addition, by monitoring the performance of small groups and talking to students while they work, teachers can identify student insights and obstacles. These sources of information give teachers a more complete picture of student thinking than is possible when relying on quizzes, class discussions, or tests.

Fourth, mentors can make professional development more effective by scaffolding teachers as they develop skill in inquiry teaching much as the WISE learning environment scaffolds students. By modeling inquiry teaching for specific science topics, mentors can illustrate the process of developing questions that highlight conundrums and point students in productive directions.

Fifth, mentors can identify promising inquiry teaching strategies and use pivotal cases to make these strategies visible and accessible. The mentor introduced a pivotal case by contrasting the process of answering a question 16 times for each group and instead interrupting the class to resolve the issue for all the groups.

Finally, by recognizing the links and connections between meaningful learning, inquiry teaching, complex science projects, and technology-enhanced learning, researchers can strengthen science understanding. When teachers link classroom learning from projects, learning environments, museum visits, textbook exercises, and laboratory investigations, they help students view themselves as making sense of science, critiquing new information, and reformulating their ideas. Ultimately, we need not only to link these varied aspects of science learning but also to align assessment with effective science instruction so that tests emphasize the goal of meaningful, coherent understanding.

AUTHOR'S NOTE

This material is based upon work supported by the National Science Foundation under Grant Nos. 9873180, 9805420, 0087832, 0311835, 55000247, and 9720384. Any opinions, findings, and conclusions or recommendations expressed in this material are those of the author and do not necessarily reflect the views of the National Science Foundation.

This material was partially prepared while the author was a Fellow at the Center for Advanced Study in the Behavioral Sciences with support from the Spencer Foundation.

The author appreciates helpful discussions of professional development with the Web-based Inquiry Science Environment (WISE) project. Special thanks go to Doug Kirkpatrick, who patiently explained the process of science teaching, and to Jim Slotta, who has collaborated on this project.

The author appreciates help in production of this chapter from David Crowell, Scott Hsu, Deanna Knickerbocker, and Tram Tran.

CHAPTER 4

Curriculum-Focused Professional Development: Addressing the Barriers to Inquiry Pedagogy in Urban Classrooms

Nancy Butler Songer

Teachers across the nation, particularly self-starters we call "mavericks" (Songer, Lee, & McDonald, 2003), continue to provide pockets of success of classroom-based meaningful learning with technology (MLT). As one example, Detroit Public School middle school teachers associated with the University of Michigan's BioKIDS research project (www.biokids.umich.edu) guide sixth-graders' use of weather-imaging software toward forecasting live storms and other meaningful uses of technology that, combined with an inquiry-focused learning environment, result in significant improvements in comprehension of basic weather concepts (Songer, Lee, & McDonald, 2003). Interestingly, not only do these teachers help students understand basic weather concepts, but their careful guidance of knowledge development with learning technologies also provides motivational learning opportunities in science (Mistler-Jackson & Songer, 2000). Research results associated with technology-rich learning environments like these suggest that learning technologies that are used carefully can be important tools in guiding today's students in complex reasoning in science and other content areas.

While these successes with learning technologies exist, they are not commonplace. They often cluster in resource-rich schools, serving students who are, largely speaking, not at risk for school failure (Songer, Lee, & Kam, 2002). This chapter discusses strategies that contribute to the promotion of meaningful learning with technology, with a focus on meaningful uses where the technology is integral to the curricular program. The examples discussed draw from implementation in resource-poor urban classrooms that, by and large, support students at risk for school failure. Through a discussion of what works in resource-poor urban environments, this chapter also invites a discussion of better means of moving beyond pockets of success clustered in resource-rich schools toward more widespread implementation of meaningful uses of technology across a range of classrooms, teachers, and audiences.

I begin with a description of the constraints we have observed to meaningful learning with technology in the middle school classrooms of one large urban district with a high rate of poverty, followed by a description of a professional development partnership we have developed to address these constraints. The partnership description includes an overview of the driving ideas behind the design of the teacher workshops, curricular programs, and key players. Following the discussion of the partnership, I outline several lessons learned within this partnership over the past 3 years.

WHAT CONSTRAINTS CHALLENGE MLT
IN URBAN CLASSROOMS?

While many teachers across the nation struggle to incorporate technology into their classroom activities in meaningful ways, teachers in low-income, resource-poor urban classrooms often face particularly daunting challenges. Over the past 3 years, our research project has focused on the promotion of meaningful learning with technology within one large, resource-poor urban school district (Songer, Lee, & Kam, 2002; Songer, Lee, & McDonald, 2003). Although we have achieved success in several different ways, one of our important findings was the identification of several constraints to meaningful learning with technology that inhibit an ability to realize successful MLT outcomes. These constraints included both technology-focused issues common in any school using new technologies, as well as issues commonly experienced in any resource-poor urban classroom. Regardless of their origin, these constraints needed to be addressed before meaningful learning with technology could be realized in our classroom settings.

The first category of constraints observed focused on technological resources and experiences. In our urban school district, we observed very poor Internet reliability in many classrooms and buildings, as well as a high degree of inexperience among teachers with technology outside of the classroom (Songer, Lee, & Kam, 2002). To challenge these constraints directly, we designed our Web-based learning tools to be available both on the Internet and on stand-alone CD-ROMs so that the learning activities could continue even when reliable Internet connections were not available. In addition, we provided a series of ongoing summer, weekend, and after-school professional development opportunities to help teachers become more comfortable with the tools in their classrooms.

A second category of constraints observed were those unrelated to the technology directly, but often associated with resource-poor schools in general. These constraints include inadequate space, materials, and equipment; large class sizes of 35 or more students; teachers with little autonomy; teachers who felt unsupported by administrators; and a large percentage of teachers with insufficient background in the content knowledge they teach, such as science (Songer, Lee, & Kam, 2002). Although some of these constraints were beyond our control, our research team worked hard to address issues of space, materials, and equipment through loans and equipment sharing whenever possible. We also invited school administrators to our professional development workshops to encourage greater understanding and support within teachers' own buildings. To address weak science backgrounds, we focused portions of our professional development workshops on the specific science content addressed in the curricular units so that, once again, teachers could experience learning about weather forecasts or biodiversity themselves, encouraging their ability to become more comfortable fostering such learning in their classrooms.

Current research indicates that it is easy to view resources such as materials, space, and money as crucial inhibitors to MLT, but that a focus on resources provides only limited understandings of how to improve MLT on a larger scale (e.g., Cohen & Ball, 2002; Songer, Lee, & Kam, 2002). Although we were concerned with resources and support in facilitating MLT in urban classrooms, we need research and guidelines that go beyond the presence or absence of particular resources toward insights into how resources should be used toward meaningful learning with technology and strong learning outcomes.

The role of technological tools in learning is the third area of constraints we observed in our work. Adopting a curricular focus to examine MLT in urban classrooms, our research team consistently realizes evidence of strong student learning outcomes associated with instructional programs that integrate technology as a central learning resource (e.g., Songer, Lee, & Kam, 2002; Songer, Lee, & McDonald, 2003) as contrasted with outcomes from a technology-rich program focused on proficiency with technological tools. Our emphasis on curricula and learning goals shifts our research questions toward what kinds of guided inquiry instruction help students in urban schools to realize strong learning with technology. How much "guidance" is needed, and what roles do teachers and technology play in this guidance?

Our shift to the role of curricula in promoting meaningful uses is also supported by current research on MLT. Becker (2000) found that although computers are nearly ubiquitous in America's classrooms, the ways in which learning technologies are used varies considerably between students from low- and high-income backgrounds. Whereas students from high-income backgrounds often use technology for problem-solving and higher-order thinking activities, students from low-income backgrounds often use technology for more mundane, repetitive tasks. In another study of schools in California, Cuban (2001) found that although computers were present and used by many at home, less than 5% of the teachers studied used programs with technology integrated into regular curricular activities. Collectively these results suggest that despite the presence of computers in schools, many students, particularly those from low-income backgrounds, are not experiencing meaningful learning with technology as a part of regular classroom activities. Adopting a focus on professional development and research around curricular programs might provide important insights into meaningful uses of technology that lead to strong learning outcomes.

WHY CURRICULUM-FOCUSED PROFESSIONAL DEVELOPMENT?

One of the earliest decisions made in our shift to curriculum-focused professional development as a means to achieve MLT was to select a highly focused population. The research discussed here represents our work within one urban district, one age group (middle school), and one content area (science). Even within this focus, we were faced with the implementation of meaningful learning among 33,000 students and teachers within 50 different schools.

The urban population was chosen as a focus for several reasons. First, we recognized current research documenting the growing number of children enrolled in America's urban districts, where large class sizes, social and disciplinary problems, and low involvement from parents challenge teachers' abilities to foster meaningful learning through technology (Agron, 1998). Second, we recognized that urban students represent a large proportion of minority students nationwide (67%) and a large percentage of students eligible for free and reduced-price lunch (52%; Young, 2000). Both of these populations are often overlooked in studies focusing on meaningful learning with technology. For our work, we focused on middle school students within the eighth-largest school district in the country, the Detroit Public Schools (DPS). While we run curricular programs that are coordinated among hundreds of schools nationwide, our focus on DPS has shifted our population of participants to include a majority of diverse schools from 1999 on (see Table 4.1).

Over the past several years, we have come to realize that the benefits of our urban district–university partnership include (1) a focus on science curricula as the vehicle for meaningful use of technology as opposed to the development of content-neutral technology skills; (2) classroom activities driven by research on how children learn; and (3) ongoing, sustained relationships. Each of these is discussed below.

SCIENCE CURRICULA AS THE VEHICLE FOR MEANINGFUL LEARNING WITH TECHNOLOGY

With DPS middle school teachers, we adopted a model of professional development that focused on curriculum as the agent of change (e.g., Ball & Cohen, 1996; Blumenfeld, Fishman, Krajcik, Marx, & Soloway, 2000; Songer, in press; Songer, Lee, & Kam, 2002). Our approach is supported by a National Science Foundation–funded partnership that includes both the Detroit Public Schools and the University of Michigan. Our partnership, Learning Technologies for Urban Schools (LeTUS), holds promise for impact because of the many benefits of a multiyear district–university partnership.

In our approach, the university and district partners meet regularly to discuss, design, and implement standards-based, technology-rich curricula focusing on science topics essential to that grade level and outlined

TABLE 4.1. Number of Schools Participating in Weather Program by Percentage of Minority Students (1996–2000)

School Population	1996	1997	1998	1999	2000
Number of schools with <20% underrepresented minorities	17	No Data	44	38	101
Number of schools with >20% underrepresented minorities	14	No Data	31	96	103

by district curriculum guides. We recognized that while we held a strong interest in using technology in meaningful ways, we viewed the learning goals—both science content and science inquiry—as the driving force behind all professional development work in the partnership.

How did we use learning goals and standards-based curricula to foster rich professional development experiences with technology for teachers? We developed a model for professional development called CERA: Collaborative construction of understanding, Enactment of new practices in classrooms, Reflection on practice, and Adaptation of materials and practices (Blumenfeld et al., 2000). In this model, the central work of the professional development workshops and study groups is the collaborative construction of understandings around particular science units, including units focusing on ecology and biodiversity, weather, simple machines, water quality, and communicable diseases. All partners participate in our workshops, including teachers, researchers, and school administrators. After detailed discussion and work with these curricular units, teachers and university personnel work together to implement modified or new practices in classrooms, including making sure the teachers are well supported in the implementation of the new technologies toward learning goals. After classroom practices have occurred and student outcomes are realized, teacher study groups and workshops focus on guided reflection on their practices so that improvements of both the curricular resources and the practices can occur in future iterations. In all of these activities, all partners are equal participants, and all voices are equally valid. In these ways, the LeTUS model of professional development provides an environment in which teachers, administrators, and researchers engage in dialogue and develop collaborative understandings of inquiry-focused curricula and the appropriate use of technological innovations towards learning goals.

MIDDLE SCHOOL SCIENCE CURRICULA AND HOW CHILDREN LEARN

Our work with LeTUS focuses specifically on technology-rich middle school science curricular programs. Why do we focus only on professional development within one discipline, science? This decision is grounded in the extensive research on how children learn, including how children learn best with technological tools (Bransford, Brown, & Cocking, 2000). Foundational research on learning states that enduring understandings occur when learners obtain a deep foundational knowledge of concepts and facts placed within a meaningful context and organized in such a way that they can apply it to new questions in the future (Bransford et al., 2000, p. 16).

In our work, this idea means that in order to provide opportunities for deep, conceptual understandings of science through and with technology, students need to spend enough time with the concepts so that they can engage with scientific questions in some depth, work with scientific data toward patterns, and build explanations from their data toward claims and scientific conclusions. Learning technologies can play essential roles in these steps, as will be illustrated with specific examples later in this chapter. In each case, an essential starting place is a focus on how the technology is used to guide learning toward central concepts, as opposed to a focus on proficiency with technology or amount of time with the tools.

Another reason to select a specific discipline and audience was to encourage clear evidence of student learning. An important LeTUS partnership priority is to improve the number of students reaching satisfactory levels on state and national standardized tests in science. Research results for DPS from 1997 to 1999 indicated that although 37% of fifth-grade students performed at a passing level on the state standardized test, only 13% of eighth-grade students passed (www.detroit.k12.mi.us/data/2000data/testscores.htm). A major goal of the LeTUS partnership was to realize stronger learning outcomes than these through technology-infused curricular activities. Early results demonstrate strong learning gains as hoped (e.g., Songer, Lee, & McDonald, 2003).

LeTUS stakeholders, who also value the goal of making science relevant to students' lives, saw meaningful uses of technology as one vehicle to obtain relevance. DPS students are largely African American (91%), and a majority of students tend to come from moderate- to low-income households, with approximately 70% of DPS students eligible for free or reduced-price lunch. Like many urban children nationwide (e.g., see Barton, 1998), many DPS students tended to see existing science classes as irrelevant to their lives, neighborhoods, and communities. With such discontinuity, perhaps it is not surprising that only a very small number of urban students hold favorable attitudes toward classroom science (25%; Atwater & Wiggins, 1995). Our previous research (e.g., Lee & Songer, 2003) suggests that technological tools can be one good means for helping students to find more relevance in classroom science through carefully scaffolded visualizations, online dialogue with scientists, and real-time data collection.

ONGOING, SUSTAINED RELATIONSHIPS

Another central tenet of our approach is the establishment of ongoing relationships. The professional development workshops are not one-shot deals, but 2 weeks of concentrated work with science units each summer, followed by monthly Saturday workshops throughout the school year when that particular curricular unit is taught in classrooms. Teachers' work consists of ongoing dialogue about the curricular units, including dialogue focusing on learning goals, pedagogy, science content, management, and technological use and support. Cohorts of teachers enacting the same curricular program are supported by several individuals, including one university researcher assigned to each teacher, peers enacting the same program at the same time who meet in small study groups on weekends, and a team of LeTUS technology support personnel to assist in smooth implementation of network technologies, CD-ROMs, and Personal Digital Assistant (PDA) resources. Therefore, LeTUS personnel provide professional development resources in a sustained, ongoing manner. Professional development workshops and study groups foster discussions in and around classroom implementation so that each teacher can find assistance and means to interpret and rework the curricular program for his or her own audience toward the high standards we have collaboratively established.

Our professional development model is also growing in its own knowledge base. After 3 years of work within DPS, most of our teachers have enacted our curricular programs at least two times, thereby serving as essential resources for newcomers on the curricula, pedagogy, and technology. At this time, the LeTUS partnership has implemented seven science curricular units between fifth and eighth grades and has worked with approximately 50% of the middle schools in the district.

In summary, we support curriculum-focused professional development as a cornerstone for meaningful learning with technology. In the LeTUS model, teachers, administrators, and university researchers experience learning- and content-focused professional development over multiple years and multiple curricular units, all within the same schools and toward the same high goals. Our model of professional development is also consistent with current research on reform that stipulates that large-scale educational development projects addressing multiple aspects of the school system in concert are necessary to realize sustained reform (Vinovskis, 1997).

MLT LESSONS LEARNED THROUGH CURRICULUM-FOCUSED PROFESSIONAL DEVELOPMENT

Our professional development model uses curricula and technologies focused around congruent learning goals to help urban teachers challenge the constraints of meaningful learning with technology. What have we learned from 3 years within the Detroit Public Schools? The next sections address this question through four lessons learned, illustrated with examples from our own classrooms.

Lesson One: Use Strong, Inquiry-Fostering Curricula Integrated with Technology

As discussed earlier, the focus of professional development workshops is enactment and reflection on the inquiry-fostering curricular units. What do these foundational curricular programs look like? We have designed units of 6 to 8 weeks of inquiry-based activities that follow an activity structure known to foster enduring inquiry understandings among K–12 students (Songer, in press; National Research Council, 2000). Our activities build rich content understandings through students' engagement in scientifically oriented questions, some of which are guided by the activities and some of which are of the students' own choosing. After questions are selected, students are guided in the exploration of this question through data-gathering, data analysis, explanation building, and real-world predictions. The following section illustrates general principles through examples from a fifth-grade curricular unit.

Our newest unit is called BioKIDS: Kids' Inquiry of Diverse Species (Songer, Huber, Adams, Chang, Lee, & Jones, 2002). In this standards-based unit focusing on ecology and biodiversity, students explore questions of species abundance and richness relative to the collection of animal data in their own schoolyard. Students collect animal data using PDAs, small handheld computers commonly used for organizational activities such as keeping phone numbers or a daily calendar. In our case, the class set of PDAs has been loaded with a piece of software called CyberTracker (http://www.cybertracker.co.za/), an icon-based software tool developed by professional animal trackers to track the location and diversity of African animals in the field. Using a version of CyberTracker that we have rewritten to contain only Michigan-regional animals (see www.biokids.umich.edu), each student takes on the persona of a real African animal tracker to explore the question, What animals live in my schoolyard? To track and record the animals, the Detroit fifth-graders are equipped with binoculars, collection jars, butterfly nets, field guides, and magnifying glasses, along with the PDAs and the Michigan-based CyberTracker sequence. These budding zoologists find, record, and identify about 50 animals in their schoolyard in each 50-minute period. When specimen-gathering is complete for the day, PDA data are downloaded to a central classroom computer through the synching process, allowing animal data to be available for analysis and reflection in each of two possible display formats. As shown in Figure 4.1, students' data can be displayed on aerial photographs of the

FIGURE 4.1. Display of Selected Student-Collected Cyber-Tracker Data on Aerial Photograph of the Schoolyard

schoolyard so that students can ask questions about animal location, interdependence, and ecology.

In all our inquiry-focusing activities, learning technologies such as CyberTracker are used exclusively to promote deep conceptual understandings of science concepts and scientific reasoning, such as building explanations from evidence. In the BioKIDS activities, for example, CyberTracker is used to gather data, summarize data, and provide tangible evidence of species location and characteristics. Each of these roles is essential in supporting fifth-graders' development of inquiry reasoning skills such as "using appropriate tools and techniques to gather, analyze and interpret data," and "think critically and logically to make the relationship between evidence and explanations" (National Research Council, 2000, p. 19).

Lesson Two: Integrate Software Through Cognitive Transformations

Complementary to our first lesson is the careful integration of the technology, ensuring that all uses for the technology advance student understandings toward challenging learning goals. In our example of PDA animal data collection and analysis, the role of technology was to support science inquiry learning rather than another goal such as a reward after the curricular unit or a remedial drill-and-practice resource for those needing additional skills training. PDA data collection and analysis are meaningful uses of technology that are embedded in the unit and that contribute

toward student understanding of the science content and scientific thinking skills. In this unit, using technology is essential to obtaining an understanding of biodiversity, explanation-building, and data analysis. Similarly,
the learning goals of understanding ecology, biodiversity, and explanation-
building are made more meaningful and relevant to students as a result
of the technology. To quote one teacher's view of this idea, "To use technology to let them explore and find answers for themselves—that was one
of my goals, and I think that was something they really enjoyed . . . it [the
technology] brings it, [the learning], more into their world."

An essential step toward obtaining strong, inquiry-focused uses of
technology is realizing that transformations are required to turn technological resources into powerful cognitive tools. The following section briefly
outlines the steps we performed to transform our technological resources
into powerful tools for learning.

Our first transformation was of the digital resources themselves. Early
on, we recognized the educative potential of the CyberTracker software
for allowing even young children to participate in the gathering of animal
data over a particular geographic region. To realize this potential, however, we needed to transform the original CyberTracker sequence created
for professional animal tracking in Africa into a learning resource for fifth-
graders focusing on tracking Michigan-based species (e.g., we did not expect to be able to find too many *kwagga*, the Afrikaans word for zebra,
around Detroit). As a result, we worked with computer programmers and
zoologists, especially Dr. Phil Myers of the University of Michigan Museum
of Zoology, to rewrite the CyberTracker code, resulting in a data collection sequence that supported fifth-graders' ability to collect accurate data
on Michigan-based animals.

The transformation of CyberTracker consisted of us asking three basic
questions: Who is our intended audience? What is our learning goal?
What level of support of guidance is needed? To address the questions
of audience and learning goal, we identified goals that were consistent
with the National Science Standards (National Research Council, 1996)
and the Michigan Curriculum Framework science benchmarks (Michigan Department of Education, 1996, pp. 80–123) for this age group. Figure 4.2 provides a sample of the science content and scientific inquiry
goals we identified as central to our purposes.

In examining the level of guidance needed, we looked carefully at the
kinds of data students gathered with CyberTracker and then we developed
scaffolded curricular activities that would utilize these data toward achieving specific inquiry goals, such as "building explanations from evidence"
(Songer & Wenk, 2003). Knowing that many children have trouble distinguishing salient information from irrelevant data when looking at au-

FIGURE 4.2. Science Content and Inquiry Standards Addressed in the BioKIDS Program

- Food webs identify the relationships among producers, consumers, and decomposers in an ecosystem.

- Millions of species of animals, plants, and microorganisms are alive today.

- Students need to develop an awareness and sensitivity to the natural world, including an appreciation of the balance of nature and the effects organisms have on one another, including the effects humans have on the natural world.

thentic science data (H. Lee & Songer, 2003), we also recognized that our data collection interface would need to be organized in a simple and powerful way so that students could easily locate the information they wanted.

Following these guidelines, we reworked the CyberTracker sequence of data into a simpler sequence focused on a selected subset of data on each specimen identified, including the kind and location of the animal, the number of animals, and the habitat in which they were found in their schoolyard. Figure 4.3 displays a sample database record illustrating the number of animals and the kinds of animals observed in three schoolyard zones. Records of animals observed are used by students in answering science inquiry questions about species abundance, richness, and diversity.

A second transformation necessary to support meaningful learning with technology was the organization of a set of technology-rich curricular units into a coordinated program with consistent and repeated use of technological tools. Research in science education, such as that discussed in the Science Education Standards (National Research Council, 1996), documents that fostering complex thinking among K–12 students and teachers takes time. In our current climate of intense accountability on standardized tests heightened by the threat of school failure, often teachers have only a few days to promote meaningful use of any given technological tool. Use of technological tools is rarely coordinated to support a larger goal or designed to build productively on past experiences.

Our research suggests that we should combat this problem directly through coordinated sequences of units that use technological tools in common ways and toward common goals. Our ongoing research focuses on working with cohorts of students as they use coordinated curricula and technology during their fifth-, sixth-, seventh-, and eighth-grade years.

FIGURE 4.3. Display of Student-Collected CyberTracker Data as Observed in Three Schoolyard Zones

CyberTracker Zone Summary

Animal Name	Zone A	Zone B	Zone C	Zone I	Other zone	Micro Habitat	Total Abundance for Each Animal
🦎 Northern spring peep	0	0	0	0	100	- In water - On plant - On something hard - Other microhabitat	100
🐦 American crow	0	0	0	2	0	- On something hard	2
🐦 Black-capped chickad	0	0	0	1	0	- On plant	1
🐦 Blue jay	0	0	0	1	0		1
🐦 Bonaparte's gull	0	1	0	0	0		1
🐦 Dark-eyed junco	0	0	0	1	0	- On plant	1
🐦 House finch	0	0	0	2	0	- On plant	2
🐦 House sparrow	0	11	0	0	0		11
🐦 Northern cardinal	0	0	0	1	0	- On plant	1
🐦 Ring-billed gull	10	0	0	0	0		10
🐦 Rock dove	0	0	0	0	0		0
🦌 White-tailed deer	0	0	0	0	0	- On plant	0
🦫 Woodchuck	0	0	0	0	0		0
🐍 Unknown snake	0	0	1	0	1		2
Unknown	300	11	12	0	0	- On plant - On something hard	323
Total Animal Abundance	322	27	30	14	112		505
Total Animal Richness	5	11	6	12	4		30

Parallel assessment systems have also been designed that are sensitive to knowledge development over multiple units and years (Songer & Wenk, 2003). For example, several units might emphasize inquiry thinking, "building scientific explanation from evidence," using different science data collected through the same or different technological tools. More advanced units will expect analysis of more complex data and the development of more sophisticated explanations. For example, we expect to utilize the Model-It software to model key components of weather in the sixth-grade weather unit and components of water quality in the seventh-grade unit, but the analysis and explanation-building in the later years are expected to be more complex.

Lesson Three: We Need Clear Evidence of Success of MLT

In order to make compelling arguments about the value of MLT, researchers and educators need to provide clear evidence that students have learned important concepts and developed rich understandings. What kinds of evidence of "meaningful use" might serve as compelling evidence?

To address these questions, we have designed measures of MLT based on learning theories of how children learn (e.g., Bransford et al., 2000) and current research on measuring student understandings (Mislevy et al., 2002). Our assessments measure three kinds of understandings that are often intertwined: knowledge of science content, knowledge of scientific reasoning skills, and meaningful use of technology. Our assessment instruments come in three formats, including multiple-choice items released from national or international tests, open-ended items, and practical exam items requiring students to visit stations to do practical problem-solving activities with technology tools like CyberTracker. Many assessment tasks are designed to evaluate particular reasoning skills, such as "building explanations from evidence," which can involve science content, inquiry thinking, and meaningful use of technology to perform successfully. In addition, recent work in the development of assessment systems to evaluate the development of scientific inquiry has resulted in an organization of assessment tasks at three levels of complexity (simple, moderate and complex). Figure 4.4 illustrates a simple and moderate assessment task used to measure students' ability to build explanations from evidence associated with biodiversity. For more information on our assessment design, see Songer and Gotwals (2005).

Research results demonstrate that even after the first unit, students who have utilized our curricular program rich in content and reasoning scaffolds demonstrate significant learning gains over students who did not utilize our curricular programs to learn about biodiversity, with more than 40% of urban students in the treatment condition demonstrating the highest level of competence in reasoning about complex problems in biodiversity on posttest items without any scaffolds or guidance (Songer & Gotwals, 2005).

Our research continues to fine-tune our assessment tasks to become more valid and reliable measures of content, inquiry, and meaningful use of technology. While this work is ongoing, our efforts to develop measures of fluent use of technology in particular contexts is an important advance in that it complements the more common practice of measuring students' fluency with tool use. Our work also helps advance understanding of appropriate roles for technology within standards-focused programs.

FIGURE 4.4. Biodiversity Questions Mapped to Simple and Moderate Complexity Levels of Scientific Reasoning and Scientific Content

---

Step One Simple Question

A biologist studying birds made the following observations about the birds. She concluded the birds would not compete for food.

Bird	Food	Feeding	Where they feed
Bird 1	berries	dawn/dusk	trees, middle
Bird 2	berries	dawn/dusk	trees, lower
Bird 3	berries	dawn/dusk	trees, upper

What evidence supports her conclusion?

    a.   insects are plentiful
    b.   they feed at different times
    c.   they feed in different parts of the trees
    d.   they lay eggs at different times

Step Two Moderate Question

Shan and Niki collected four animals from their schoolyard. They divided the animals into Group A and Group B based on their appearance as shown below:

Group A: Group B:

They want to place this fly   in either Group A or Group B. Where should this fly be placed?

A fly should be in   Group A /Group B
                         Circle one

Name two physical characteristics that you used when you decided to place the fly in this group:

(a)

(b)

Lesson Four: Promote Flexible Means for Meaningful Uses of Technology

Our final lesson ends with the idea, or more correctly the ideal, of using technology to support complex thinking. In science education, a common belief is that classrooms using technology for science inquiry should appear noisy and driven by students' own questions. An ideal classroom might consist of small groups of students engaged in a variety of self-guided activities, with the teacher moving from group to group acting as a resource and guide. For many teachers this image is not realistic within the constraints of their schedules or schools. As a result, teachers might feel that they cannot support MLT because they cannot conform to such an idealistic image. We believe that the definition of what MLT looks like in classrooms needs to be broadened to include many examples and formats. In our work, we redefine technology-rich inquiry activities to fit a class size of 35, a common size for urban schools in our region. We advocate teaching the same essential components of MLT, but we encourage variations that allow teachers or students to adapt the support structures or format of presentation when needed. We see these variations as bearing some similarity to the variations discussed for certain cases of complex reasoning, such as inquiry reasoning in science or critical thinking in history. In these cases, researchers recognize that guidance and scaffolding are essential to guide students in the development of the critical thinking and reasoning skills desired. In inquiry science, recent National Science Standards documents (National Research Council, 2000) present variations of what it means to perform inquiry science such as "engaging in scientifically-oriented questions." On one extreme, students are very self-directed and are posing questions themselves. On the other extreme, learners are engaged with questions provided by teachers, technological tools, or other resources. While the latter example is often not viewed as a rich example of scientific inquiry, research demonstrates that structured, scaffolded manifestations of engaging with questions not only are most productive for learners new to inquiry reasoning, but provide necessary guidance for future learner-directed reasoning activities (Songer, Lee, & McDonald, 2003). In another example, students in our sixth-grade weather program use our Internet browser and visualization software to obtain live weather maps before making forecasts of tomorrow's weather. We learned that our sixth-graders needed very specific guidance to locate salient weather features; otherwise, students' ability to forecast live storms was not possible (H. Lee & Songer, 2003). Again, specific guidance was necessary to guide first experiences with inquiry reasoning and set important reasoning foundations for more independent activities.

These examples remind us that we need to continue to develop multiple exemplars of classroom-based MLT that we can share within professional development communities so that teachers in a variety of environments can have strong and successful models to follow. We believe such an approach can help a wide range of teachers to be effective as agents of meaningful learning with technology without being discouraged by narrow or unattainable views of how to use technology in their classroom.

CONCLUSIONS

Meaningful learning with technology involves the cognitive transformation of technologies and curricular products into powerful tools for learning. Such transformations involve coordination between the learning goals and the resources used to foster those goals, including the curricular activities, professional development workshops, and technologies themselves. Also important, it takes time to foster deep conceptual understanding of concepts and meaningful uses of technology, often much longer than a one-shot exposure. Students and teachers need multiple exposures and sustained experiences with a given technological tool to develop deep conceptual understandings of the content associated with the meaningful use of the technology. Sustained relationships among teachers are also needed to support longitudinal learning with technology, and to support best practices associated with the coordinated curricular units and assessment tools.

CHAPTER 5

Seeing the Meaning "Hidden" in History and Social Studies Teaching

ROBERT B. BAIN

In the last few years, "deep understanding" and "meaningful learning" have emerged as key phrases for educational reform. Used across various school improvement movements, these phrases touch upon long-standing desires to set the instructional horizons beyond memorization or rote learning. As instructional goals, deep understanding and meaningful learning encourage teachers to teach beyond typical exam expectations to help students acquire useful knowledge with robust connections to authentic intellectual and cultural activities. Like other educational phrases, such as "active" or "cooperative" learning, deep understanding and meaningful learning are powerful rallying points. After all, who could oppose teaching that helps students develop meaning or understanding?

However, like many other widely accepted educational concepts, these ideas run the risk of becoming mere expressions that stand for much, but provide little substance for the practitioners who must figure out how to achieve such lofty goals. Ironically, schools might be adopting "meaningful learning" and "deep understanding" without engaging in the substantive conversations and investigations that promote deep meaning and understanding about these ideas themselves.

This chapter pauses to consider meaning and understanding in the teaching of history and social studies. I will focus the majority of my remarks on history education and not social studies. Since history is a central feature of social studies education, most of my comments will apply to the entire field of social studies in schools. However, an essential feature

Meaningful Learning Using Technology, edited by Elizabeth A. Ashburn and Robert E. Floden. Copyright © 2006 by Teachers College, Columbia University. All rights reserved. Prior to photocopying items for classroom use, please contact the Copyright Clearance Center, Customer Service, 222 Rosewood Dr., Danvers, MA 01923, USA, tel. (978) 750-8400, www.copyright.com.

of my argument is that meaning-making in social studies employs *disciplinary* means to develop and build connections across facts and concepts, identify and verify facts using evidence, and create and test warrantable assertions.

Different disciplines, as Hirst (1965) and Schwab (1978b) have argued, develop the habits of mind and cognitive procedures to create meaning within their fields. Although social studies seeks (or claims) to be an integration of many distinct disciplines (National Council for the Social Studies, 1994), I am not confident that such a goal has yet been achieved. Therefore, I find it more difficult to locate patterns of meaning-making within the social studies field than I do in history or one of the social sciences, such as political science, psychology, sociology, geography, or economics.

Three questions shape this chapter: First, what do we know (or seem to know) about meaningful learning in history classrooms? That is, what appear to be the common understandings about history teaching? Second, what more is there to meaning-making and understanding in history than has been commonly discussed? Or, to use a key metaphor for this chapter, what are the hidden characteristics that make history meaningful for historians and history students? And, finally, given the technology focus of this volume, how might instructional tools—those with and without plugs—support meaningful learning in history?

WHAT DO WE KNOW ABOUT MEANINGFUL HISTORY TEACHING AND LEARNING?

So, what do we know about meaningful history teaching and learning? Judging from popular conceptions of school history, teaching (and learning) of history in the United States have not always been particularly meaningful, thoughtful, or interesting. At the very least, history education is cursed by bad publicity. Is there another teacher more satirized than the history teacher, typically pictured droning on and on and on, haunting students with litanies of irrelevant facts to memorize? Unfortunately, such bad press may not be totally unwarranted. For at least a century, educational critics and school reformers have pointed to high school history teaching as the model par excellence of meaningless, fact-driven instruction. Consider, for example, the introduction to a series of nineteenth-century books on teaching, edited by psychologist G. Stanley Hall:

> History was chosen for the subject of the first volume of this educational library because, after much observation in the schoolrooms of many of the

larger cities in the eastern part of our country, the editor . . . is convinced
that no subject so widely taught is, on the whole, taught so poorly. (Hall,
1886, p. vii)

Popular culture joins educational critics in depicting ways in which history and social studies teachers turn their content into a dry compilation
of names, dates, and events. In this view, social studies classes often look
like Ben Stein's now-famous rhetorical economics recitation in the movie
Ferris Bueller's Day Off:

> In 1930, the Republican-controlled House of Representatives, in an effort to
> alleviate the effects of the . . . Anyone? Anyone? . . . The Great Depression,
> passed the . . . Anyone? Anyone? The tariff bill? The Hawley-Smoot Tariff
> Act? Which, anyone? Raised or lowered? . . . raised tariffs, in an effort to
> collect more revenue for the federal government. Did it work? Anyone?
> Anyone know the effects? It did not work, and the United States sank deeper
> into the Great Depression. Today we have a similar debate over this. Any-
> one know what this is? Class? Anyone? Anyone? Anyone seen this before?
> The Laffer Curve. Anyone know what this says? It says that at this point on
> the revenue curve, you will get exactly the same amount of revenue as at
> this point. This is very controversial. Does anyone know what Vice Presi-
> dent Bush called this in 1980? Anyone? Something-d-o-o economics. "Voo-
> doo economics." (Internet Movie Database, 1990–2005)

Such a view of teaching—caricature though it may be—embodies the
concern that, as Hall wrote more than a century ago, "[t]he high educational value of history [and social studies] is too great, to be left to teachers who merely hear recitations, keeping the finger on the place in the
text-book, and only asking the questions conveniently printed for them
in the margin or the back of the book" (Hall, 1886, p. viii).

Poor teaching leads to the second piece of common wisdom about
school history: Student learning has not always been filled with meaning.
Ironically, for all the emphasis teachers seem to place upon facts, most state,
national, and international tests reveal how little students remember. Students confuse key events in U.S. history, failing, for example, to locate such
important historical events as the Civil War within the appropriate century (Ravitch & Finn, 1987). Young adults' ignorance and confusions are
a *Tonight Show* staple, with Jay Leno going out into the street to ask simple
questions about history, geography, and government, and eliciting an even
simpler answer—for example, "Oh, Europe? It's on the northern border
of the United States." Teachers have collected student malapropisms, providing some humor in the midst of growing concerns of educational failure—for example, "Gravity . . . is chiefly noticeable . . . in the Autumn

when the apples are falling off the trees" (Lederer, 2003, para. 36) or "Drake circumcised the world with a 100 foot clipper" (Lederer, 2003, para. 23). Facts, facts, and more facts—it appears that teachers obsess over them while students do not know even the most elementary information.

Of course, beyond such popular conceptions and criticisms, educators know that history and social sciences are more than the mere accumulation and transmission of facts. Scholars understand that the social studies disciplines provide unique ways of coming to know the social world, providing distinctive approaches to gathering, using, and interpreting data, and offering meaningful explanations to understand our individual and collective experiences. Likewise, most teachers know that learning these subjects involves more than merely memorizing facts, but also involves active meaning-making by students. Just as scholars employ disciplinary habits of mind, so meaningful learning involves students working with distinctive historical or social problems, concepts, and intellectual processes.

However, this move from meaning-making within the history and social science fields to meaning-making within the classroom has been fraught with difficulty. Often the move from scholarly history to school history is marked by the assumption that "students learn best and most usefully . . . [when] being asked to master the conclusions of scholars about questions the students only dimly comprehend" (R. H. Brown, 1996, p. 267).

Recently professional organizations, curricular standards, and the instructional literature have taken a very different stance, arguing that students understand the social studies disciplines best when they are engaged in disciplinary meaning-making themselves. A consensus is emerging around the idea that "doing" a discipline is critical to learning it. In history, this in part means using primary sources to pursue history's "big" questions. Using primary sources has now become the sine qua non of history teaching and assessment. Document-based questions, first formulated by Advanced Placement history tests, have become one of the most widely used tools to assess students' capacity to think historically. Primary-source excerpts populate textbooks or form the valuable and popular supplements. The *Magazine of History, Social Education,* and other teaching journals now include primary-source-based lessons in each issue. This move toward the "doing" of history by framing big questions and using primary sources is an encouraging attempt to make history more meaningful by making it parallel the active practices of the discipline of history. It is an important step in moving us away from the simple transmission of facts, names, and dates.

Still, it is important to ask, Is there more to doing history and social studies than analyzing evidence to answer driving questions? Beyond using sources and questions, what else makes history's content meaningful?

What else helps to create meaning from what at times appears to students as laundry lists of discrete and disconnected facts?

IS THERE MORE? LEARNING TO SEE HISTORY'S SECOND RECORD

When trying to understand and improve a practice, it makes sense to look to expert practitioners. Therefore, in trying to help students develop meaning from discrete historical facts, it makes sense to look to people who occupationally work to make meaning of the social world—historians, sociologists, geographers, economists, and political scientists. Each belongs to a community that has developed a disciplinary "tool kit" filled with established modes of inquiry, evidentiary criteria, and accepted patterns of analysis (Bain & Ellenbogen, 2001). Considering the ways historians and social science scholars use information in their work can help teachers understand *how* meaning develops and is framed. In short, social studies teachers at all levels can benefit by trying to understand the meaning-making structures of the subjects they teach—the concepts and processes used to develop meaning within the respective fields.

Disciplinary scholars work with two types of knowledge: one is the content (or substance) of the discipline and the other is its organizational/ conceptual structure. Although both are essential, it is this second type of knowledge that is critical for meaning-making and forms the center-piece of this section. There are a number of ways to represent disciplinary knowledge. I have found that one of the most useful, particularly for history teachers, comes from the work of philosopher and historian Joseph Hexter who asserted a very useful distinction between the two different "records"—the first and second—that historians work with and on (1971). Although writing specifically about history, Hexter's ideas about the first and second records help illuminate all the social studies.

The first record, Hexter argues, consists of the events, the content, and the substance of the surviving past. This is the "stuff" of historical and social scientific study. However, this record of the past or the social world is merely "a set of points" that, no matter how "closely arrayed they may be, all by themselves they do not make a [meaningful] pattern." The meaning and pattern, Hexter argues, are added to the facts and are

> always the work of a historian or of someone acting in the capacity of a historian. . . . It always involves an inference. The points themselves do not have the dimension of history and cannot alone legitimate the inference. To legitimate it the historian himself must supply something. Without that

something there can be no history, and that something must come from the second record, since there is no place else for it to come from. So without resort to the second record there can be no history at all. (1971, p. 82)

This distinction—between the subject's first-record "stuff" and the second-record intellectual processes that give meaning to the "stuff"—is a crucial distinction for teachers to see, understand, and use in teaching all the social studies disciplines. Indeed, it appears to be the critical element that keeps history and social studies learning from being just "one damn thing after another." What makes the distinction complicated is the ease with which students and teachers can typically see the first record—the factual, event-laden flora and fauna of the social world—while the second record is often tacit and difficult to see. Yet, as I shall demonstrate, failing to recognize the disciplinary second record condemns students to confusion or forces them to use their own second record to create meaning that might run counter to that of the field.

To illustrate how the second record brings meaning to substance, I will use a modest series of examples of first- and second-record thinking. To begin, I created a list of historical "stuff": a randomly generated list of first-record facts, events, documents, and names from U.S. history (see Figure 5.1). These words are in no logical order or organizational pattern. If you see an order or meaning, then you are bringing your own "second record" to these words. I listed these with no meaningful organizational pattern in mind.

However, in the five examples that follow (Figures 5.2–5.6), I used different second-record concepts to create meaning out of this "stuff." In Figures 5.2 through 5.6 below, I brought different conceptual layers of organization to the same set of items and thus imposed new meanings on the same terms. Begin by looking at the restructured list in Figure 5.2. Can you see the connections that led to my structuring these 12 items into seven categories? Take your time, as it may not be immediately obvious how I restructured the first-record items. The pattern in the chart is not explicit. No label tells you how I structured the terms or organized them to provide new meaning. Here, as in all the examples that follow, the first record stays visible while the second record remains implicit and embedded in the organizational structure. Figure 5.2 might prove particularly difficult because the relationship between the words in each category is not obvious. Often people look at the separate elements, the terms and names, repeatedly without being able to see a unified or connected whole. Of course, that is one of the points of this demonstration. Often our students experience history in school without being able to see the links that connect discrete elements to give them meaning. Therefore, students often

FIGURE 5.1. First Record of "Stuff" from
U.S. History

Progressive Era
Lincoln
Columbus
Woodrow Wilson
Civil War Period
Colonial Era
Antebellum Period
Seneca Falls Resolution
Revolutionary War Period
Declaration of Independence
Emancipation Proclamation
Exploration and Discovery

FIGURE 5.2. How Is This Historical
"Stuff" Organized?

Lincoln
Columbus
Woodrow Wilson
Progressive Era
Colonial Era
Civil War Period Antebellum Period Seneca Falls Resolution
Declaration of Independence Emancipation Proclamation Exploration and Discovery
Revolutionary War Period

fix their sights upon the separate and discrete elements. Meaning comes with and through the second record.

When you are finished thinking about Figure 5.2 (we will return to it later), look at the remaining examples in Figure 5.3 through Figure 5.6. Try to figure out their connections and order. Are some more evident and easier to see than others? What were the hidden second-record patterns in these examples? Skipping over Figure 5.2, I will begin with Figure 5.3, in which I arranged the terms in *chronological* order. Did it seem obvious and, therefore, easy? Don't minimize the intellectual work needed to see these relationships. If you recognized the chronological order, you brought a number of understandings to both the terms and the order—at bare minimum, you knew enough of the terms and their approximate dates and were at least somewhat familiar with social studies "stuff."

In Figure 5.4, I organized the terms by *type*, placing all the people in one category, the documents in another, and the eras in a third. For example, Wilson, Lincoln, and Columbus—historically quite different— shared a grouping because they were people. Easy? You were able to see the meaning *if* you knew the *type* of object each term represented.

What if I ignored the semantic meaning entirely and treated each term as a word made up of separate letters? How might I then organize these words? In Figure 5.5, I used the first letter of each term or phrase and arranged the items *alphabetically*. To see this, you did not have to bring any separate understanding about the term's temporal place in history or object category, but rather had to recognize them as English-language words and know that we could structure them alphabetically. A similar pattern guided this organizational structure in Figure 5.6, where I again grouped items by *type, except* here the number of words in each phrase defined the category, i.e., one-, two-, or three-word phrases. Often people's prior understanding of the words' meaning interferes with their making sense of this list, leading to internal dialogues such as, So, what could Columbus and Lincoln have had in common? Why would Woodrow Wilson be in the same category with the Antebellum Period or Colonial Era? Might it have something to do with wars? Prior meaning, your tacit second-record connections, might have hindered your seeing the connections that I made in Figure 5.6 and interfered with your recognizing the organizational pattern or structure embedded here.

You can see that the first-record facts remained constant, but how I treated them changed. Given what I could guess about the second-record meaning you might bring to the list, I was able to organize the terms in increasingly more difficult patterns; that is, except for Figure 5.2, typically the most difficult pattern to see and the one we tackled first.

FIGURE 5.3. *Example 1*: How Is This Historical "Stuff" Organized?

Exploration and Discovery Columbus
Colonial Era
Revolutionary War Period Declaration of Independence
Antebellum Period Seneca Falls Resolution
Civil War Period Emancipation Proclamation Lincoln
Progressive Era Woodrow Wilson

FIGURE 5.4. *Example 2*: How Is This Historical "Stuff" Organized?

Lincoln Woodrow Wilson Columbus
Colonial Era Revolutionary War Period Civil War Period Exploration and Discovery Antebellum Period Progressive Era
Emancipation Proclamation Declaration of Independence Seneca Falls Resolution

FIGURE 5.5. *Example 3*: How Is This Historical "Stuff" Organized?

Antebellum Period
Civil War Period
Colonial Era
Columbus
Declaration of Independence
Emancipation Proclamation
Exploration and Discovery
Lincoln
Progressive Era
Revolutionary War Period
Seneca Falls Resolution
Woodrow Wilson

FIGURE 5.6. *Example 4*: How Is This Historical "Stuff" Organized?

Columbus Lincoln
Antebellum Period Colonial Era Emancipation Proclamation Progressive Era Woodrow Wilson
Civil War Period Declaration of Independence Exploration and Discovery Revolutionary War Period Seneca Falls Resolution

Now that I have treated the items as linguistics objects—organizing them alphabetically or by number of words in the phrase rather than as terms with historical meaning—look again at Figure 5.2. Do you see the pattern now? If not, look at Figure 5.7, where I have provided clues in the form of numbers next to each item. The numbers might have given you the clue you needed to see the grouping by *syllabic* pattern. In fact, I grouped the items by the total number of syllables in the words or the phrases.

These examples somewhat playfully reveal ways in which second-layer knowledge operates upon substance or content to give it meaning. Lee (2005) refers to these hidden organizers as the "rules of the game," the ideas that silently govern patterned action. Imagine playing or watching a baseball game *without* understanding the concepts that constitute action—such as walks, runs, balls, strikes—or the procedures that warrant actions—such as four balls equal a walk, three strikes equal an out, nine innings can equal a game. For someone without knowledge of these "hidden" rules, baseball would be a confusing mix of people walking, running, and going on and off the field with no discernable reason. One might sense that players' actions have a logic and, given the cheers and boos of the crowd, are meaningful; but without knowing the second-record connections, baseball would be very difficult to understand—exactly my experience

FIGURE 5.7. Revisiting Figure 5.2 (With Clues)

Lincoln (2)
Columbus (3)
Woodrow Wilson (4)
Progressive Era (5)
Colonial Era (6)
Civil War Period (6)   Antebellum Period (7)   Seneca Falls Resolution (8)
Declaration of Independence (9)   Emancipation Proclamation (9)   Exploration and Discovery (9)
Revolutionary War Period (10)

in trying to make sense of cricket or many of our students' experience studying history or social studies.

The second record influences every aspect of historical understanding and, consequently, of instruction. As the examples show, different systems provide different meaning to the same items. Indeed, shifting the organizational scheme alters features we pay attention to in a collection of facts. In one instance we note temporal features, while in another we attend to the linguistic elements. Thus, the second record is important and powerful because of its capacity to transform the shape and meaning of other historical facts and ideas.

Historians, historiographers, and a growing community of researchers in history and history education have identified a number of *vital* second-record concepts that give shape to history: *time, change, cause and effect, significance, accounts, evidence,* and *empathy* or historical *perspective-taking*. Although beyond the scope of this chapter to explore in depth, it is worth the effort for teachers to understand how these move history beyond a "one damn thing after another" collection of facts. There is a rich body of accessible scholarship exploring each of these concepts (see for example Lee, 2005; Lee & Ashby, 2000; Seixas, 1994). Understanding how experts in a field build meaning is a necessary feature in teachers' history and social studies knowledge.

However, knowing what makes history meaningful for expert practitioners is not sufficient for teachers. Teachers must do more than find meaning for themselves; they must help others develop such meaning. Teachers, therefore, must know how their students come to understand and find meaning in history and social studies. Here, again, the idea of the second record proves valuable because it can help teachers think about their students' preinstructional understanding of history and social studies.

STUDENTS' PREINSTRUCTIONAL IDEAS ABOUT TEXT, EVIDENCE, AND CAUSE

Our students are not blank slates when it comes to making sense of the social world, past and present. Students have their own second-record ideas that they employ when facing new experiences and information. They have developed logical ways to describe and explain the world, a logic that is often quite different from that of adults and historians. Indeed, the cutest and most humorous moments in talks with children, from Art Linkletter's *Kids Say the Darndest Things* to Jay Leno's *Tonight Show* to our own, occurs when children explain their thinking to reveal a distinct logic about the way the world works. For teachers, however, such comments are not so cute when these revelations follow instruction designed to deepen student thinking; for example, "Greeks believed in myths. Myths are female moths" (Lederer, 2003).

Teachers must be able to recognize, uncover, and work with students' preinstructional understandings of history and its methods, their ideas about causation or significance, or their assumptions about human behavior in the past and the present. Differences between the understandings of students and adults are not simply a by-product of the amount of knowledge or first-record facts they control, but rather of the way they organize information, ask questions, or employ intellectual tools. The differences reside in the second record. Hallden calls this web of students' preconceptions of history an "alternative frame of reference" (1994a). He makes the distinction between incorrect ideas arising from misunderstandings in instruction, that is, Columbus sailed before Cheng Ho, and "incorrect" ideas emerging from the "autonomous frameworks" that the students have developed for thinking about their experiences. Consequently, a student's incorrect answer or difficulty in understanding may not simply be a miscomprehension. Rather, it "may be a correct statement, if it is considered within a different system for describing and explaining the world. The answer may be consistent with other beliefs, but within a different context from that presented in the instruction" (Hallden, 1994b, p. 43).

Ideas that appear to teachers as illogical might make perfect sense when considered from the students' alternative frame of the social world. Further, behavior that on the surface appears similar might actually have very different meanings for students and social studies teachers. Consider how students and scholars—in this case, historians—read historical sources.

Differences Between Students' and Scholars' Views of History

Evaluating sources is an essential tool for historians and social scientists. History instruction and assessment have recently seen a rise in emphasis upon the use of primary sources. The document-based essay question (DBQ), which tests students' historical thinking by asking them to read and analyze unfamiliar primary sources, has become a dominant mode for assessing students' thinking, for example, on Advanced Placement exams and state proficiency tests such as the Michigan Educational Assessment Program test. As tests increasingly incorporate primary sources, it follows that more teachers look to use them in the classroom. It appears sensible because by using primary sources students are "doing" the work of historians and social scientists and thus are engaging in an "authentic" disciplinary activity.

But maybe the activity is not quite so similar. That, at least, is one im-
plication emerging from the research of Sam Wineburg (2001). Wineburg
demonstrated important differences in the way high school students and
historians read texts and approach sources (Wineburg, 1991b). Wineburg
taught a group of high school history students and a group of historians
how to employ the think-aloud method of reading, a research methodol-
ogy asking people to verbalize their thoughts while reading text. Then he
gave each group a set of primary source documents from the U.S. Revolu-
tionary War to read while expressing their thoughts out loud and compared the ways each accomplished the task (Wineburg, 2001, p. 64). The
students had completed successfully a U.S. history course and in some cases
had a greater factual knowledge of the events under study than did some
of the historians, particularly those whose specialty was not U.S. history.
Yet factual knowledge did not seem to affect how each group read the
sources. The historians employed multiple strategies while reading. They
corroborated sources within the document set, consciously attended to who
had created the source and the time of its creation, and worked to construct a larger context to situate the documents. All the historians tried to
corroborate, discover attribution, and contextualize each document and
the entire set. They engaged in a multilayered dialogue between the documents and their own questions, trying to understand the minds of those
they were studying while weaving tentative interpretations that successive readings challenged or refined.

And the students? They handled the documents as they did any text,
simply reading for information. They rarely paid attention to a document's
author, to the relationship among sources, or to the larger context surrounding the evidence. Students read documents in the order given and
from top to bottom. Unlike historians, students made their assessments
of the sources "without regret or qualification" (Wineburg, 1991b, p. 83).
In other words, they approached historical texts as vehicles of information,
reading simply to get the facts. Historians, on the other hand, "seemed
to view texts not as vehicles but as people, not as bits of information to
be gathered but as social exchanges to be understood" (Wineburg, 1991b,
p. 83).

These differences, Wineburg concluded, were more complicated than
differences in factual knowledge or reading skills. Rather, he argued that
the differences were "sweeping beliefs about historical inquiry, or what
might be called an epistemology of text. For students, reading history was
not a process of puzzling about authors' intentions or situating texts in a
social world but gathering information, with texts serving as bearers of
information . . . Students may have 'processed texts,' but they failed to
engage with them" (Wineburg, 2001, p. 76). Students did not share histo-

rians' disciplined understanding of text, and so naturally applied their autonomous frameworks and experiences to their reading.

There is a hidden pedagogical danger, then, in pushing students to become more active and do the work of historians. As more teachers follow the credo of "students as workers," we might be fooling ourselves, confusing the outward trappings of a disciplinary activity such as reading primary sources with the harder-to-see thinking that defines the activity in a disciplinary community. While demonstrating the overt elements of the desired behavior, students really may be doing (thinking) something quite different. Indeed, they may bring a different second-record stance toward history that silently shapes or even undermines how they perform "authentic" historical tasks.

Such underlying ideas influence students' understanding of the instructional activities we design, even when the activities use the discipline's big questions and primary sources. In an ongoing analysis of my high school students' work, I found that my ninth-grade world history students entered class with a clear conception of history, its purposes, and its processes (Bain, 2000a). In describing their understandings in the first days of class, students mixed homilies about history's value with dry images of the history classrooms that could have been taken from a Dickens's novel. For my students, history consisted almost entirely of facts about the past that are "always true." World history is "the study of different cultures . . . [having] to do with the study of maps." It is a "written record of events that happened in chronological order." For one student, history entailed objects drawn from the past: "if you got a pencil two days ago, you use it today, so now you are using history." History's value rests in its ability to inoculate us against errors, for example, "history repeats itself because we do not learn from our mistakes." When giving proof of these repetitive patterns, students give broad examples, for example, "there is always war." One student advises, "You cannot change history, but you can make history" (Bain, 2000a).

In other words, my students brought with them to the classroom a view that the past was filled with facts that historians retrieved for them to memorize in ways that somehow inoculate them—and us—against errors in improving the present. In a sense, my students had a positivist view of history. For them, history was a mirror of the past, and thus historical facts existed independently of the historian and could speak on their own. In the mind of these students, the historian's job is to gather information, analogously, say, to that of a photographer, who brings back "true" pictures of distant times, peoples, and places (Shemilt, 1983). Before I even started teaching history to my students, I often felt adrift in a sea of assumptions about the discipline that threatened to engulf the deeper, meaningful exploration of the past.

Ironically, students typically share a stance toward historical under-standing with their textbooks. History textbooks do not typically repre-sent history's uncertainties, "the fact that the story told is partly unknown and partly reconstructed from indirect sources"; or history's controver-sies, "the fact that different versions of the same story may exist and may be discrepant or even contradictory" (Britt, Rouet, Georgi, & Perfetti, 1994, p. 71). Textbooks, Crismore (1984) found, lacked the linguistic markers, such as "may," "might," or "possibly," that reveal the interpre-tative nature of historical thinking, filled with judgments and uncertain-ties. Rather, textbook language covered up the authors' uncertainties, interpretations, or leaps to conclusions. This reinforces students' habits of reading for facts instead of reading for interpretations or to understand the mind of the author. "What happens," Crismore wonders, "to critical reading (learning to evaluate and make judgments about truth condi-tions) when hedges . . . are absent? When bias is not overt (as it is not in most textbooks) are young readers being deceived?" (Crismore, 1984, p. 279). Such texts reinforce the ideas students hold about history as an accumulation of past facts.

Given the correspondence between the students' presuppositions about the nature of the discipline and the structure of textbooks, it should come as no surprise that students often see textbooks as more reliable and free of bias when compared to other sources (Gabella, 1994). Students held the textbook with the highest regard as an exemplar of historical knowl-edge (Gabella, 1994). The "credibility of a source varies inversely with apparent human craftsmanship"—a presupposition of which teachers who are trying to have students think like historical artisans must be aware (Crismore, 1984, p. 279).

This is in almost direct opposition to the ways students try to explain historical change and causation. Here human agency takes the upper hand, pushing structural factors, such as economics, politics, or ideology, to the side. A number of studies revealed how history students gravitate to the personal to explain historical events. For example, Carretero and his col-leagues (1994) in Spain asked students in the sixth, eighth, and tenth grade and graduate history majors to rank order examples of personal, political, economic, ideological, or global explanations for the pivotal events of 1492 in world and Spanish history. When comparing the re-sults, Carretero discovered that history graduate students valued struc-tural explanations, for example, changes in international trade, over personal explanations of human wants or desires. The history majors tried to locate personal actions *within* larger structural contexts. However, precollegiate students consistently ranked personal agency, intentions, and desires as the most compelling explanations for historical changes.

Most surprising was how little change in causal reasoning occurred between grades 6 and 12 (Carretero et al., 1994).

This presents a powerful challenge for history teachers seeking to push their students to understand large-scale structural changes and their impact in history, a particularly important goal for secondary history teachers. Even if the textbooks or lessons include structural explanations, students are likely to translate structural trends into personal desires or personify abstract categories, for example, "the middle class wanted." In one study, Hallden (1994b) interviewed and observed a teacher whose major focus during a unit was large-scale political change in Sweden. However, this line of thinking was almost totally absent from the students' writing or in their conversations about class. A transcript from class discussion showed students steadily using personal explanations to answer the teacher's structural questions. Hallden concluded that although the teacher presented events "mostly by reasoning at the structural level," the "students try to contextualize given information through their personalized concept of history" (p. 35). Working with different and competing second records, teachers and students did not share the deeper meaning of the inquiry. At best, students learned to use the language of the teacher without using the meaning. At worst, students got lost in the teacher's language, whose meaning was hidden from their view.

History students, although studying the far away and long ago, may still be thinking in the here and now. They may be using their personal, temporal, racial, gender, ethnic, or regional memories to give meaning to what and how they study in history. For example, Professor Peter Stearns (1999) has described patterns he noticed in his university world history course, where students' assumptions about the West and modern life quietly shaped their experiences in the course. Lee and Ashby (2000) described students who consider people in the past as generally less intelligent than those in the present, displaying a "temporal-centrism" that makes historical empathy very difficult. T. L. Epstein (1997) has identified differences in the views that white and black students have toward history. White students in Epstein's study thought that textbooks, teachers, and the library were the most trustworthy historical sources, whereas the African American students thought that families, teachers, and movies could be trusted, rarely mentioning textbooks or libraries. Although sitting in the same classroom and participating in the same lessons, students bring to and take from instruction very different understandings (Epstein, 1997).

As these studies clearly demonstrate, students have their own second-record ideas about history as a discipline and about what counts for evidence, explanation, or veracity. Students' preinstructional conceptions typically live far from the underlying ideas and beliefs of historians. Failure to consider students' disciplinary assumptions when planning or enacting instruction is a risky enterprise for dedicated history teachers. It is particularly crucial for beginning teachers. Beginning teachers are often concerned with behavior—their own and that of their students. When pressed to consider knowledge and understanding, novice teachers are concerned about their own knowledge, behavior, and actions. Without some prompting and guidance, teachers typically ignore students' thinking.

Just as historians' underlying second-record views make meaning of their disciplinary work, so do students' conceptions shape the meaningful activities in which they engage. Therefore, teachers must go beyond designing instruction around big questions and primary sources, but must also attend to students' second-record understanding of *evidence, cause and effect, significance,* and *history* itself. At minimum, teachers must probe student thinking to make visible students' second-record ideas, because these will shape the meaning of even the most engaging historical problem or engaging primary sources.

Teaching in Light of Students' Ideas

It is tempting simply to urge teachers to be aware of how students might approach historical documents and sources. Such advice is complicated when we consider Yeager and Davis's study of how history teachers themselves approached historical texts (Yeager & Davis, 1996). In replicating Wineburg's (1991b) study with teachers, Yeager and Davis found little evidence that teachers regularly corroborated evidence, looked for attribution, or constructed context when reading multiple sources. Although there was variation among the teachers in the study, the majority approximated the reading habits of the high school students in Wineburg's study. Yeager and Davis agreed with Wineburg that the main issue was not the "acquisition of a fund of historical knowledge," as "[e]ach [teacher] appeared to know a great deal of historical information," but rather it was teachers' beliefs and ideas about history that proved critical (Yeager & Davis, 1996, p. 161). Such research raises important questions about teachers' underlying beliefs of their subject matter. If teachers see history and the social sciences as a mere accumulation of facts or stories, how will they be able to help students develop meaning beyond that of those facts or stories? If teachers' views of the second record do not approximate those of the disciplinary experts, then teachers might (unwittingly?) transform curricular or pedagogical moves designed to promote student meaning-making back into lessons that merely transmit facts. Preservice and inservice education, then, must reveal and challenge teachers' ideas of the subject matter and its instructional challenges.

Does this mean that we must wait until teachers and their students develop more sophisticated ideas about primary sources *before* engaging in active, disciplined inquiry in studying history? That is, before effectively using primary sources or essential questions, must students (and, of course, teachers) already see history as more than a simple search for facts? Must they approach history as a way of thinking that demands particular skills, for example, corroboration or significance, *before* they can develop such meaning?

My experience as a history teacher as well as a sociocultural researcher points to ways to use and develop instructional technology—tools *with* and *without* plugs—to embrace what Bereiter (1985) has called the learning paradox: that, to develop sophisticated meaning in a discipline, students must already have sophisticated meaning. Such instructional tools allow history teachers to recognize students' naive views of evidence and significance, yet support them in developing disciplined meaning in history and social studies. I address the use of such discipline-specific thinking tools in the rest of this chapter.

TOOLS WITHOUT PLUGS TO SUPPORT
SECOND-RECORD THINKING

Five years ago, both my youngest daughter and I packed up and moved from a high school in Ohio to college at the University of Michigan. Ilana moved to Ann Arbor to join the 1998 freshman class, while I was becoming a junior faculty member in the School of Education after 26 years as a high school history and social science teacher. As you could predict, both of us packed "stuff" for which we had little use (our Ohio State T-shirts, for example, turned out to be a liability in Ann Arbor). However, both of us discovered after 4 years of college that the most important things we carried with us were the *tools* we developed while in high school.

Actually, the most important teaching tool I carried with me was the concept of "tool" itself. First introduced through the work of Vygotsky (1978), the idea that tools mediate all higher mental functioning helped me rethink a critical instructional problem. Indeed, the idea has shaped all my subsequent teaching and scholarship on teaching (Bain, 1997, 2000a).

What was the instructional problem that the concept of tools helped me meet? Like many teachers, I was committed to using active pedagogy to help students develop discipline-specific habits of mind and conceptual understanding. Essentially, I trusted that by "doing" the discipline in my classroom—that is, learning history by doing history or learning sociology by doing sociology—my students would acquire more sophisticated habits of mind. They did not. Such higher-level thinking was difficult for students to do, practically unnatural (Wineburg, 2001). Active learning alone did not seem to improve their thinking dramatically.

The call for active learning, while essential, begs the instructional question about the ways students actually engage with authentic activities, such as reading primary sources to investigate the past. As discussed above, most history students, like most adults, read text for information, scanning it for relevant facts, whereas historians "habitually" go beyond facts, actively working to use authorial perspective, context, and other evidence to weave an interpretation. I tried to teach such thinking skills—most high school history teachers at minimum hand out sheets explaining "how to read primary sources"—yet my students typically did not use them outside my watchful eye or forceful reminders. Although engaged in the trappings of doing history by reading primary sources, students rarely internalized the historical stance toward the practice.

Of course, a few students would master these sophisticated intellectual skills and most could appropriate the language of the historian, for example, "primary source." However, the majority of students' performances revealed how difficult it is to graft new "expert" ways of thinking *over* their old novice ways. In a sense, I had committed what I have elsewhere called the *tabula rasa fallacy*, a logical mistake that assumed my students had no preinstructional habits for dealing with primary sources, conducting inquiry, or drawing conclusions from evidence (Bain, 2000b). If students were so blank, it followed that timely exposure to disciplinary practices would produce positive results. However, my experiences showed that such instructional *imprinting* did not work. Students' preinstructional habits were deeply ingrained, not easily replaced even by authentic disciplinary activities.

Something was missing from the "learning by doing" prescription. The problem rested in my taking a practice from a community of scholars—for example, reading primary sources—and transplanting it into a body of student novices. Scholarly tasks embedded within an expert community draw meaning from the *group*'s frames, scripts, and schemas. However, students who are learning a discipline do not yet share such disciplinary understandings. The features that sustain a practice within the community of scholars rarely exist within a classroom. Consequently, although students may initially accept the transplanted activity—for example, reading the primary sources or conducting an inquiry—they typically reject the higher mental functioning carried by the practice. Thus the activity often left their naive or scholastic habits intact (Gardner, 1991). I had to do more than lift the practice from the scholarly discourse community; I had to transplant the "sociocultural prerequisites" of these practices as well (Kozulin, 1998). Here is where the ideas of sociocultural tools became so instructive.

Kozulin (1998) defines such sociocultural, cognitive tools as "those symbolic artifacts—signs, symbols, texts, formulae, graphic-symbolic devices—that help individuals master their own natural psychological functions of perception, memory, attention, and so on" (p. 1). Theoretically, sociocultural tools bridge the gap between individual acts of thinking and the more sophisticated cognition located in a community's practices (Kozulin, 1998). Tools assist learners in performing many more competencies than they could independently. "Until internalization occurs, all performance must be assisted" (Tharp & Gallimore, 1988).

Intrigued by the theory, I worked to translate these ideas into my teaching practices. I read widely in epistemology and in discipline-specific cognitive studies to identify critical but often hidden features of the disciplinary practices we used in class, for example, working with primary sources. To make those features visible for students, I created history-specific tools by embedding that thinking into classroom artifacts and interactions to support students as they "did" history. I developed a host of history-specific visual prompts, linguistic devices, discourse, and conceptual strategies to help students learn content, analyze sources, frame historical problems, corroborate evidence, determine significance, or build historical arguments. We designed posters to assist in determining historical significance and invented and used symbols—H_{EV} and H_{AC}—to capture the critical differences between history-as-event and history-as-account (see Bain, 2000a, for a more detailed description of these tools). Surrounded by these supports, students regularly used the posters and terms—in class and on homework or tests—to make sophisticated distinctions in weighing significance or assessing competing historical accounts. Over the semester, students decreased their reliance upon the tools while continuing to use the intellectual distinctions the tools symbolized.

Helping students use historians' heuristics when working with primary sources was another site where cognitive tools proved fruitful. By modifying students' discourse procedures to reflect the strategies historians use when reading primary sources, I established reading procedures that enabled a group of students to read and question sources *together* in ways they did not do on their own (Bain, 2000a). The key was a disciplinary-specific division of labor where each pair of students became a particular type of historical question or questioner, that is, "corroborator" or "sourcer." Within these roles, students questioned classmates about documents. While some questions aimed at reading comprehension, for example, identifying confusing language, most of the questions were specific and central to historical inquiry. Thus, students posed questions that expert historians might ask, interrogating classmates about a source's creator, its intended audience, and evidence that supports or challenges its assertions. Although I equipped students with questions that structured what the class considered, they decided when and how to ask the questions and, more significantly, how to use the texts to work out the answers with their classmates.

Different from a typical group activity in which the group divides the content of a topic, here the division of labor was based on the thinking needed to engage in a complex intellectual task. Using discipline-specific questions to interrogate one another and the texts helped students avoid their preinstructional habit of treating historical text only as a site for facts. Structuring the discourse patterns enabled the students as a group to participate in a difficult historical analysis in advance of their capacity to do so individually. Over the term, students took on more than one questioning role until most students engaged in the reading without needing the ascribed questions. Instead of my lowering standards or allowing novices to merely mimic experts, the cognitive tools were able to carry most of the intellectual load so students could participate fully in a disciplinary practice (Cole, 1996).

I began to see the classroom as a "considerate" environment: one that challenged students to do difficult work but was considerate enough to provide them with the tools they needed to do such work. Some colleagues argued that I was giving students "crutches," fostering a dependence upon the artifacts and discourse procedures. Rather than reject the analogy, I embraced it. Few people use crutches unless they need them, and most people cast them aside when they do not. So it was with my classroom tools. When the posters, discourse strategies, or terms got in students' way or slowed their thinking, they stopped using the supports. However, the tools remained available for those times or students who needed assistance.

To help my students learn to think like historians—to help them employ history's second record—I designed various types of visual, linguistic, and discourse tools specific to the practices and tasks I was asking students to perform as they "did" history and social studies. However, these tools were limited to the classroom, that is, they did not extend beyond the limits of classroom time and space. However, my emerging experiences with new electronic technology enabled me to transcend some of those limits to give students access to cognitive tools outside the classroom.

TOOLS WITH PLUGS: CREATING CONSIDERATE
TECHNOLOGY FOR LEARNING HISTORY

Electronic technology has made historical and social scientific resources more accessible to students, teachers, and historians. Without minimizing the serious gaps in technological equity across school districts, it appears that we have realized the potential of new technology to deliver instantly vast amounts of historical material and virtual historical experiences. "Google" the words "history resources for students" and you will get almost 3 million English-language hits, while "history resources for teachers" yields nearly 2 million sites. Although the quality and usefulness of these sites varies widely, it is clear that the Internet has put access to information of truly historic proportions literally at the fingertips of historians, history teachers, and history students. For historians and history teachers, such innovation is cause to rejoice. Getting efficient access to materials has been an enduring and endemic problem for historians and history teachers. However, for generations of history students who experienced history and social studies classes as "giant data dumps" (Rosenzweig & Thelen, 1998), electronic access to more sources does not hold the key to more meaningful understanding.

Electronic technology, however, can offer students more than access to vaults of information. In this section, I argue (and demonstrate) that computers and the Internet can become powerful instructional tools in the sense discussed by Vygotsky (1978) and Kozulin (1998), rather than mere "gophers" for primary sources. Redesigned by history teachers, the new technology can become a sociocultural tool that can bridge the gap between students' novice acts of thinking and the more sophisticated cognition located in a discipline's practices (Kozulin, 1998). In other words, teachers can redefine and shape the computer into a history– or social-science–specific tool to help learners engage in meaningful history and social scientific thinking. It can enable teachers to *mediate* and *support* student historical thinking, even when students are working independently or outside class.

How might computers provide such support for students' meaning-making in history or the social sciences? What form might technology take to help students meaningfully study the past? In answering these questions, I want to reconsider the second-record issues we have already discussed, the reading of primary sources, and ask, How might technology help students use more expert historical thinking—to use corroboration, sourcing, and contextualization—as they approach and use primary sources in studying history?

As a high school history teacher, I developed a set of electronic tools to assist students working in my world history class. The examples I am

discussing come from work I began as a high school history teacher and
have subsequently developed, refined, and expanded through collaborations at the University of Michigan. While teaching high school history in
1997–98, I developed a number of Web tools to support ninth-grade students studying world history (Bain, 1999, n.d.).

One tool that I constructed used the hypertext capabilities of Web
pages to explore ways technology could support students as they read
primary sources. In this instance, I attempted to extend the discourse procedures we used for reading sources (described above). Although the
system described above worked quite effectively, it did not extend to students' independent work. With no special training in html or Web design, I began to experiment to see how the computer might support
students' thinking about historical sources, even when working outside
class or our classroom discussions.

In the most successful design, I built a frame around the historical
sources to hold scaffolds that students could use as they read. Figure 5.8
shows a picture of a Web page I built around a section of Olaudah Equiano's
(1791) autobiographical account of slavery and freedom, *The Interesting
Narrative of the Life of Olaudah Equiano or Gustavus Vassa, The African* (Bain,
1999). Figure 5.9 shows a more reader-friendly version of the same page.
The text sits in the center of a frame of navigation tools and, most importantly, learner-centered, history-specific supports. How did this help students develop meaningful connections to the evidence and sources they
used?

First, and most immediately, students encountered phrases to the left
and right of the text that reminded or prompted them to use various cognitive procedures while reading the historical source. A number of the
prompts helped students make sense of the document in front of them on
the computer screen. The frame on the left urged students to:

- Identify key vocabulary
- Create a storyline or summary
- Select and organize key ideas
- Identify the author
- Determine the type of source

Borrowed from metacognitive reading procedures (for a discussion of
these see Bruer, 1993), these prompts aimed at helping students make
meaning of any text or source by encouraging them to identify confusing
language, define hard-to-understand words, summarize key points, and
predict patterns. While recognizing the importance of reading literally to
establish meaning, the prompts in the left frame do little to reflect the

FIGURE 5.8. Sample Web Page

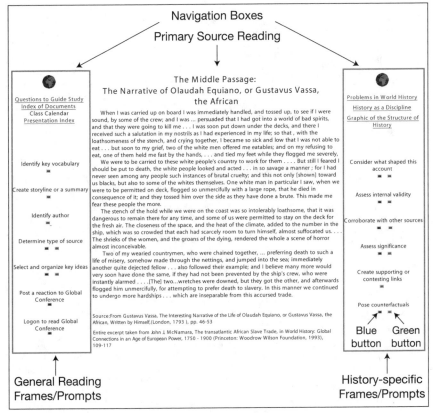

Source: Bain, 1999.

disciplinary-specific ways in which historians analyze sources. They are, rather, generic supports to help students read for comprehension.

The discipline-specific supports essentially reside on the frame to the right of the text. These prompts encouraged students to think like historians, to analyze as they read the sources.

- Consider what shaped this account
- Assess internal validity
- Corroborate with other sources
- Assess significance
- Create support or contesting links
- Pose counterfactuals

FIGURE 5.9. More Reader-Friendly Version of the Same Web Page

Questions to
Guide Study
Index of
Documents
Class Calendar
Presentation
Index

Identify key
vocabulary
Gr
Create storyline
or a summary
Gr
Identify author
Gr
Determine type
of source
Bl Gr
Select and
organize key
ideas
Bl Gr
Post a reaction
to Global
Conference
Bl
Logon to read
Global
Conference
Bl

The primary source reading is framed by scaffolds to help students analyze the text. Green buttons give students questions to help analyze text. Blue buttons take students back to work earlier in course where we first studied and tried to make sense of historical analysis. Try the blue button for "determine type of source."

The Middle Passage:
The Narrative of Olaudah Equiano, or
Gustavus Vassa, the African

When I was carried up on board I was immediately handled, and tossed up, to see if I were sound, by some of the crew; and I was ... persuaded that I had got into a world of bad spirits, and that they were going to kill me ... I was soon put down under the decks, and there I received such a salutation in my nostrils as I had experienced in my life; so that , with the loathsomeness of the stench, and crying together, I became so sick and low that I was not able to eat ... but soon to my grief, two of the white men offered me eatables; and on my refusing to eat, one of them held me fast by the hands, ... and tied my feet while they flogged me severely,

We were to be carried to these white people's country to work for them . . . . But still I feared I should be put to death, the white people looked and acted . . . in so savage a manner ; for I had never seen among any people such instances of brutal cruelty; and this not only [shown] toward us blacks, but also to some of the whites themselves. One white man in particular I saw, when we were to be permitted on deck, flogged so unmercifully with a large rope, that he died in consequence of it; and they tossed him over the side as they have done a brute. This made me fear these people the more.

The stench of the hold while we were on the coast was so intolerably loathsome, that it was dangerous to remain there for any time, and some of us were permitted to stay on the deck for the fresh air. The closeness of the space, and the heat of the climate, added to the number in the ship, which was so crowded that each had scarcely room to turn himself, almost suffocated us . . . . The shrieks of the women, and the groans of the dying, rendered the whole a scene of horror almost inconceivable.

Problems in
World History
History as a
Discipline
Graphic of the
Structure of
History

Consider what
shaped this
account
Bl Gr
Assess internal
validity
Bl Gr
Corroborate
with other
sources
Bl Gr
Assess
significance
Bl Gr
Create
supporting or
contesting links
Bl Gr
Pose
counterfactuals
Bl Gr

Source: From Gustavus Vassa, *The Interesting Narrative of the Life of Olaudah Equiano, or Gustavus Vassa, the African, Written by Himself,*(London, 1793), pp. 46-53   Excerpt taken from John J. McNamara, The transatlantic African Slave Trade, in *World History: Global Connections in an Age of European Power, 1750 - 1900* (Princeton: Woodrow Wilson Foundation, 1993), 109-117

Contact: Bob Bain at bbain@umich.edu

Available at www.umich.edu/~bbain/display/courseshs/historyproblems/atlantictrade/
equiano2.htm

Note: "Gr" and "Bl" refer to the green and blue buttons on the Web pages.

For each primary and secondary source, I provided prompts to help students employ sophisticated, expert tools to read, analyze, and develop meaning from the sources. The frame encouraged students to ask questions about the source, about its creation, creator, use, and context. It surrounded the student with reminders to look for internal contradictions or suggest other sources that might support, expand, or contest one's understandings of the source under investigation. The frame provided memory aids to help students formulate disciplinary questions and think more strategically about the source.

It is important to remember that these were scaffolds, supports available to assist students to perform cognitively challenging tasks. The frame *did not* teach these intellectual skills. As historiography, educational scholarship, and experience demonstrate, students have a difficult time developing the intellectual habits of corroboration, weighing significance, posing counterfactuals, assessing bias, and explicating perspective. Further, their everyday thinking about these often complicates their learning (Wineburg, 2001). Therefore, teachers must *explicitly* teach each of these intellectual processes to students. It is important to remember that the computer scaffolding does not substitute for instruction, but rather supports students in developing disciplinary habits after they have had at least initial instruction in each procedure.

For example, early in the semester I introduced students to the importance of corroborating sources and looking for internal validity. We began with students' experiences to introduce and demonstrate the importance of these procedures. Then we practiced these using a number of handouts, situations, and examples. Corroboration became one of the questions students posed to one another as we read document sets together in the classroom. In other words, the electronic scaffolds supported thinking *after* we worked on these thinking procedures in class, through explicit instruction and with explicitly purposed materials.

However, all teachers know that even with the most explicit and thoughtful instruction, some students (indeed, often most students) do not remember or cannot transfer such learning to new situations. Even with a prompt suggesting that they corroborate or determine what factors shaped an account, students do not automatically connect the scaffold to earlier instruction. Here is another place where the computer can serve as a tool to link students to the lessons, notes, and classroom artifacts in which they first learned a procedure. That is, not only can the technology remind students of previous instruction, for example, corroborate this source, but it can "send" students back to the time, lessons, and artifacts that first taught the procedure to them.

To accomplish this, I added a button (blue on the Web page but desig-
nated with a "Bl" in Figure 5.9) below each historically specific scaffold/
prompt that students could use to reconnect to the specific materials we used
to teach or explain that second-record procedure. For example, if a student was not certain about the different types of historical sources—
primary or secondary—the blue button under the "Determine the type of
source" prompt would take them to the handout used in the first week of
class that explained the meaning of primary and secondary sources. Beyond
archiving classroom artifacts, lessons, or handouts for review, the computer
enabled me to link those prior experiences to later experiences. Students
thus could revisit earlier instruction and employ it meaningfully when
needed later in the course. Although not meant to replace the teacher or
classroom discussion, the frame and the button simulate the questions a
facilitator might ask to help the student focus more strategically on the
source, the type of thinking an expert might do around the source, *and* the
experiences that introduced students to the discipline-specific strategies.

In a sense, these links made visible the thinking of expert historians
who could explain why corroboration was important, what it means, and
how one corroborates. The technology captured the voices of historical
experts and allowed students to call upon such expertise as needed.

Of course, asking strategic questions—even those scaffolded carefully—
does not mean that students will be able to answer those questions for a
particular source. For example, remembering to ask about authorial intentions or perspectives—questions generated by the "consider what generated
this account" prompt—does not mean that one can read that source and
recognize its perspective. Students might need supports to use the strategy
for a specific document or source. Each scaffold/prompt, then, had another
button—the green button (or "Gr" in Figure 5.9)—that took students to a
set of questions or answers to support their analysis of a specific text.

For example, if students wanted more help in reading for authorial
perspective, the appropriate green button would take them to critical information about the author and some specific reading suggestions:

- Look at the adjectives the author used to describe his experience.
  How would you describe those adjectives?
- How did you feel reading this? Do you think the author wanted
  you to have that feeling? Why?
- What does the author think about what she describes? How do you
  know?
- Why do you think the author wrote this passage? Why do you think
  that? What in the text or what you know about the author or event
  leads you to this idea?

In short, technology enabled me to make the scaffolding process more dynamic, transcending the limits of the classroom tools I discussed in the previous section. The frame around the source surrounded students with disciplinary-specific supports, making the help available when and to the degree needed. Reading with this enhanced, student-friendly electronic document with its teacher-constructed cues was a very different activity than reading the same document on paper or on another Web site. In a sense, it placed a historian and a teacher by the student's side while reading. The cognitive prompts with links back to earlier lessons and forward to questions specific to the source established a virtual conversation between the novice and the expert. The embedded questions placed voices outside the text inviting students to think as historians by "endowing . . . inanimate texts with voices and proceed[ed] . . . to engage these voices in conversation" (Wineburg, 1994, p. 126).

This short discussion only briefly explores the productive features of electronic technology in helping students engage in learning that is more meaningful. The examples discussed above did not demonstrate ways we used the electronic technology to extend classroom discussions or to make visible students' historical thinking. These are all critical features in developing meaningful learning in history and social studies, and teachers can enhance them through strategic design and use of electronic tools. While incomplete, I hope this discussion at least encourages teachers to experiment with technology, to push it beyond its capacity to bring materials to students, and to employ it as a sociocultural tool to support students' meaning-making. In short, teachers should try to use the computer as a tool to support students' historical thinking.

CONCLUSIONS

To make teaching and learning in history and social sciences more meaningful, teachers must attend to the features that make content meaningful in the first place; that is, teachers must pay attention to the "stuff" that content experts bring to the content to make connections between and among the historical or social scientific facts. At minimum, this means teachers must pay attention to questions of evidence, significance, causation, consequence, periodization, explanation, and the construction of the accounts in the content they teach. Teachers must also be prepared to take stock of students' preinstructional understandings of these same features; that is, teachers should try to understand the "stuff" that students bring to the content that might support or hinder their more sophisticated meaning-making.

Teachers can then use their understanding of the content and of the range of students' anticipated interpretations to design learning environments that are both knowledge-centered *and* learner-centered. (See Bransford et al., 2000, for a discussion of these ideas.) An important feature of thoughtfully designed learning environments is the availability of appropriate disciplinary-specific tools—both with and without plugs—to help students engage in thinking that is both a prerequisite and a consequence of meaningful learning.

This is not a small task for educators, because it requires the willingness to develop a substantial understanding of learners, of learning, and of the content they teach. It also requires teachers to expand their capacity to design, assess, and share the cognitive, instructional tools they use to help students deepen their understanding. Districts and schools committed to make meaningful learning more than a catchphrase will have to support teachers in this enterprise through strategic, coherent, and long-term professional development focusing upon knowledge, learners, assessment, and teaching. I am confident—a confidence born of experience and research—that we will benefit from such an effort. I know that our students will.

CHAPTER 6

Mapping the Terrain for Meaningful Learning Using Technology in Social Studies

ELIZABETH A. ASHBURN, MARK BAILDON,
JAMES DAMICO & SHANNAN McNAIR

Maps are tools for helping us navigate from here to there. They also offer new vistas, paths of possibility, and expanded horizons. Historian John Lewis Gaddis compares the craft of the historian to that of a cartographer. The cartographer's skills of creating patterns and relationships help give meaning to the ambiguities and complexities of a terrain by reducing "the infinitely complex to a finite, manageable, frame of reference" (2002, p. 32). This metaphor of maps is useful in addressing the question of what teachers need to know and be able to do to teach for meaningful learning using technology. It provides images and language that can help educators understand what it means to navigate this "infinitely complex" terrain of students' achieving enduring understandings of content (in multiple social studies disciplines in this instance) and of using technology in ways that foster understanding (Jonassen et al., 1999; Wiggins & McTighe, 1998; Wiske, 1998).

Given the broad terrain for learning in social studies, constantly changing learning contexts, and the opportunity for technology to both simplify and complicate the terrain, skills in using maps and other tools for navigation are helpful. More importantly, teachers need to know how to map the location of learning at any given moment, so that instructional decisions build on the context in ways that move students effectively toward learning goals. The options for these instructional paths are infinite within this terrain for learning in social studies because of the nature of "here" (beginning with students' current knowledge, experience, needs, and interests), "there" (achieving enduring understandings of complex ideas, skills, and content in multiple disciplines), and the diversity of possible content and paths for the learning journey. Mapping in each moment the location of students in the terrain is critical to know what subsequent instructional steps will scaffold and guide them toward a particular journey's end. As the report from the National Research Council's Committee on Developments in the Science of Learning states, "Knowing where one is in a landscape requires a network of connections that link one's present location to the larger space . . . [I]t is the network, the connections among [learning] objectives, that is important" (Bransford et al., 2000, p. 139).

To map something means to establish or concisely describe with clarity *like* that of a map. This is different from *making* a map, which denotes creating an actual representation of a static area in some physical form. Concisely describing the location within "a network of connections" in the learning terrain illuminates possible moves toward the objectives. Mapping skills, then, are those that enable the identification of the terrain's particular features, the determination of one's location in the terrain, and the articulation of relationships among the features, the location, and the objectives in ways that inform instruction.

To further explain the importance of mapping for navigation, an example may be useful. When one of the authors realized that she was unable to get to a known destination efficiently because she was traveling through unfamiliar territory, she called en route to a colleague to ask for directions. Her colleague, of course, was unable to respond until she knew the author's location. Being unfamiliar with the terrain, the author had to perceive and then explain clearly the key features of her location. Not unlike the classroom context, her sense of urgency to make a navigational decision was intensified because of rush-hour traffic, the number of lanes, and the need to know where to turn. Because she knew key features to attend to—such as street names for the one she was on and the one just crossed, the railroad tracks in the distance, and her relationship to her starting point—and she had a mental model of street maps in general, she was able to create a set of information that located her position to get directional help.

Project TIME's approach to teaching for meaningful learning using technology offers a framework and a set of tools to help teachers do this kind of mapping in the instructional process. In this chapter, we respond to the question of what teachers need to know and be able to do to teach for meaningful learning using technology by discussing how a major component of this project addressed the question. Although the discussion is built around the example of Project TIME, we think that the general principles and ideas apply more broadly. (See the Introduction and chapter 1 for further description of Project TIME's work.) The project's framework and set of tools help locate with greater clarity the features and details of particular moments in the journey through the learning terrain in ways that indicate progress toward student understanding and how the path might need to change, what perspective might need shifting, or whether backtracking might be needed.

First and foremost for mapping the journey, teachers need to know and understand key features of the terrain for learning. The space of the terrain is what needs to be navigated, from here to there—from students' prior knowledge and understanding based on their experiences to specified learning outcomes. The terrain for learning considered in this instance is the social studies disciplines. Typically, this terrain is determined by particular content defined by state curriculum frameworks accompanied by student learning standards and benchmarks. Often implicit within the frameworks and standards are big ideas and methods of the disciplines. Project TIME's approach has emphasized these latter two components as explicit features to be addressed intentionally. The meaningful learning attribute of content centrality focuses on big ideas and methods of the discipline, in addition to subject matter content (see chapter 1). Because they are key to locating points for connection along the learning journey, they form a stronger and clearer definition of the terrain for meaningful learning.

Second, teachers need tools for mapping learning contexts, which, unlike roads and mountains, are constantly changing in the classroom. Project TIME has focused on three kinds of mapping tools, each of which delineates details that are important for locating at any particular point where students are on the learning journey. The tools Project TIME has used that help teachers map the learning journey are:

1. A clearly defined four-step process of disciplined inquiry: explore and develop questions; gather and evaluate information; analyze and interpret data and information; communicate new understandings. Students' engagement in active inquiry is one of the six attributes in Project TIME's MLT framework (see chapter 1).
2. A unit of instruction: the Mexico and Migration unit. This unit defines a sequence of learning tasks and assessment guidance as a route to reach a specified set of learning goals. Similar in concept to mapping an automobile journey, it lays out a model for how a

journey might be made when technology is integrated into learning experiences characterized by the MLT attributes.

3. A set of technology tools that contribute to moving efficiently and effectively through this complex learning terrain (see Appendixes A and B).

In the next section, we describe these tools and the three features of the terrain for learning. Then, using data from one of the project evaluation case studies, we describe ways in which one teacher used these tools and mapped the course for his students through the learning space defined by these key features. We also include some of his reflections on how he understood the development of his own knowledge and skill as he taught the Mexico and Migration unit. Finally, we reflect on ways in which Project TIME districts have supported teachers in developing these kinds of understandings and skills in teaching for meaningful learning using technology.

KEY FEATURES OF THE LEARNING TERRAIN

Big Ideas

Big ideas, as Project TIME has used the term, are defined by two important characteristics. First, they are core conceptual frameworks and principles that experts within the discipline recognize as powerful for interpreting the social and physical world. Research on the knowledge of experts indicates that it "is not simply a list of facts and formulas that are relevant to their domain; instead, their knowledge is organized around core concepts or 'big ideas' that guide their thinking about their domains" (Bransford et al., 2000, p. 36). Second, big ideas open windows within students' worlds by making the complex more accessible through reframing and renaming students' experience. Big ideas act both as lenses that can relate, integrate, and transcend isolated concepts and bits of information, and also as glue that can make coherent connections between the subject matter content and students' personal experience.

In the overview to Project TIME's Mexico and Migration unit, the importance of big ideas is explained:

In this unit, students explore their life experiences within the context of big ideas central to the social sciences and relate their own experiences to the unit's subject matter content. The intention is that they will begin to develop the big idea lenses of social scientists. Most students are unlikely to have developed such large mental models. To help students organize their knowledge around big ideas, this unit starts by connecting students to their lived experiences—in the classroom and school, as well as personal histories—and by scaffolding the development of these big idea lenses in ways that make sense to them. It then relates these personal contexts to the unit's subject matter content and, finally, to applications in the world beyond.

Three big ideas ground the subject matter content in the Mexico and Migration unit: *history as story, space becomes place,* and *culture as human creation.*

- Through *history as story*, students come to understand that history is controversial because differing accounts and interpretations exist about what happened in the past. Throughout the unit, students are encouraged to consider why different stories exist about the same segment of history and to think about what these multiple perspectives afford them in making sense of the world as individuals and citizens.
- Through *space becomes place*, students see how individuals and groups claim spaces and make them their own places governed by their own rules. Students come to understand how individuals and groups define identity, membership, and relationships through different uses of space. They are also encouraged to examine how these different spaces are shaped by issues of gender, race, class, nationality, and power.
- Through *culture as human creation*, students are introduced to culture as a dynamic and relative framework that changes with time and context. This lens helps students explore questions about how humans create culture, why cultures change, and how individual and cultural identities are intertwined.

Within these three conceptual frames, the lived experiences of students are used to help them understand subject matter, and subject matter is drawn upon to help students understand their lived experience. These ideas provide focal points for connections that help students make sense of complex content and experience. They encourage students to think about their own stories, spaces, and cultures; consider multiple perspectives; and make connections between their experience and the experiences of others, such as Mexican immigrants. Big ideas "help students 'learn their way around'" the discipline, to connect specific content knowledge to a larger network, "to understand an overall picture that will ensure the development of integrated knowledge structures and information about conditions of applicability" (Bransford et al., 2000, p. 139). By compelling learners to engage with the content in ways that have meaning for them and to connect the content to big ideas, students come to think broadly about the world and themselves in the world, develop understandings of their own and others' views of the world, and re-see the world in novel ways. As lenses, big ideas can be applied across disciplines and to issues beyond the classroom.

Subject Matter Content

Local, state, and national standards have been designed generally to provide a guiding vision for defining the content of what students are expected to learn and be able to do in each discipline. Social studies subject matter is a broad terrain for learning that includes multiple disciplines: history, civic education, geography, political science, economics, psychology, sociology, and anthropology. In Michigan, for example, standards and benchmarks are organized around seven strands: history, geography, civics, economics, inquiry, public discourse and decision-making, and citizen involvement. Within these 7 strands, 25 standards define the lay of the subject matter landscape (Michigan Department of Education, 1996). Teachers, however, must still make strategic decisions about the specific content and scope of units of instruction and activities for learning.

The Mexico and Migration unit models one particular set of strategic decisions about content. Designed for the sixth-grade curriculum, which in Michigan includes Latin America, it has also been adapted by Project TIME teachers for use in fifth- and eighth-grade contexts. The unit was developed by first defining the enduring understandings that are both desired as learning outcomes and related to the big ideas (Wiggins & McTighe, 1998). Key concepts and information were then selected for the unit that are important for achieving those understandings and that offer rich possibilities for making connections to students' personal experience. The content for learning tasks also addresses significant questions about long-standing dilemmas and problems and provides for multiple perspectives and interpretations.

Throughout the Web-based unit (most of the content for learning is accessible online, including video clips of interviews, photographs, various Web sites, and online databases), students study content about Mexico and migration as it relates to their own questions within the context of the unit's learning goals. For example, they investigate the El Paso/Ciudad Juarez border region, studying rural-to-urban migration and Mexican migration into the United States. They examine how rural and urban cultures blend and how borderland cultures emerge and develop. In particular, they consider the expansion of *maquiladoras* (assembly plants) that have developed in northern Mexican cities such as Ciudad Juarez. They also explore the controversies surrounding issues of water use in this border region. Students grapple with key historical content, including the Mexican-American War of 1846–48, the Treaty of Guadalupe Hidalgo, and the Gadsden Purchase, to further develop understanding of present-day border issues between Mexico and the United States.

Paying attention to this feature of the MLT terrain, then, means selecting particular subject matter content and organizing it for instruction in ways that develop students' enduring understandings, connect to students' personal experiences, and provide for multiple perspectives afforded by the technology.

Methods of the Discipline

Because social studies is a multidisciplinary field, historians and social scientists commonly use a variety of methods to create knowledge. Historians gather, organize, analyze, and interpret information about the past related to significant issues and questions, assessing various kinds of historical evidence and interpreting the evidence to produce narratives and other kinds of accounts of history. Political scientists and sociologists often use polls and surveys to marshal evidence for their claims. Geographers work with maps to understand spatial relationships. Other methods of investigation used by social scientists include interviews, social and psychological experiments, and ethnographic observations of human behavior and patterns of interaction. These methodological processes contribute to the development of knowledge in the disciplines that make up the social studies, and are, therefore, part of the terrain for student learning.

When students learn to use methods of the social studies disciplines, they are learning how to work with information in systematic and disciplined ways. They are learning how historians and social scientists gather and organize information, establish evidence and claims, and formulate reasoned interpretations and tentative conclusions (Bransford et al., 2000; Wineburg, 1991b). In using these methods, students develop understanding about what counts for evidence and knowledge in disciplinary communities. They are then able to use these methods to construct their own knowledge and understanding in subject matter.

In the Mexico and Migration unit, teachers work with students to develop facility with five social science tools: direct observation, interviews, surveys, tables and graphs, and maps. Students are expected to use these tools as they conduct their own investigations into the content area of

Mexico and migration. Teachers need to know how to relate these disciplinary methods to students' development of content knowledge as well as to the big ideas, and how technology can support the use of these methods within the process of disciplined inquiry. These are key features for navigating the terrain of thinking, doing, and knowing in social studies.

MAPPING TOOLS

Teachers need to understand and be able to use tools that help navigate the complex terrain of learning in the social studies disciplines. The navigational tools that Project TIME has found useful are: (1) a well-defined process of disciplined inquiry, (2) a curriculum unit with lessons that model the six MLT attributes and guide teaching for meaningful learning using technology, and (3) technology tools that support meaningful learning. Each clarifies components of the highly complex process of teaching for meaningful learning using technology. A four-step inquiry process provides a simple conceptual organizer to guide the development of higher-order thinking skills in learning particular content. The model curriculum unit demonstrates the nature of MLT attributes and how to embed them in social studies instruction. The technology tools provide an infrastructure that makes the journey of learning through this complex terrain possible and manageable.

The Process of Disciplined Inquiry

Disciplined inquiry is a powerful tool that enables making connections among standards-based content, big ideas, and methods of the discipline. Levstik and Barton define inquiry as "the process of asking meaningful questions, finding information, drawing conclusions, and reflecting" and disciplined inquiry as the purposeful act of seeking information or knowledge, investigating significant and important questions, and constructing knowledge "within a community that establishes the goals, standards, and procedures of study" (2001, p. 13). Disciplined inquiry as a navigational tool helps to identify the current locations of students' thinking in relation to their prior knowledge, the content to be learned, and big ideas and methods of the discipline, and provides a cognitive vehicle for directing the journey toward the desired ends.

Disciplined inquiry requires sophisticated cognitive processes (Wineburg, 1999). Teachers' skills in modeling and scaffolding these processes are critical for students in learning to

. . . actively try to solve problems, resolve dissonances between the way they initially understand a phenomenon and new evidence that challenges that understanding, put collections of facts or observations together into patterns, make and test conjectures, and build lines of reasoning about why claims are or are not true. (Thompson & Zeuli, 1999, p. 346)

Disciplined inquiry is also an important part of standards-based reform initiatives in the social studies. In Michigan, for example, inquiry is one of the seven core strands that frame the curricular standards and benchmarks. Students are to conduct investigations by formulating clear questions, "gathering and organizing information from a variety of sources, analyzing and interpreting information, formulating and testing hypotheses, reporting results both orally and in writing, and making use of appropriate technology" (Michigan Department of Education, 1996).

Consistent with findings from the National Research Council, the inquiry process that undergirds the Project TIME curriculum unit provides a model that makes explicit the kinds of thinking done by experts in history and the social sciences at a level of complexity appropriate for middle school students (Bransford et al., 2000, pp. 41–42). Students accomplish the unit's learning goals by following a four-step inquiry process embedded in the unit: (1) developing investigative questions; (2) gathering data and information and evaluating them for relevance and credibility; (3) analyzing and interpreting the information; (4) developing an interpretive account, which often raises new questions. Using the process of disciplined inquiry in teaching history, for example, teachers help students "work with various forms of evidence, deal with issues of interpretation, ask and adjudicate questions about the relative significance of events and the nature of historical agency, and cultivate a thoughtful, context-sensitive imagination to fill gaps in evidence trails when they arise" (VanSledright, 2002, p. 1092). This process supports students to learn how to classify and categorize evidence in many ways; check and cross-check evidence for building contextualized interpretations; make judgments about authorship, perspective, and the validity and reliability of evidence; and "fill in the blanks" by providing important contextual information that helps one make sense of evidence.

The Map: A Curriculum Unit

A Web-based curriculum unit on Mexico and migration (see Appendix A) is the map that specifies the direction for the journey in a particular learning terrain. A curriculum unit development team at Michigan State University College of Education collaboratively designed the unit with Battle

Creek–area educators and piloted it in several middle schools. The Mexico and Migration unit was designed to model the use of technology to support meaningful learning. The unit specifies the content for instruction and learning outcomes related to Mexico and migration. Aligned with state standards and benchmarks, these learning outcomes include developing students' abilities to craft investigative questions, locate relevant data and information and evaluate their credibility, use social science methods, interpret information, make claims based on relevant evidence, and communicate their understandings of the Mexico and migration content. The journey toward these learning outcomes requires students to investigate collaboratively questions of personal and social significance.

A main focus of the Mexico and Migration unit is for students to develop skills with the intellectual and technological tools of the social studies disciplines—that is, to learn to think like social scientists. This mind-set includes an understanding of how knowledge is constructed in the social science disciplines. It also includes developing what Bransford et al. (2000) describe as experts' abilities to reason and solve problems. These abilities

> depend on well-organized knowledge that affects what they notice and how they represent problems . . . The fact that experts are more likely than novices to recognize meaningful patterns of information applies in all domains . . . An emphasis on the patterns perceived by experts suggests that pattern recognition is an important strategy for helping students develop confidence and competence. These patterns provide triggering conditions for accessing knowledge that is relevant to a task. (p. 48)

The Mexico and Migration Unit provides a map for disciplined inquiry in a particular content area to assist teaching that develops this mind-set.

In Part I of the Mexico and Migration unit (which was subsequently separated into the unit on inquiry; see Appendix A), students develop familiarity and skill with the inquiry process and with how to use technology to support this process. In Part II, students learn to connect their personal experience and historical data using the three big ideas, *history as story*, *space becomes place*, and *culture as human creation*. In Part III of the unit, students conduct investigations about Mexico and migration on the basis of their own questions and construct interpretive accounts of their findings in the form of multimedia historical narratives.

With the processes of disciplined inquiry and the use of technology embedded throughout, the unit allows space for the teacher to guide students in selecting paths of inquiry that are most compelling and meaningful to them, while simultaneously supporting in-depth investigations of standards-based subject matter. As many have noted, "curricula that emphasize breadth of knowledge may prevent effective organization of knowledge because there is not enough time to learn anything in depth" (Bransford et al., 2000, p. 49). This curriculum unit supports in-depth learning by organizing instruction around big ideas and by providing tools that structure the learning process in ways that are consistent with disciplined forms of inquiry. By learning to use the tools that are an integral part of the unit, students can develop the habits of mind and competencies for in-depth learning in other areas.

Effective and Efficient Technology Tools

Teachers need to know how to select and use technology tools that support meaningful learning to navigate a path to deeper student understanding (see chapter 7).

Project TIME's technology tools bring life to the social studies content and methods of the discipline, as well as immediacy and efficiency to the inquiry process and student learning tasks. Teaching and learning in the Mexico and Migration unit are supported by wireless Internet-connected laptops, 1 or 2 per student, and innovative Web-based software developed by Project TIME. The Meaningful Learning Toolbox (MLToolbox) includes iJournal and iMail. iJournal supports student reflection on particular questions about the content and how it relates both to their own experience and to the big ideas. iMail is an internal e-mail program that supports efficient collaboration and communication among students and with the teacher. Another component of the MLToolbox is the Inquiry Station. As an interactive Web-based application, it enables students to search an internal database of clips (i.e., video, sound, pictures, Web sites, and text); gather and store text and image clips from the Internet in a database; and select and assemble clips from the database into Web page interpretive accounts that tell a story or explain findings. In the Mexico and Migration unit, for the final performance task, students conduct Web-based research and construct multimedia historical narratives using the Inquiry Station. These products can then be easily shared within and across classes.

The technology tools developed by Project TIME support students' sense-making of important social studies content, especially as students select and evaluate Web-based information. These technology tools help stimulate student questioning, efficiently provide multiple perspectives about content being investigated, and foster students' making connections to the world beyond the classroom. In Project TIME classrooms, teachers often used a computer connected to a projection device to model and scaffold the kinds of thinking required in disciplined inquiry. In addition to modeling by making their own thinking public—for example, in evaluating

Web sources for credibility and relevance—teachers can also easily make student thinking visible by sharing iJournal and iMail responses.

USING KEY FEATURES OF THE TERRAIN AND MAPPING TOOLS TO NAVIGATE FOR MEANINGFUL LEARNING: EXAMPLES FROM THE CLASSROOM

Case studies were conducted by the Project TIME evaluator of four teachers to provide images and details of what is both possible and problematic in teaching for meaningful learning using technology. We have used data from one of those case studies for examples described in this section. David Johnson, a sixth-grade language arts/social studies teacher at Beadle Lake Elementary School, was one of the 10 social studies MLT model unit teachers in Project TIME. His undergraduate degree from Earlham College was a double major in elementary education and psychology; his master's degree in school administration is from Michigan State University. He has taught for 30 years in the Harper Creek Community Schools (MI) district.

We enter Dave's sixth-grade classroom to describe how he used the MLT model curriculum unit, the inquiry process, and technology tools to navigate the learning terrain with his students. In preparing to teach the unit, Dave admitted that he was unsure about inquiry-based teaching and acknowledged that he was essentially a technophobe. Neither inquiry nor technology had been part of his teaching of social studies. As he began to teach the unit, he was impressed with his students' skills in using the wireless laptop computers to explore a variety of Web-based multimedia resources related to unit content. As his own comfort level with the technology increased and his students grew more engaged and adept with the technology, he was able to focus on supporting them to use the technology to investigate their own questions.

Navigating the terrain involves identifying moments in instruction that are critical for bringing students systematically to the desired learning results. Understanding these critical points helps the mapping process: where are we now in relationship to where we need to be, and what are the next steps in instruction to move us in the desired direction. Data from Dave's classroom suggest some key points of student learning that call for skill in mapping instruction: (a) using students' own questions as learning goals, within the boundaries of the curriculum unit; (b) developing understanding of criteria for good investigative questions in social studies and how to apply these criteria; (c) searching efficiently for Internet information; (d) selecting credible information that is relevant to the investigation; (e) developing understanding that conclusions are tentative; (f) interpreting data and information; (g) working collabora-tively; and (h) developing habits of mind and constructing mental models that enable students to critically examine evidence and claims.

Over 2 years of teaching for meaningful learning using technology in the Mexico and Migration unit, Dave grappled with instructional challenges at each of these points. In his 2nd year, he noticed that his mapping skills had increased; he saw features of the terrain he had previously missed, he guided students through complex terrain with more confidence, and he discovered better paths to reach the learning goals. How he negotiated these challenges is described below in three areas: (1) developing a com-munity of inquiry using technology, (2) formulating student questions that warrant investigation, and (3) guiding students to see, use, and understand big ideas.

Developing a Community of Inquiry Supported by Technology

Developing a community of inquiry involves, for many educators, chang-ing mental models of education (see, for example, Brophy & Alleman, 1998). Integrating technology provides a catalyst for this change. In the first part of the MLT model unit, guidance is provided for shifting the per-spective of teaching and learning to one of collaborative acts of interaction with the content, in which students' questions are used to direct their learn-ing in standards-based curriculum and technology is used to expand the possibilities for their question.

As Dave discovered, developing a community of inquiry in the class-room takes time and patience. A major pedagogical challenge for him in accomplishing this focused on students' existing habits of classroom work. His students were accustomed to hearing or reading about an idea or con-cept once or twice, producing some related written work, and then mov-ing on. Although he modeled curiosity and "digging deeper" and constantly reflected, reframed, and restated students' questions and theories, students at the beginning had difficulty separating from their previous strategies for learning. They sometimes expressed puzzlement and boredom or became overwhelmed and shut down. As Dave reported, this took the form of "looking and looking" for articles of interest on Web sites with little sense of how they would know when they found it. Students would "print, print, print" pages of documents in an effort to come up with a "product." Dave realized the sources of their discomfort in moving to a way of learning that not only required their taking individual responsi-bility for engaging with the content in new ways, but also compelled them to work with one another to make sense of a large amount of information. In the 2nd year of teaching the unit, Dave reported being better able to manage the connections between the content and the inquiry process so that student learning in small groups was more focused. For example, Dave stated that controlling the number of Web sites used by each inquiry group prevented overlap of materials across groups and led to better sources with more time for collaborative analysis of information from those sources.

The unit's clearly specified process of disciplined inquiry and related habits of mind that support inquiry were key for Dave in locating where students were in any particular moment in learning to think like social scientists about the content. He stated that he never doubted their ability to "get there," and he recognized that their dependence on textbooks, obvious answers, and a surface approach to content was an understandable and also changeable "stuck place." Over time, Dave increasingly saw the value for students' learning of being a community of inquiry and found more opportunities for building the community. He reported:

> One of the best places in the Mexico and Migration Unit to build the community of inquiry is when the class narrows the huge list of questions they have developed. I used the projector to display the questions to the students; this allowed the whole group to see thinking change as students tried to influence each other's perspectives about the questions they wanted to investigate. Using their personal persuasive skills, students promoted their favorite questions. Using the criteria for good investigative questions, they skewered their classmates' questions with adroit skill during these dialogue sessions. Many of my more reflective students benefited greatly from these conversations and also became models for "quick answer" students. Students voted on the deletion and/or acceptance of every question on the list until we reached consensus on our final investigative question and subquestions. The use of the inquiry habits of mind [as defined in the unit, e.g., considering multiple perspectives, developing a critical stance toward claims and evidence, and searching for connections and relationships] reached very high levels for all students during these sessions.

As Dave persisted in using the inquiry process and the technology to support students in changing their habits of mind and also their classroom habits of work, students became more comfortable with listening to one another and with working together to interpret information and make decisions about learning tasks.

Using technology in ways that support a community of inquiry was another pedagogical challenge. At first, Dave reported that he "couldn't see the parts of the unit at times due to all the technology trees." In the

2nd year, he said, "The picture became clearer to me about when to use the projector to model, to reflect student thinking, or to display data to the class; when to work with particular groups on a program such as Inspiration; or when to just write on the dry erase board." Dave saw that building a community of inquiry using technology required changes in the physical setup of the classroom, in how students accessed and recorded information, and in how he related to his students.

Collaborative work that involved each student working on a laptop required different space arrangements. As Dave stated, "The addition of so much equipment into classrooms not constructed for it is a challenge. Just compare the beautiful labs at the local community college to my small 'egg crate' classroom designed in the 1950s." He moved out rectangular tables and moved in hexagonal tables, rearranging the classroom several times and asking students for their ideas about how the space could be used more effectively to collaborate in the inquiry process. He deserted his traditional desk and created an area suited to "guide" students with his laptop, overhead projector, and easel pad technologies. After 2 years, he reported, "I feel more comfortable using the overhead projector, and I know more about how to effectively use my teacher station iMACs now," he said, and "my space has become my place." More often than sitting in his own place, however, Dave sat with small groups to build classroom community, listening to students' ideas, coaching their online investigations, and checking for understanding.

Another aspect of this challenge in using technology to support students' collaborative inquiry dealt with gathering and storing information related to the investigative questions. At first, he and the students felt a need to have a hard copy of everything they found online, using the wireless printer located in a corner of the room. This became unmanageable over time. Ultimately, they found that the better way was to locate information, "read it, then cut and paste" what was pertinent. Not only did moving away from hard copy save the students' time, it also required them to be more selective about what they chose to use. Cultivating this selectivity not only eliminated the volumes of paper but also developed students' inquiry skills, compelling them to think early on about the connections between the information and their investigative questions. As a result, group conversations about interpreting the information were substantially more focused.

Dave learned from the experience of the 1st year with the unit to be less helpful to his students with the technology, letting them work through by themselves, for example, the process of getting the laptops started and logging onto the network. Initially he had been more directive, and he found that this "enabled" students' dependence on him. As he allowed them to engage in more problem-solving on their own, and encouraged them to assist one another, they became competent with the technology more quickly. Moreover, Dave noticed how this change affected relationships among students in a way that strengthened the classroom community:

> This is one of the things that does come out—the students who are more comfortable [with technology] help others. It is really neat to see the "division" go away, girls helping guys, guys helping girls, not just friends helping friends. I see that as a real difference in how they help one another with laptops versus textbooks. Maybe when help is facilitated by the laptop, then when we return to looking at a piece of text, for example, that will carry over.

This change in course, Dave reflected, was informed by his understanding of the inquiry process and the curriculum unit, both of which support developing students as competent thinkers and problem-solvers within a community of learners.

Formulating Student Questions That Warrant Investigation

Questions are at the heart of meaningful learning using technology, as students learn to pose and pursue investigative questions that matter to them. A significant pedagogical challenge lies in ensuring that these questions connect deeply to the unit's standards-based content. Students might ask a lot of questions, many of which may be only tangentially related to the curriculum's learning goals. A teacher needs to scaffold, coach, and guide students in developing investigative questions that align with goals of the unit.

Dave used the inquiry process, the curriculum unit, and technology as tools to meet this challenge. Dave found that his students initially needed a great deal of support to ask investigative questions. Students were not accustomed to asking questions, and when given the opportunity did not necessarily ask questions that engaged them meaningfully with subject matter. Dave coached his students in using criteria outlined in the unit for investigative questions (e.g., possibilities for criteria include: the question has no single answer; deals with important or controversial topics in the discipline; and requires analysis, interpretation, evaluation, and other types of complex thinking). These criteria, along with particular learning tasks in the unit, provided strategic opportunities for Dave to scaffold his students' skills as investigative questioners. For example, one learning task requires that the students analyze photos of the Mazahua, an indigenous group in Mexico, and their experiences migrating to Mexico City. Students worked in pairs, using laptops to access photographs from Web sites and other unit resources, gleaning information, making tentative hypotheses, and writing questions about each photo. Students also composed iJournal entries on their laptops, recording new questions they had about the Mazahua and their migrations. Dave moved from table to table responding to student work. Much of the small-group discussion focused on the nature of students' questions, with Dave coaching students to clarify their questions and consider other questions about the photos, the Mazahua, and migration.

After the students gained some facility with using the inquiry process, the curriculum unit resources, and the technology, Dave led the students in developing, revising, and refining an overarching whole-class investigative question about Mexico and migration. From the list of possible investigative questions the students generated, some questions were quickly discarded because they did not hold students' interest. Dave then guided students "to see patterns in the areas their questions covered" to come up with an overarching question. This entailed coaching students to reword their questions carefully to align with the criteria for investigative questions. After much discussion and debate, the students eventually elected to investigate the following overarching question: How do Mexican immigrants cause changes in the United States?

The next step was to divide this question into subquestions. With an emphasis on "seeing patterns" within the overarching question, Dave guided students to the following three subquestions through discussion, debate, and voting—what Dave called "features of participatory democracy":

- Should the flow of Mexican immigrants to the United States be controlled?
- What are the reasons Mexicans sneak across the border, and how do those reasons cause changes in the United States?
- How do Mexican immigrants cause changes in the United States' laws against discrimination?

Working in groups of six, students conducted online research related to their subquestion and then connected their analyses and findings with the other groups' work. The culminating step was assembling their work into a whole-class product.

Arriving at one overarching investigative question with subquestions was neither easy nor quick, yet technology helped Dave manage this challenge. He used an LCD projector as a tool to display the students' questions. This anchored the discussion in students' thinking, enabling the class to discuss and make revisions on the computer while they applied criteria to the questions and discussed ways to refine the overarching question and develop subquestions. Dave recounted this learning event:

> When we talked about the questions and went from rather simple questions to the "how" and "why" questions, they constructed better questions as we went along. Narrowing the 30 to 40 questions to 20, then 10 and then 4 included a tremendous amount of constructing and learning [through discussion and debate]. They liked to vote, and most of the time went with a majority vote, although sometimes they chose to discuss to consensus. There was a lot going on, lots of participation, and kids who are usually less visible participants were involved, saying, "here's the vote, do we keep this one or delete it?" There was something there that really caught hold and made for a really good learning experience.

Scaffolding students to ask and investigate questions that are both interesting to them and rooted in disciplinary content is a core instructional challenge. Dave used the inquiry process, the curriculum unit, the criteria for investigative questions, and technology as tools to guide students through this process. Although Dave acknowledged that the students needed significant amounts of guidance to develop their investigative questions, he was pleasantly surprised with the quality and depth of his students' thinking. He noted that in the past when using textbooks, students had not asked "these types of higher-order, complex questions."

Dave noted that technology played a pivotal role in this shift. As a result of exposure to a diverse array of complex texts and multimedia resources through the Internet, he concluded that the students were more actively engaged with information and thus prompted to ask more meaningful questions. After developing their investigative whole-class question and subquestions, students were ready to locate and evaluate sources of information that addressed their investigative questions.

Guiding Students to See, Use, and Understand Big Ideas

The students' journey with Mexico and migration content is defined and shaped by the way Dave used the curriculum unit, the inquiry process, and technology as tools to scaffold students' learning. A core pedagogical challenge associated with doing this work entails how Dave guides students to see, understand, and use the big ideas—*history as story, space becomes place, and culture as a human creation*—to deepen their understandings. This is a formidable challenge for two reasons: teaching with big ideas is not the norm in classrooms, and teachers receive little guidance to do this work.

Standards and benchmarks in social studies, as well as in other disciplines, lay out the content that needs to be addressed and how using methods of the discipline can enable students to learn this content. Yet these standards and benchmarks do not use big ideas as larger conceptual frames to structure learning tasks. Consequently, as teachers like Dave work to guide students in using big ideas to deepen their learning, they simultaneously wrestle with the challenge of deepening their own understandings of these big ideas and how to use them in instruction. This section highlights the ways Dave used the curriculum unit, inquiry process, and technology as tools to scaffold students' understandings of the big ideas and then describes Dave's own learning journey with big ideas, emphasizing his developing proficiency with introducing and reinforcing big ideas at strategic points in his teaching.

The inquiry process and technology provide an infrastructure for the learning tasks in the Mexico and Migration unit. After Dave's students learned about the inquiry process early in the unit, they wrote family migration stories. Using methods of the discipline, they interviewed family members and assembled this information in charts, graphs, and tables on their laptop computers. The depth and breadth of the family migration stories varied. Some students were able to interview parents, grandparents, and other extended family members, compiling a wealth of data to support their accounts, whereas other students had less access to family migration data (e.g., parents or grandparents could not be interviewed). Despite these differences across individual students, collectively the class generated a lot of information with their family migration stories.

Next, Dave scaffolded students analyzing this information by creating a chart with headings for three types of migration stories: (1) city-to-city, migration accounts within the state; (2) state-to-state, migration stories within the country; and (3) country-to-country, the international migration accounts. Students then shared parts of their migration stories and assigned them one of these categories; Dave recorded their responses on the table as it was projected for all to see. One reason Dave used this chart stemmed from his developing experience with the inquiry process as a tool to support students' learning. He had noticed that many of his students struggled with the analysis phase of the inquiry process; they were often unsure how to organize the information they had collected in order to analyze and interpret it. This three-part chart guided students with this analytical task.

Stressing the importance of "getting everyone's story represented," Dave noted that working with this chart enabled his "students to see comparisons across their stories," which provided "a natural way" to make connections to the big idea, *history as story*. At this point, his students began to recognize that their work (collecting interview data and representing this information in charts, tables, and graphs) resembled the work of historians, and they saw and heard how the differences across their migration stories could parallel the differences across the accounts or stories that historians create. During these discussions, Dave also sought opportunities to bring the big idea of *space becomes place* into the conversation. Sometimes he prompted students with questions that emphasized the different ways in which the interviewees worked to make new spaces that they migrated to, their own special places. Other times, Dave heard aspects of *space becomes place* embedded in the students' stories; this provided opportunities to reflect their thinking to them and make the big idea visible. With examples such as, "Tiffany [student] just described how she moved into this new town or space and has tried to make it her own special place . . . ," Dave showed students that their thinking was connected to big ideas. As students became more adept at using the inquiry process and at listening for the big ideas, Dave observed, "There were some times when the students brought the big ideas right into the discussion with their own questions" or ideas.

After guiding students to gather and make sense of interview data and make connections to big ideas, Dave used the curriculum unit as a tool to coach students in comparing their own migration stories to content in the Mexico and Migration unit. Students viewed video clips and transcripts of Mexican Americans who shared their stories of crossing the border from Mexico into the United States. The students also studied the migration story of the Aldaba family as they migrate from rural Durango, Mexico, to the northern Mexican border city of Ciudad Juárez. (The story of the Aldaba family appears on the videotape *Mexico Close-Up*, which is part of the Children of the Earth series from Maryknoll World Productions, 2000.) Students were able to relate content in the unit, such as the experiences of the Aldaba family, to their own family experiences. One student, for example, shared an incident:

> . . . when I moved from one farmhouse to a place in the city. I am used to having a farm with lots of room, but now I am in a small house, and . . . we need some more room. Like the Mazahua moving into this small apartment where they don't have much room, but they were forced to move, [because of] bad water. The Aldabas had to move also because of bad crops—it was pretty cramped up.

This student also related to the video interview with Irma, a Mexican immigrant to the United States, and added, "like where they had to move from Mexico to Lansing—to this one-room apartment." (The videotaped and transcribed interview with Ìrma was conducted and produced by Project TIME.) For this student, the unit resource served as a tool to deepen her understanding of Mexico and migration content by making connections between her own experiences and the stories of Mexicans and Mexican Americans.

Throughout the unit, Dave used the curriculum unit map as a tool to scaffold students' learning as they compared and contrasted their own family migration stories with the accounts of the Mexican and Mexican American families in the unit. This also afforded Dave opportunities to reinforce connections to big ideas. With his goal to enable students to see how the big ideas could provide lenses to guide their understandings, Dave employed a range of pedagogical strategies, from asking direct questions to providing time for students to introduce the big ideas without explicit guidance from him. The following example highlights how one student articulated her understanding of Mexico and migration content through the big idea *culture as human creation*. During an interview with the project evaluator, this student described her experience traveling to Mexico.

> I went to Mexico and I found someone who was selling candy bars to help Mexican families—and he lived in Mexico for a while and he moved to the U.S. for about five years, and he is moving back to become a minister. I am relating this to culture as human creation—because he was saying that Mexicans want to move to the U.S. with their culture—they like their lifestyle but don't have jobs and educational opportunities for their children. Like some of the older—grandparents and all others that come to the U.S. like to find other Mexicans for the younger people to marry to keep their culture.

This example highlights at least an emergent understanding that culture is dynamic, changing with time and context, and imbued with tensions as a group of people work to embrace changes yet preserve their traditions and values. Throughout their study of Mexico and migration, students learn to deepen their understandings of the big ideas by exploring connections between their own experiences and the Mexico and Migration unit content.

Dave reported that his own awareness and understanding have been deepened by using the Mexico and Migration unit, the inquiry process, and technology. These tools have offered him strategic opportunities to learn more about how big ideas can foster students' deeper understandings of Mexico and migration as well as other social studies content. In one interview, Dave discussed his own learning about big ideas through his involvement with Project TIME in the last few years. He said, "At first I kind of understood them [big ideas] at a surface level, but as time has gone on, I've been able to get more depth of understanding. . . . We're always trying to get kids to what we think are big ideas, but they've never been defined like this." Dave cited how developing his facility with the inquiry process, the curriculum, and the technology enabled him to teach with big ideas more effectively. For example, along with immersing himself with the range of technology tools employed in the unit, Dave stressed how he has worked to develop his understanding of the inquiry process through studying the curriculum unit and reading professional books, such as Levstik and Barton's *Doing History: Investigating with Children in Elementary and Middle Schools* (2001).

For Dave and his students, the big ideas represented a new way of thinking about and doing social studies. Standards and benchmarks in social studies lay out the content to be covered, yet it is the big ideas that frame and organize this content and serve as guideposts on the learning journey. As Dave deepened his understandings of the big ideas, he became more adept at seeing and using strategic points where he could guide students to see, use, and understand these big ideas to deepen their own learning. With increased confidence and competence with the inquiry process, the curriculum unit, and technology, Dave reports that he now uses big ideas more "naturally" with his students, often framing or reframing what students discuss in terms of big ideas, and sometimes "sitting back a bit" and letting students initiate and use the language and lenses of big ideas to explore and demonstrate their understandings.

SUMMARY AND IMPLICATIONS

Steering the course for meaningful student learning using technology in the subject matter terrain of social studies is a complex task. In addition to including several disciplines, curriculum frameworks and standards in the social studies typically consist of a collection of topics to be covered without a structure that connects the broad array of content to be learned. Understanding big ideas in the disciplines and how they can provide these connections for learners, as Dave pointed out, is a different way of thinking about teaching and learning. Integrating into curriculum and instruction both the technology of Internet-connected laptops and inquiry-based collaborative learning using students' questions is new for many teachers. Using the methods of the discipline and the inquiry process in ways that contribute to developing students' habits of mind that are characteristic of social scientists' thinking is another aspect of complexity in this navigational task.

To deal with this complexity, Project TIME's work has focused on (1) shifting the instructional perspective to include in the terrain for learning attention to big ideas and the use of methods in the disciplines, and (2) providing tools for mapping and guiding students' learning. In addition to content knowledge, then, teachers need to understand the big ideas and methods of the discipline and how to use them to develop student understanding of content. They need to be able to map the location of students' progress at any particular moment on the nonlinear and hard-to-predict learning journey and to address the consequent pedagogical challenges in ways that effectively and efficiently move students forward to understanding challenging content and working with complex problems. They must be able to use the inquiry process within a curricular infrastructure to provide a sense of direction for instruction as a way to integrate learning experiences for students and as a guide for using technology.

Developing the knowledge, understanding, and skill to do all of this, as Dave's story suggests, occurs over time. It also requires taking risks to experiment, taking time to reflect, and having a community of colleagues to support this risk-taking and professional learning. Dave has had time for learning and reflection in a community of colleagues through the structure and resources of Project TIME. He and his colleagues met for 2 hours every other week over 2 years, with leadership from the Michigan State University social studies team. In addition to providing feedback to the unit developers that led to improvements in the unit and software, they dealt with struggles using the technology, the meaning of big ideas, the challenges of doing inquiry with middle school students, and how to assess students' understanding of the content.

The majority of the 10 teachers who were involved in this experience valued it highly for developing their knowledge and skill in teaching for meaningful learning using technology. They expressed a desire to continue as a community of professional learners and presented a proposal to district leaders for how this might occur. In the final year of Project TIME funding, district leaders wrestled with how to sustain this kind of professional learning format. The lack of common periods during the day for colleagues either within or across districts to gather, the cost of substitute teachers (both financially and to students), and the various commitments of teachers after school (which are often school-related) are three substantial obstacles to making this a reality.

A substantial body of research continues to accumulate confirming that a professional learning community is key to building an environment for meeting the significant challenges in increasing teachers' knowledge, skills, and opportunities to improve instruction (Borko, Wolf, Simone, & Uchiyama, 2003). This is very difficult work. As a Project TIME superintendent stated,

> The hard and complex task of teaching for meaningful learning using technology will only get accomplished with strong leadership from building principals and district instructional leaders. And it's the superintendent's job to remove other competing priorities so that this most important work gets done.

Until districts and states make the serious commitments necessary for restructuring the professional life of teachers, the vision for developing the knowledge and skill required to teach for meaningful learning using technology will be constructed piecemeal and painfully slowly. Building a vision, however, for how these innovations might profoundly affect teaching and learning, and creating a shared understanding of the operational details required to achieve this vision, contribute to a significant foundation for progress.

CHAPTER 7

Technology and Teaching:
A New Kind of Knowledge

RAVEN S. McCRORY

Science teachers have been innovators and leaders in the use of technology for many decades. They have used technology in labs and physical experiments, hands-on activities, field trips, and data collection. Science teachers pioneered the use of handheld devices in schools in the 1980s, using probes and microcomputer-based labs to collect data. Yet even today there is evidence that, overall, science teachers along with teachers in other disciplines are not making effective use of the digital technologies now available in classrooms and schools. In some cases, teachers do not have adequate access to technology or adequate support to be able to use it effectively. But even teachers with support and access do not seem to use computers in the ways predicted and advocated over the last 2 decades (Cuban, 2001). Teachers themselves report that they are not well prepared to use new technologies even when they have access and support (Becker, Ravitz, & Wong, 1999).

What do teachers need to know to use technology—particularly computers and the Internet—in ways that promote meaningful learning? The argument of this chapter is that knowledge at the intersection of pedagogy and technology is missing and that the missing knowledge is not what we might expect. Teachers need knowledge in two broad categories. First, they need to be able to identify and develop technologies into tools for meaningful learning. This means knowing what technology offers for such learning and what effective use looks like in practice. Second, they need a useful portfolio of technologies that engage students in meaningful learning. This means knowing about specific tools and resources that they can use in their teaching. Rather than more technical knowledge—about emerging technologies, networking, or hardware—teachers need knowledge of curriculum-based technologies that work with both the ways teachers teach and what students need to learn. This chapter will use examples from science education to make these points, although the argument could be made for any subject, at any grade level.

LESSONS FROM THE CLASSROOM

Teachers themselves provide evidence that what they need is not technological expertise, but rather a useful portfolio of technology resources. From my observations of numerous teachers using computers in their classrooms, five important lessons about teaching with technology stand out:

1. Knowing how to *use* computers is not the same as knowing how to *teach* with computers. A teacher can be an early adopter or a "techie" *and* a good teacher and yet not teach effectively with technology. There are many versions of this:
   - An early adopter can be so enamored of the technology that she teaches technology rather than her subject.
   - A competent computer user may know the tools for his own work (e.g., word processing and e-mail), but not the cognitive tools for teaching his subject matter.
   - A teacher with a lot of training may know technologies to which she does not have access—for example, although she may know how to make computer models with STELLA (Richmond, 1985–2005), the software may not be on the school's computers.

2. Technology is specific: grade level, subject, computer configuration, and computer availability are among the variables that completely change what is desirable and what is possible in a particular classroom. Thus, it is difficult to provide generic education for teaching with technology. Teachers need to know how to use specific software for specific purposes; general knowledge of technology is not adequate. Even if teachers have general knowledge of technology, they still need to convert that knowledge into specific ways to use specific technologies in their classrooms. Being an expert with Excel and being an expert social studies teacher do not automatically endow a teacher with knowledge of how to use Excel to teach social studies.

3. Teachers do not need to know it all. They need a repertoire of technologies with which to teach: software, Web sites, and data sources, as well as computers, printers, and other devices like cameras and scanners. Teachers do not need to have it all; they need a selection of only those items that fit with their curriculum and that are available in their school or classroom. Not every teacher needs to use every technology.

4. Teaching with technology is time-consuming, hard work for a teacher. It is not sufficient to set up a lesson, turn on the computers, and let the students go to work. To gain the benefits of technology, teachers need to help students engage with the complex ideas and processes that technology makes possible. In most cases, technology does not teach on its own. Interaction among students and between students and teacher is required to make sense of what technology offers. Teachers must have subject matter knowledge, pedagogical knowledge, and technology knowledge and engage in extensive planning. They need to know not only what the technology will do, but also what students are likely to do with the technology. They need to anticipate problems with technology and with pedagogy and be able to respond to those problems in the moment. In essence, they need to rehearse their teaching with technology ahead of time, the way in which expert teachers develop mental models of teaching routines and activities to rehearse other kinds of teaching. But most teachers have not had the opportunity to develop those kinds of mental models or engage in rehearsals for teaching with technology. Technology is new, and because it changes so rapidly, it tends to stay new year after year.

5. Computers change too fast for teachers to worry about what they are *not* doing. Both teachers and administrators need to focus on doing what can be done with the technologies available, not on pushing the envelope. Technology currently available in schools offers enormous possibilities for meaningful learning across the disciplines. Even if the technology continues to change as rapidly as it has in the past decade, the only way teachers can use it effectively is to create relatively stable repertoires of technology uses that serve important curricular ends and that can be sustained over time.

All of these factors imply that teachers should not be expected to be technology experts. First, given the variability of the contexts in which teachers teach, it is hard to imagine general technological knowledge that has wide application across settings. Second, given the rate of change of technology, it is unrealistic to expect that teachers could keep up with and be true experts in the latest technology. Finally, the demands on time for knowing any particular technology in any meaningful way are huge. Teachers have more valuable ways to spend their time than on understanding the new features in the latest system software or trying out new software packages released for classroom use. Some teachers will do these kinds of things, but a teacher who becomes a technical expert will continue to be the exception, not the rule. What do teachers need to know? The argument that follows proposes three areas of knowledge important for effective teaching with technology: (1) knowing what technology offers for meaningful teaching and learning within a particular content area; (2) knowing what effective use looks like in practice; and (3) knowing a portfolio of technologies that can be used for meaningful learning within a content area. These three areas are addressed in the sections that follow, using examples from science education.

WHAT DO TEACHERS NEED TO LEARN
ABOUT WHAT TECHNOLOGY CAN OFFER?

There are two broad categories to describe what teachers need to learn about what technology offers: what it offers for student learning and what it offers for teaching. A convenient way to talk about what technology offers is to use the idea of *affordances* (Gibson, 1977). An affordance is something that is made possible, although not necessarily required, by an object such as a technology. So, for example, a chair affords sitting, and so does a flat rock high on a mountain. Affordances will be used here to indicate such characteristics of technology—possibilities that may or may not be realized in practice. Proposed here are four affordances for learning and five affordances for teaching:

Affordances for Learning	**Affordances for Teaching**
Representation	Boundaries
Information	Stability
Transformation	Authority
Collaboration	Pedagogical Context
	Disciplinary Context

The affordances for learning are similar to the Project TIME classification of technology uses (see chapter 1), but differ in that they focus on what the technology itself offers rather than on how it is used. The following sections explain these affordances and what they mean for teacher learning.

Affordances for Learning

Technology for education can afford opportunities for students to engage in meaningful learning in four categories:

- *Representation*: Providing representations of ideas and processes that are difficult or impossible to represent without technology
- *Information*: Providing access to data and content
- *Transformation*: Changing the nature of tasks in which students engage
- *Collaboration*: Facilitating communication and collaboration with peers and experts

None of these is an automatic result of using technology. They are, however, affordances that describe what technology can offer and are the bases for the tremendous enthusiasm for technology in the education community. Project TIME categories—inquiry, communication, construction, and collaboration—describe various ways in which users (students and teachers) might take advantage of these affordances. For example, a student engaged in inquiry might seek information or collaborate with others. A student engaged in construction might use computer-based representations or software that makes it possible to create new kinds of representations, transforming the nature of the task. And so on. The affordances for learning are described in detail below.

Representation: Providing representations of ideas and processes that are difficult or impossible to represent without technology. For example, technology can be used to speed up time through simulations of processes that would ordinarily take place in real time. Using modeling and simulation programs such as ModelIt (HI-CE, 2003–2005) or StarLogo (A. Epstein, Wahba, & Tau, 2004), students can build models of complex systems such as stream ecology or a predator–prey system. Doing this work can help students understand important concepts in the topical area (e.g., the food chain in a predator–prey model) as well as important processes of scientific investigation (e.g., dependent and independent variables or using graphs to represent data).

Another example is probeware. With handheld devices like calculators or personal digital assistants (PDAs) connected to digital probes, students can measure and record data such as the pH level, temperature, and oxygen content of water in a nearby stream. In a laboratory setting, probes connected to computers can be used to record temperature change or other variables, yielding real-time output of graphs. Clearly, doing these activities is only worthwhile in the context of units of work that provide students opportunities to make sense of the data collected and the ideas and processes entailed by these activities. But certainly these technologies make it possible to avoid some of the pitfalls of activities that depend on data collection—time-consuming and inaccurate data collection and graphing, for example.

Simulated dissections provide another example of representational technology for science learning (Hill & Hughes, 2001–2004; Hipscham, 1993). Scientifically accurate simulations of dissections of frogs, cow eyes, sheep brains, and fetal pigs can be found online, and others are available on CD-ROMs. Although dissections can be done without computers, there is often controversy surrounding use of real animals, and there is also some evidence that students learn a great deal from the simulated dissections, especially when used in conjunction with real dissections (Cavanaugh, 2002).

The affordance of representation is central to the use of technology in inquiry, providing access to ideas that have been difficult to teach and learn. In addition, this affordance of technology can bring authentic scientific tools into classrooms. Visual, interactive representations can help students grapple with big ideas in ways that are not possible with conventional tools.

Information: Providing access to data and content. Using the Internet, students can have access to data that were previously impossible to use in classrooms. For example, up-to-the-minute weather data, images from the most recent National Aeronautics and Space Administration (NASA) missions (*Human Space Flight*, 2005), and current earthquake data from around the world are readily available on the Web. Students can find content about topics that would have been very difficult to study before the advent of the Internet—for example, information about zebra mussels in the Great Lakes or reports on the predicted water levels and snow cover in Lake Superior (Brandt, 2005). Access to information is important in at least two ways: First, it makes it possible to study things that are interesting and motivating to students. Second, it provides content for schools that are resource-poor and perhaps dependent on old and outdated textbooks.

Transformation: Changing the nature of tasks in which students engage. Doing lab work in science classes has historically been a matter of following recipes for getting through a specific series of steps and reaching a known conclusion. Authentic processes of science—particularly experimentation and data collection and analysis—have played only a small role in science classrooms, in part because of the time they require. Technology has made it possible for students to engage in these processes by speeding up time and automating data collection. As described above, tools like ModelIt, handheld devices, and probeware radically change what students can do and what they can learn in science classes; they are not merely doing the same things better, they are doing things they could not do before. They can do what scientists do—collect and analyze data, test hypotheses, design experiments, draw conclusions—because of tools that reduce some of the constraints of the classroom and of the developmental barriers to such work. For example, technology can let students use the ideas and processes of calculus well before they have the mathematical knowledge to do and understand calculus (Roschelle, Kaput, & Stroup, 2000).

Collaboration: Facilitating collaboration with peers and experts. Some of the earliest uses of technology in science education were collaborative data-collection activities. A National Geographic Society (NGS) Web site, for example, connected kids around the world through activities in which students collected and shared data such as acidity measurements of local rainfall. Today, such activities continue through NGS and other projects, including Kids as Global Scientists (One Sky Many Voices, 2001) and project GLOBE (Globe Program, 2005). A favorite site for collaborative projects is Journey North, a Web site where teachers can sign up to participate in observations of migratory populations, sharing data with students across the country and world (Journey North, 2004). Another example of this affordance is the Jason project, in which classes participate virtually in scientific explorations, including, for example, the journey to Mars (Ballard, 2005). In these journeys, students can communicate with scientists in the field, ask questions, make suggestions, and "watch" as the explorations unfold. It is by participating in collaborative scientific activities that students learn that science itself is a collaborative human effort to make sense of all that is in our world and in the universe.

These four affordances—representation, information, transformation, and collaboration—explain the impetus for using technology in education. With technology, students can do things that were previously impossible and learn content that was inaccessible to earlier generations of students. What teachers need to know is what each particular technology—a software program or Web site, for example—affords for student learning. That is, teachers need to be able to recognize the affordances of a technology as part of evaluating its usefulness for learning and planning for its use, asking the question, "What is it about *this technology* that will support students in engaging with the big ideas of the discipline?"

Another aspect of understanding what technology offers is considering how it supports teaching. That is taken up in the next section.

Affordances for Teaching

The second category of affordances of technology relate to teaching. We can create a list of ways in which technology might improve the work of a teacher—for example, automating student records, facilitating communication with parents, or keeping track of lesson plans—but general management and organizational affordances are not our focus here. The question here is, in what ways can technology support the work of teaching for meaningful learning? For example, if we think of traditional resources as technologies, textbooks support teaching by providing a map of the content to be covered along with an authoritative version of that content. The chalkboard supports teaching by providing a persistent, stable place to record ideas. It is proposed here that technology, from pencils to computer software, can support teaching across five dimensions:

1. *Boundaries*: What are the topics the technology supports and where will students work on them?
2. *Stability*: To what extent, and at what pace, will the technology change over time?
3. *Authority*: To what extent does the technology provide authoritative content?
4. *Pedagogical Context*: To what extent, and with what tools, does the technology support managing, monitoring, and evaluating student work?
5. *Disciplinary Context*: To what extent and in what ways does the technology provide a coherent flow of ideas in the domain or structure the development of skills or processes?

Not all technologies provide supports in all dimensions, and adding technologies is not necessarily a better solution. Instead, these affordances represent trade-offs: In the abstract, technologies that provide *none* of these supports make the work of teaching more difficult, placing more demands on the teacher. Technologies that provide *all* of these supports could make meaningful learning, and particularly learning through inquiry, less likely by overstructuring the environment. What teachers need to know is what to look for when they are deciding when and how to use a particular technology and what might be needed to adapt it to their classroom. This list of dimensions is one way of thinking about the affordances of technologies for supporting the work of teaching. Teachers can consider these affordances as they evaluate and adapt technologies to their classrooms.

Boundaries: What are the topics that the technology supports, and where will students work on them? For a technology to be useful, it must fit somewhere into the curriculum. Many technologies, including chalk and the Internet, neither specify how they fit into a particular curriculum nor match well with any specific curriculum. Someone (often the teacher) has to make the match. Using the Internet as an example, one common use in classrooms is to have students "do research." This activity can mean having students work in a relatively unbounded domain and in an unbounded "space" where they can encounter content from A to Z. These two kinds of boundaries—the intellectual boundary around topics and the spatial boundary around the location of student work—can be more or less open-ended, depending on the technology and how it is incorporated into the classroom. A worksheet is highly bounded in both respects, for example, whereas the Internet does not necessarily provide either (although some Web sites provide both).

A technology can aim clearly at a particular niche in the curriculum, focus on a particular topic, and provide a workspace where students interact. On the other hand, a technology can lack boundaries. A data set on the Internet, an open-ended research assignment, or a visual representation tool are examples of technologies that lack one or more kind of boundary. The presence or absence of technology-created boundaries suggest different work for teachers. For example, to use a visual representation tool effectively, the teacher must fit it into particular places in the curriculum, making it useful for a specific purpose by putting it into a bounded use. Some technologies provide very clear boundaries. WISE: Web-based Inquiry Science Environment (University of California, Berkeley, n.d.) and Journey North, for example, give teachers support by bounding the work students are expected to do and the location where they do it. Yet both provide opportunities for open-ended inquiry. ModelIt does not bound the topic—it can be used to model any process, including social processes. But it does bound the location and nature of student work. There is no "best" version of boundaries to support teaching, but it is a dimension that should be considered when designing activities for meaningful learning.

Stability: To what extent, and at what pace, will the technology change over time? Conventional materials do not change much, and they do not change rapidly. Teachers can count on them year after year and thus can invest time and effort to develop effective uses. Technology—

especially Web-based technology—can be just the opposite, changing from day to day and certainly not to be relied on for years in the future. Other technologies change or disappear when a company changes hands. Many wonderful programs from Minnesota Educational Computing Consortium (MECC), for example, never made the transition to the company that bought MECC in 1995. Some of the best technologies for science education are very stable and relatively long-lived. ModelIt (HI-CE, 2003–2005), StarLogo from the Massachusetts Institute of Technology (MIT) Media Lab (Epstein et al., 2004), and Project Globe (Globe Program, 2005) are examples of technologies that a teacher can count on. Teachers need to know and consider the implications of the stability of technologies they decide to use. If they choose technologies that are likely to disappear, they may have to find something different the next year.

Authority: To what extent does the technology provide authoritative content? Deciding whether curriculum materials present information that is true or false, reliable or unreliable, or relevant or irrelevant is not a routine activity in classrooms using conventional resources. Even though there is evidence that textbooks often contain incorrect information, teachers are free, or even encouraged, to count on textbooks as authoritative. Technology turns this upside-down. Information obtained on the Internet can be anything whatsoever. In science class, information created through the use of technology—for example, a student-created model—may not be a valid representation of the science. Teachers need to know a lot of science to deal with the issue of authority, whether they determine for themselves or help students learn to determine what is scientifically valid. While this may be good—for example, by altering students' and teachers' views of the nature of science—it requires different knowledge, skills, and allocations of time on the part of the teacher. Some technologies provide support in this area. For example, data from known scientific agencies and projects—NASA, the American Meteorological Society Web site (American Meteorological Society, 2004), or the One Sky Many Voices project (2001)—provide authoritative, reliable information for science education. This is a dimension that a teacher needs to consider when using a technology: Is it authoritative? If it is not, how will the issue of scientific accuracy be dealt with?

Pedagogical Context: To what extent, and with what tools, does the technology support managing, monitoring, and evaluating student work? One of the most difficult things about teaching with technology is pedagogy. How does the teacher manage this teaching? Keeping track of student work, figuring out what students are doing, and responding to questions are all made more complex when some kinds of technologies are in use. For example, if students are working on computers, and if they are doing open-ended activities in which they work at their own pace or on their own topic or model, the teacher may have few ways of assessing what they are doing or how they are doing. Some technologies and materials provide many more supports for teachers. In a well-known study, Carter found that expert teachers could draw accurate conclusions about classroom activities from pictures of classrooms (Carter, Cushing, Sabers, Pamela, & Berliner, 1988). Teachers rely on seeing what is on students' desks, how it is configured, who is working together, what page in the book is open, and more. In a virtual environment, many of these clues are not present or are in such abbreviated form (e.g., one screen at a time) that they are difficult to interpret. Yet some technologies provide such clues for teachers. For example, in ModelIt, with which students develop a model over time, the software provides a current version of student work, and by observing (albeit expert observing), the teacher can tell what each student has been doing.

Technologies that support teachers in this category are those that both make student thinking visible and capture a record of student thinking. Many technologies, especially Web-based technologies, make it difficult for the teacher to gather data about student work through observation and interaction. For example, using a Web-based data set, each student may be looking at entirely different data; the teacher may see only a single screen with no apparent history of what the student has done before. In addition, the data may be unfamiliar to the teacher, especially if it is a large data set. In such a case, the teacher needs to anticipate the desirability of using supplementary materials (structured notebooks or question sheets, for example) for students to record and track their work.

As with the other affordances for teaching, there is no best way for technology to support pedagogy. However, a range of possibilities have differing implications for what a teacher needs to know and do to teach effectively.

Disciplinary Context: To what extent and in what ways does the technology provide a coherent flow of ideas in the domain or structure the development of skills or processes? Disciplinary context refers to the coordination of the technology with the curriculum and the discipline, including developmental appropriateness, coherence of topics, and relevance and accuracy with respect to the domain. At their best, textbooks and conventional curriculum materials pay attention to the order and flow of topics, to the age- and developmental appropriateness of content and activities, and to current understandings in the discipline. Schwab describes the process of creating curriculum as "discovering in scholarly materials curricular potentials which serve the purposes which have been envisaged in the light of detected student needs; then, assessment of the probable advantages of one potential against others as a means toward educational benefits" (Schwab, 1978a, p. 380). He and many others who have studied curriculum development describe this as complex, knowledge-intensive work. Yet when teachers use the Internet and other technological resources, they may find themselves in the position of doing this work on their own, with little support from the tool itself or from outside the classroom. This places great demands on teachers' subject matter knowledge. Some technologies provide more support for the disciplinary context than others. For example, Web sites like Journey North or Project Globe have extensive resources for teachers to help them place these activities in context. Tools like the units in WISE or One Sky Many Voices address particular topics in the curriculum and make well-developed connections to the discipline. Other technologies provide little connection to the discipline. Some, such as word-processing or concept-mapping software, are designed to be open-ended tools for use across disciplines and topics.

Although there is no best configuration for technology with respect to these five affordances, having none of them is a recipe for chaos rather than deep learning. An extreme example of a lesson with none of the five affordances might be an open-ended assignment to do research on the Internet about a topic of the student's choice. In such a case, students may have minimal boundaries on either what Web sites they use or what topic they work on. The materials they encounter and use may change or even disappear from one day to the next. They may unknowingly use incorrect or unverifiable information, and the teacher may not have any way of knowing what students have done or what they need to do next. Their actual progress and work may have little or no relationship to the discipline in question. Of course, one can imagine an open-ended research assignment for which a teacher establishes much more structure than is described above, and thus creates affordances of the technology through her own skill as a teacher. The affordances, however, are not features of Internet technology but rather are determined by its use in the classroom. At the other extreme, prescriptive technologies, whether "drill-and-kill" software or programmed texts, provide little opportunity for meaningful learning through inquiry. What is needed with respect to these affordances is balance: enough support for teaching through one or more of these dimensions to make the teaching feasible, but not so much that learning is narrowly prescribed. Some technologies provide superb support for teaching by making student thinking visible; providing a record of student work;

and at the same time supporting inquiry-based, open-ended activities. Teachers who learn to look for and recognize these affordances in technologies they consider for classroom use will be better able to adapt technologies in ways that make them work for meaningful learning.

WHAT DO TEACHERS NEED TO LEARN ABOUT WHAT EFFECTIVE USE LOOKS LIKE IN PRACTICE?

The ideas above suggest some of the opportunities made possible by technology through representation, information, transformation, and collaboration, and some of the ways technology can support the work of teaching. However, none of these affordances can or will happen without the mediation of a knowledgeable teacher. In the end, use of technology in practice rather than a list of affordances for teaching and learning is what determines effectiveness. Technology alone does not teach. Worse, if it teaches, what it teaches may not be what we want it to teach. Students certainly learn from television, from computer games, and from Internet browsing and chatting. But in schools, and particularly in the meaningful learning with technology (MLT) framework, we want students to learn particular kinds of things, and in some cases quite specific things. The focus is on content central to the discipline. This coordination of teacher intention and student learning requires *teaching*—the mediation and intervention of a knowledgeable other. Teachers teach, and they are an essential part of the sense-making process that must go on for students to learn disciplinary content in meaningful ways.

What do teachers do to teach effectively with technology? Effective teachers pay attention to six critical elements for teaching with technology: affordances, integration, content, appropriateness, effort, and time. Effective uses of technology can be recognized by the presence of these elements. This section details these elements that contribute to effective use of technology in classrooms.

Affordances: Effective uses of technology do things that are uniquely possible with, or enhanced by, technology. Effective use of technology means taking advantage of what technology can do that is difficult or impossible to do without technology. It is not enough to replicate past methods of teaching unless something pedagogically significant is gained in the process. Effective use means representing complex ideas in new ways, accessing significant information, changing the nature of tasks, and communicating differently. Word processing, surfing the net, or checking e-mail may not be effective uses of computers in a science classroom.

Although these are important functions that students need to be able to do, they do not necessarily contribute to meaningful learning of science. The first question that should be asked about any use of technology in a classroom is, What are students learning from or with this tool that is better learned with the tool than without it? If the answer does not include a serious objective for learning content within the focal discipline, the use of technology should be called into question.

Integration: Effective uses of technology do things that address specific curricular needs; the uses are *integral*, not *peripheral*. Integral uses of technology do things that are central to the curriculum and include all students. Adding a research project on astronomy for the sole purpose of letting students gain some experience with looking for images on the Web is peripheral. Incorporating images from NASA into a unit investigating the properties of light—as in the WISE unit "How far does light go?"—is integral for a teacher whose curriculum includes light. Using a modeling or simulation tool to "play" with a model of a predator–prey relationship as a reward for early completion of work is peripheral. Although it may benefit the few students who get to do it (or it may not, depending on how it is used), it could not be a fundamental part of the course or it would be used to engage all students. On the other hand, having all students work on models of the local watershed using ModelIt as part of a unit on water quality is an integral element of the curriculum (Singer, Marx, & Krajcik, 2000).

Content: Effective uses of technology focus on content, not on technology. It is easy to get sidetracked by technology, in part because computers and networks are so unreliable and fragile. When computers crash or the network goes down, when one of 15 computers has different settings than the others, or when the software configuration is different on each computer, a teacher is practically required to deal with technology problems. Enough of these issues can send even the most dedicated and well-intentioned teacher over the edge between teaching content and teaching technology. If students need help using the technology every minute, it does not take long for a teacher to either give up on the technology altogether and return to conventional tools or give in to the need to provide technical support and deal with all the problems.

Another reason that teachers teach technology rather than subject matter is that the content in technology-based activities can be very messy and hard to manage. This has to do with affordances of the technology for teaching and learning described above and with design of the activity, but it is a pitfall hard to avoid. For example, one affordance of technology is access to information. But without extensive structuring of what information is used, how it is accessed, and what it is used for, an activity that lets students find and use information can be so hard to manage that a teacher may reasonably resort to helping students with technical issues rather than substantive ones. In this case, the teacher may begin to teach how to refine searches or what search engines to use rather than trying to figure out how to help each student substantively with the content he or she encounters. These and other technology skills may be important things for students to learn, but not at the expense of the subject matter goals of the class.

Appropriateness: Effective uses of technology are not necessarily high-tech; the tool matches the learning goal. Technology can mean a lot of different things, but in educational settings it is perhaps best thought of as comprising the tools and techniques for improving teaching and learning. The best technology for a given purpose may not be a computer or the Internet. It may be a graphing calculator, a set of blocks, or a video. It may even be a blackboard and chalk. A good example of a relatively low-tech tool for teaching very complex ideas is Jasper (Cognition and Technology Group at Vanderbilt [CTGV], 1997). Designed for middle grades mathematic classrooms, it consists of a set of videos (originally videodiscs, currently CDs) that provide stories in which complex mathematics problems are embedded. The videos are professionally produced and give a real-life setting, or anchor, for problems that could actually occur in the real world. The technology gives a representation of problems that would be hard to create in the classroom, and it provides guidance for the teacher in the form of extension activities and suggestions for use. It also makes it functionally simple for teacher or student to rewind to a specific point in the video to find data or parameters needed for problem-solving. The work of teaching and learning with Jasper and the real determinant of its success come from what teacher and students do together to engage with the ideas and problems presented in the video, not from whether it is the latest in technology advances.

Effort: Effective uses of technology entail hard work and engagement by teacher and students. Technology does not teach; teachers teach. More accurately, technology does not necessarily teach what we mean for it to teach. It has been shown time and time again that what students learn when left to their own devices with technology—from television to books to manipulatives to computers—is unpredictable, uneven, and often erroneous (Ball, 1992; Erlwanger, 1973; Salomon, 1984). The work of the teacher is to help students learn the important ideas that are afforded by the technology. The only way to do this is through dialogue, listening to what students say, watching what they do, giving them opportunities to talk about their thinking, and giving them feedback. The teacher nudges them in the right direction, helps them understand difficult concepts, and keeps them focused on the relevant data and ideas.

What do teachers need to do to teach with technology? They need to engage with students in making sense of the subject they are working on. Although that sounds easy and straightforward, in practice it is not so simple. Computers or other digital technologies add layers of complexity and, often, physical and mental exhaustion. Imagine 30 students, 15 computers, and an activity engaging students in analyzing current weather data from the Web. (For a description of such a case, see Wallace, 2002.) Students are learning to read weather maps, to understand major factors in weather forecasting, and to make simple predictions. In reality, however, the teacher is in constant motion, helping one student after another, answering the same question in 15 different ways, keeping track of who is confused and what they are confused about, making mental notes of what needs to be explained or clarified to the whole class, and making decisions about what to do next for each student and for the class as a whole (Lampert, 1995). Compare that scenario to one in which the teacher stands in front of the room projecting a map on a screen or monitor and taking the whole class through a demonstration and explanation of map-reading and forecasting. Or compare it to a scenario in which the students use maps available on the Web while the teacher grades papers at her desk. In all three of these scenarios, the Web is used to teach weather, but the effort expended by both teacher and students is vastly different.

Time: Effective uses of technology take time. Alan Kay, one of the early innovators in educational technology, talks about "hard fun," and it is a notion worth repeating (Kay, 1998). Teachers and students have come to expect technology to be fun and even easy; if you can't figure out how to use a piece of software in a few minutes, it is too hard. This comes in part from experiences with the Internet. Using a Web browser is so simple and can yield such interesting results that it has created a disincentive for doing hard work to use technology. But, in fact, some of the most beneficial technologies for classroom use are what Kay calls "hard fun." It takes a lot of initial effort, but the payoff is huge. Kay's example is the pipe organ, which could be seen as the interface from the devil. It takes a big investment of time and effort to learn to use it—two hands and two feet controlling hundreds of remotely located pipes—but the results can be stupendous: truly inspired music. In today's climate, the pipe organ might be rejected as not intuitive or easy enough, not user-friendly. Similarly, tools like ModelIt, WISE, Jasper, and nearly every significant technology for education across the disciplines require an investment of effort on the part of teacher and students to yield the meaningful learning the tools can support. Even searching the Web, although easy to do at a basic level, takes time, effort, and knowledge if it is to lead to meaningful learning (Wallace, Kupperman, Krajcik, & Soloway, 2000). In schools and classrooms where time pressure is immense, it is difficult to use such tools effectively. If we expect teachers to make meaningful use of technology in education, they need time, and they need to know that it takes time.

WHAT DO TEACHERS NEED TO LEARN IN ORDER TO DEVELOP A PORTFOLIO OF TECHNOLOGIES FOR THEIR OWN TEACHING?

Knowing what technology offers for teaching and learning and what effective use looks like in practice is not enough. Teachers also need to be able to translate that knowledge into actual uses of technology in their own classrooms. This means developing a portfolio of technologies that actually work in their unique contexts. What do teachers need to know to be able to collect this portfolio? At one level, they need to apply the knowledge outlined above to evaluate technologies that are available to them. This is easier said than done. For example, if a teacher has the Internet in his classroom, the number of possibilities can be overwhelming, making it hard even to begin a process of selecting and evaluating.

At another level, teachers need some way to bring technologies into view—to decide what to consider for evaluation. Probably the best way to make these decisions is by relying on others—school district curriculum personnel, professional colleagues, or publications that point to resources others have found useful. Another approach is to look for technologies that solve particular pedagogical problems (e.g., children's ongoing misconceptions about heat and temperature) or fit into particular places in the curriculum (e.g., the fifth-grade unit on energy). The main point is that teachers cannot know or evaluate every possible technology that might be useful, but they need to learn strategies for choosing and evaluating a few technologies until they develop a portfolio that infuses their teaching with appropriate tools.

Evaluation strategies are not difficult. A starting point is the affordances described in this chapter. What is hard is winnowing down the vast and complex array of things that might be considered and coming up with a few good ideas to evaluate and then adopt. These decisions are inherently local. As outlined above in the section on lessons from the classroom, what works for one teacher may be impossible for another. Thus, the work of finding feasible technologies may best be done in local, collaborative groups of teachers who teach in the same school or district, at the same grade level, and with similar access to and support for technology.

Once a teacher identifies a technology for her portfolio, she then has the opportunity to develop it through experience into a tool for meaningful learning. The teacher learns through her own experience how students respond to activities that use the technology, what activities are effective, what strategies and routines are beneficial, and a host of other complex knowledge about how the technology works in her classroom. This knowledge cannot be learned in general about technology: it is specific to a particular technology in a particular classroom. This is where and when the teacher really learns to teach with technology for meaningful learning.

SUMMARY: WHAT DO TEACHERS NEED TO KNOW?

The argument above suggests that teachers need to know about how technology intersects with meaningful teaching and learning, and they need a portfolio of technologies that can be used in such learning. On the face of it, it seems straightforward that if teachers know how to evaluate technology, know how to fit it into teaching and learning, and have access to a portfolio of technologies, effective use will follow. Using technology effectively for meaningful learning, however, has proven to be hard at best, and more often elusive. Research suggests that although ample technology is available to teachers and students, it is often used ineffectively or not used at all (Becker & Anderson, 1999; Cuban, Kirkpatrick, & Peck, 2001). Some have blamed this on teachers or administrators, attributing to them a weak commitment to innovation or a kind of technophobia. Others have blamed it on teacher knowledge, arguing that teachers do not know enough about technology.

These do not seem like adequate explanations. Teachers, administrators, and parents, along with policymakers and the general public, have expressed an unprecedented enthusiasm for the value of computers and networked technologies in schools (Schofield, Davidson, Stocks, & Futoran, 1997). Districts along with individual teachers have invested time and money in professional development for teaching with technology. So what are the barriers to effective use?

One problem is the unreliability and fragility of technology. Until and unless teachers can count on technology to be usable, rationality dictates that they not depend on it. If they cannot depend on it, it cannot be an integral part of their work. A second problem is access. Even though the numbers have improved—the student-to-computer ratio in the United States has decreased to about six to one (National Center for Education Statistics, 2000)—there is much evidence that teachers cannot plan to use computers when they want to in the configurations that make the most sense. For example, they may have to sign up months in advance to use the school's computer lab, and then only have use of it for a few days. Or they may have 2 computers in their classroom to serve 30 students, with other computers in teacher workrooms and the library. Neither of these scenarios readily lends itself to the kinds of technology-based activities that lead to meaningful student learning.

Another problem is the overwhelming amount of technology now available, offering so many choices and so much information that the best technologies for education are buried. Free tools like some of those mentioned above, superb Web-based activities, and important data sets are lost in the quagmire of advertising, propaganda, personal Web sites, and just plain junk on the Internet. Teachers may also receive advertising from commercial publishers selling stand-alone software or programs that supplement adopted textbooks. Teachers have limited time to find and evaluate technology, and trying out new things is always risky in classrooms.

A final problem is professional development: although there has been a huge investment in professional development for teaching with technology, the focus may have been on the wrong kinds of knowledge. Learning to use productivity tools (electronic grade books or e-mail, for example) may be important for some aspects of teaching, but such knowledge does not lead in any straightforward way to effective teaching. Learning to use a great tool that is not available is also ineffectual. Professional development needs to focus on the kinds of knowledge outlined above, including the final step of supporting teachers as they develop a suitable portfolio of technologies for meaningful teaching and learning.

CONCLUSIONS

Teachers need a different kind of technology knowledge than a banker, a lawyer, or a computer programmer might need. They need knowledge that is directly related to teaching content in the classroom. This entails knowing what a technology can offer for student learning and knowing how technology can support teaching. It also entails knowing specific technologies that fit into their classroom and that support content that is central to the discipline they are teaching. To obtain the latter, they need time with their own colleagues, in local collaborations, to figure out how to use specific technologies in ways that work in their classrooms and schools.

Effective uses of technology are specific; few if any generic uses of technology provide meaningful opportunities for students to learn. Teachers need time to identify resources or technologies, learn to use them and learn how they fit in the curriculum, develop activities that lead to meaningful learning, interact with students as they engage in meaningful learning, and reflect on their teaching.

Unfortunately, in many schools technology knowledge *per se*—knowledge of hardware and infrastructure—is still a troublesome issue because the technology is so fragile and unreliable that teachers who want to use it must be able to fix it when it breaks. Until and unless technology becomes more reliable and better supported, many teachers will, and should, make the rational choice not to use it as an integral part of their teaching. Instead of expecting teachers to have technical knowledge of the sort that can restart a network or troubleshoot a disk crash, we should expect teachers to be developing meaningful uses of technologies for their curriculum.

This view of the knowledge that teachers need to teach with technologies has implications for school district leaders. The significant issues for administrators and other school leaders are time, access, and support. Without these, all the technology in the world will not create classrooms where meaningful teaching and learning with technology happens. Another issue is expectations: school leaders must not expect teachers to do this all on their own—to become technology experts and convert that expertise to effective teaching—while administrators look the other way. Realistic and supportive expectations from administrators might be that teachers build their repertoire one technology at a time, with collaboration and support from leaders and peers and with deliberation and conversation at all levels about effective teaching and learning with technology.

In the end, what teachers need is a repertoire of "learning technologies"—each a combination of devices, software, and curriculum—that they use in their teaching, in a setting where those technologies are stable, reliable, and well-supported. In the past, a teacher's repertoire has consisted of school-provided curricula, lab materials, and supplementary materials the teacher has collected. In the future, this repertoire should include technologies that fit learning goals by addressing ideas and topics specific to their own classrooms. Teachers cannot know everything, and they cannot be expected to evaluate every new device or program that comes along. What they can do is accumulate, over time, a portfolio of stable technologies that work, supplementing and replacing them through a rational, collaborative process, aided by peers and leaders, for identifying and evaluating new resources.

CHAPTER 8

Fostering Meaningful Teaching and Learning with Technology: Characteristics of Effective Professional Development

YONG ZHAO, KENNETH A. FRANK
& NICOLE C. ELLEFSON

The past few years have witnessed a growing interest in preparing teachers to use technology. Since the release of the seminal report *Teachers and Technology: Making the Connection,* by the now-defunct U.S. Congressional Office of Technology Assessment (1995), teachers have gradually moved to the center of the educational technology stage in the United States. In the ensuing years, states began to include technology proficiency as a licensing criterion for teachers (Zhao, 2003), accreditation agencies added technology as a component of their requirements (National Council for Accreditation of Teacher Education, 1997), federal technology grant programs began to make teachers' professional development a priority (for example, PT3: Preparing Tomorrow's Teacher to Use Technology, a federal grant program devoted to supporting the preparation of teachers to use technology), teacher education programs and school districts started to build degree and non-degree programs to teach teachers to use technology, and publications and conference presentations about technology professional development began to appear in large quantities.

Preparing teachers to use technology in support of teaching for meaningful learning is not a simple task. The process, from initial contact with to fluent use of technology for teaching, is often long and painful (Fisher, Dwyer, & Yocam, 1996). Enabling teachers to use technology meaningfully requires more than affording them isolated technology skills (Burns, 2002; Zhao, 2003). Teaching for meaningful learning with technology is not simply inserting technology into the teaching sequence, but, rather, inventing new ways of teaching. Thus, helping teachers to integrate technology should not be thought of as a single event or isolated programs. Instead, teachers need a series of interconnected, situated, and sustained experiences to construct new practices through experimentation and reflection. What characterizes such experiences?

In this chapter, we present a conceptual framework that outlines the characteristics of effective professional development experiences for teachers. The design of effective professional development experiences must be based on a good understanding of what teachers need to know and be able to do in order to teach for meaningful learning with technology (MLT). In other words, we must first understand the goals of professional development. In addition, we need to understand the process by which teachers develop the capacity for teaching with technology. Thus we begin with a discussion about what constitutes teachers' capacity for teaching with technology for meaningful learning. We then discuss the developmental process of teachers' ability to use technology for teaching. Finally, we describe the characteristics of professional experiences that can facilitate the development of the capacity for teaching with technology.

DEFINING THE CAPACITY FOR TEACHING
WITH TECHNOLOGY

Driven by current educational technology standards for teachers, most of which seem to emphasize technology skills as the defining quality of the capacity for teaching with technology (Zhao & Kendall, 2003), many technology professional development efforts seem to focus only on isolated technology skills (Burns, 2002). Research, however, suggests that the ability to teach with technology encompasses a much broader set of cognitive and psychological qualities, including: teachers' knowledge of technology as a solution to their problems; teachers' beliefs about and attitude toward technology, especially with regard to its compatibility with existing practices and potential for improving student learning; teachers' knowledge about and perception of enabling conditions; and teachers' social capital—their access to assistance from others. In the following paragraphs, we discuss what enables a teacher to teach with technology in terms of knowledge, beliefs, and skills.

WHAT TEACHERS NEED TO KNOW TO TEACH
FOR MEANINGFUL LEARNING WITH TECHNOLOGY

For teachers to teach with technology, they need to have knowledge of: (1) technology as a solution to their problems, (2) enabling conditions of a technology, and (3) location of support and ways to obtain it.

Knowing How to Use a Technology's Potential to Solve Pedagogical Problems

A technology has built-in functions. These functions represent the developer's knowledge of the connection between a problem and a solution. In other words, technology is a knowledge system (Hickman, 1990). Thus technology is not neutral or unbiased. Rather, it has its own propensities, biases, and inherent attributes (Bromley, 1998; Bruce & Hogan, 1998). Its inherent attributes or functions suggest to its prospective users what problems it might solve. For example, the functions of an e-mail program strongly suggest that it is designed to solve communication problems through electronic means. Hence, for teachers to use a technology, they need to know its inherent functions. Knowledge of the functions of a technology helps teachers not only to make the connection between the technology and existing problems but also to identify new problems.

The problems identified by the developer of a technology, however, may not be the same problems that teachers face. Thus teachers often consider the built-in functions of a technology irrelevant unless they are presented as solutions to educational problems. For instance, most word processor applications today have a function for embedding annotations in a document. This function is a solution to the problem of including notes in a written document. However, simply including notes in a document is not in itself an educational or pedagogical problem. Until it is connected to educational problems such as inserting comments into students' electronic manuscripts or engaging students in peer editing, the annotation function is not considered useful by teachers. Therefore, for teachers to use technology they need to develop knowledge that enables them to translate technological potentials into solutions to pedagogical problems that are very local and deeply situated in teachers' own contexts. The knowledge is not only about what technology can do but also, and perhaps more importantly, what technology can do for them. The usefulness of a technology lies only in its uses. Thus teachers' technology knowledge consists of three progressive elements: (1) knowledge of problems that can be solved by technology, (2) knowledge of a technology that can solve their problems, and (3) knowledge of how technology can solve their problems.

Teachers who are sufficiently equipped with this knowledge should be able to decide when to use technology and when not to. They should also be able to select technologies appropriate for their current problems.

For example, the act of gathering, organizing, and analyzing data is a significant attribute of teaching for meaningful learning with technology. The Internet is a great source of information. Probes are also great tools for collecting real-life data. Excel can be used for organizing and analyzing data. Very often, however, the functions of these tools are taught without a connection to pedagogical problems. For instance, while teachers may know about Microsoft Excel and some of its functions, some teachers may use it exclusively to keep track of student grades. Rarely do we see teachers using it to support sustained inquiry, while in fact Excel holds great power for organizing and analyzing data, such as its capability for sorting and graphing data in different ways, in addition to its many statistical functions. In order for teachers to use Excel, we need to present the pedagogical problem of organizing and analyzing data and how it can be solved with Excel's data manipulation functions.

Knowing the Enabling Conditions of a Technology

Traditionally, technology proficiency has been understood as the ability to operate a piece of equipment or use a software application. However, research suggests that an additional dimension of technology proficiency plays an equally important part in proficiency: knowledge of the enabling conditions for a technology—that is, knowing what else is necessary in order to use a specific technology in teaching (Zhao, Pugh, Sheldon, & Byers, 2002). Modern computers and computer-related technologies are dependent on many contextual factors to function. For instance, an activity as simple as having students exchange writings using e-mail requires access to a functional network, networked computers, e-mail software, and perhaps even filter software. Simple knowledge about how to send and read e-mail with a single e-mail program only works when everything else functions perfectly, which is seldom the case with classroom technology. This is not to suggest that teachers need to know how to manage computer networks or install software, but it is essential that they understand the enabling conditions of certain technologies.

Knowing How to Access Social and Technical Support

Knowledge of where to go for what type of support has also been shown to be significant in enabling teachers to use technology (Zhao & Frank,

2003; Zhao et al., 2002). Although teaching for meaningful learning with technology shares many qualities with other types of innovations (Fullan, 1991), it requires teachers to be more socially sophisticated than when engaging in other types of innovations, for a number of reasons. First, today's technology, especially network-based computers, often requires resources beyond the teacher's control. In order to make computers work, teachers often need to interact continuously with technicians and administrators, two groups of people with whom teachers have not traditionally had close relationships. Thus teachers have to discover which individuals in the school or district can provide the help they need, and they have to know how to work effectively with those individuals. Second, technology-based projects can make traditionally private classroom activities public and can expose students to an environment beyond the classroom walls, disturbing well-established school patterns. Such disturbance often produces anxious parents and administrators. Socially savvy teachers are much more aware of the potential for problems and can frequently negotiate compromises among the various parties that smooth the way for successful class technology experiences. Furthermore, technology requires money and attention in today's schools. In egalitarian places with limited resources such as schools, the extra resources technology projects receive or require can easily disturb social harmony among peers. Thus, knowledge of school resources and sensitivity to the needs and priority of colleagues are helpful for successful technology integration.

WHAT TEACHERS NEED TO BELIEVE TO TEACH FOR MEANINGFUL LEARNING WITH TECHNOLOGY

Two related beliefs are critical in enabling teachers to use technology to teach for meaningful learning: (1) that using technology will bring certain benefits, and (2) that technology is compatible with existing practices.

Believing in the Cost-Benefit of Technology

Teachers are purposeful and rational decision-makers, who, in the face of an innovation, first assess its potential benefits and costs. This is not to suggest that teachers actually pull out a spreadsheet and compute the costs and benefits of a certain way to use the computer. Nor is it the case that teachers' decisions are based on complete information and necessarily optimal in terms of educational value. In fact, we would argue that very often teachers make decisions on the basis of limited information (Simon,

1957) and in response to pressure. Nonetheless, a teacher's decision is based on the calculation of costs and benefits, although that calculation may be quick and appear impulsive (Zhao & Cziko, 2001).

It is important to note that the costs and benefits are not necessarily actual but *perceived*. They can take a variety of forms: social status, salary, student achievement, and time. When a teacher faces a new way of doing things, she makes a value judgment and decision on the basis of her current knowledge, beliefs, and attitudes, which are deeply grounded in her current practices and the school culture in which she teaches. Such judgments and decisions are critical to teachers' successes, and because teachers are keystone species, their decisions affect others' uses and opportunities for success. Their calculation of results greatly affects how and how much they use computers.

Teachers' perceptions that a certain way to use the computer may lead to limited student learning, requires an excessive amount of time, might make them "look bad" before their students, or cause legal and ethical problems adds to the cost side of the equation. So does the perception that the use may demand dramatic changes in teaching practices, upset social relationships, or negatively affect a teacher's sense of identity. For example, survey studies found that although many teachers use the Internet to look for information themselves and assign students to use the Internet as a research tool, very few make use of it as a tool with which students can communicate with others (Becker, 1999; Zhao et al., 2001). This may have resulted from the perception that it is difficult to control what students do and with whom they communicate in live Internet communications, as well as from other security and legal issues. It could also be that teachers do not feel that communicating with others necessarily "teaches" anything.

In contrast, the perception that a certain use may improve student learning or the public image of the school and teacher, reduce workload, or improve social status adds to the benefit side of the equation. So does the perception that a particular use leads to more resources, salary increases, or simply better relationships with colleagues. At least one of the reasons why teachers frequently use the Internet for lesson planning (Becker, 2001; Cattagni & Farris, 2001; Zhao et al., 2001) is that it makes it easier to locate instructional resources.

Compatibility Between Teachers' Pedagogical Beliefs and Technology

In carrying out daily activities and classroom lessons, teachers draw upon their own beliefs and collected knowledge to negotiate the busy ecology of the classroom successfully. Studies of teaching and teachers' beliefs have shown that teachers who are more reflective and aware of their own pedagogical beliefs are generally more adaptive and flexible teachers (Clark & Peterson, 1986). Research suggests that successful implementation of technology innovation into the classroom is more likely to take place when teachers are highly reflective about their own teaching practice and goals, in the sense that they consciously use technology in a manner consistent with their pedagogical beliefs (Becker, 1999; Zhao & Frank, 2003; Zhao et al., 2002). When a teacher's pedagogical approach to teaching was consistent with the technology she or he chose to use, the efforts to use technology were more likely to yield positive results. This is because technology is not functionally neutral, as some have argued (Means, 1994). Although at a generic level modern computing technology is quite versatile, capable of supporting a variety of uses, specific technological applications have their own affordances and constraints (Bromley, 1998; Bruce & Hogan, 1998); certain technologies are simply better suited for some tasks than others. (For more on affordances, see chapter 7 by Raven McCrory in this volume.) When teachers choose a technology that is compatible with their pedagogical orientation, the technology is much more smoothly integrated. We found that when teachers' pedagogical beliefs conflicted with the technology they were attempting to incorporate into their classroom, they struggled to accomplish the goals of their proposed project. In these cases, projects were postponed, severely modified, or simply canceled.

This is not to suggest that technology is an obedient slave to teachers' existing beliefs and practices. In fact, the use of technology can lead to changes in teachers' beliefs and practices. Some even argue that in order to take advantage of new technologies, teachers must change their pedagogical beliefs. Such is the case in teaching for meaningful learning with technology, which in essence presents double challenges for teachers. On the one hand, they need to challenge their existing pedagogical beliefs and practices. On the other hand, they need to master the technology to support their changed beliefs and practices. Take the use of the Internet as an example. A teacher who holds a traditional teachercentric view may use it as a source of information for lesson planning. To support teaching for meaningful learning, however, using it just as a source of information is not sufficient. An inherent goal of teaching for meaningful learning with technology is learning how to evaluate the validity, credibility, and objectivity of information. The teacher will need not only to use the Internet himself, but also to teach students how to use it. Moreover, much of his teaching will not be about the technical aspects of the Internet, but rather about the nature and quality of Internet information.

DEVELOPING SKILLS TO TEACH FOR
MEANINGFUL LEARNING WITH TECHNOLOGY

Obviously, teachers need to possess some basic technology skills in order to make use of technology. However, teachers do not need to know a lot about all available technologies (Burns, 2002). Instead, we think fluency with a few technologies may be more beneficial. Teachers' technology skills can be grouped in three levels of proficiency: mechanical, meaningful, or generative. (For a related discussion of the stages of teachers' learning to use educational technology, see chapter 2 by Martha Stone Wiske in this volume.)

At a *mechanical* level, teachers' understanding of a technology is fragmented, limited, and superficial, focusing more on form than function. Teachers at this level of proficiency hold relatively stereotypical views of the functions of a technology—paralleling what is portrayed about a particular technology in popular media or by the manufacturer. Typical behaviors of teachers who understand technology at a mechanical level include following strictly prescribed steps of action when approaching a technology, attempting to memorize specific instructions on how to use a particular technology, and inability or reluctance to use new and unfamiliar technologies.

At the *meaningful* level, teachers begin to separate functions from forms. They can think of or accept alternative ways to achieve the same function. Although they begin to gain a certain situational awareness about technology, they are still limited in their ability to use or repurpose the tools in new or different contexts.

At the *generative* level, teachers have a deep understanding of technology that enables them to disassociate form from function and break away from stereotypical uses of technology. These users also have a good understanding of the contextual implications of technology and are sensitive to appropriate and inappropriate uses of technological tools.

The depth of teachers' technology skills significantly affects their uses of technology (Zhao et al., 2002). Teachers at the mechanical level of understanding often try to repeat what technical manuals prescribe or what they are taught and by whom. They are less inclined to repurpose technology for their own uses. On the other hand, teachers at the generative level of knowledge are creative and frequently reinterpret technology for their purposes. They adapt technology instead of simply adopting it.

DEVELOPING CAPACITY FOR TEACHING WITH TECHNOLOGY

The Apple Classroom of Tomorrow (ACOT) project (Fisher et al., 1996), one of the first and most extensive large-scale experiments with infusing technology in all aspects of teaching, found that teachers go through a five-stage evolution in their uses of technology: entry, adoption, adaptation, appropriation, and invention (Sandholtz & Ringstaff, 1996; Sandholtz et al., 1997). In the entry stage, teachers did not have much experience with technology—it could be said that their technology knowledge was at a mechanical level. Their focus was on changes in the physical environment and "typical first-year-teacher problems such as discipline, resource management, and personal frustrations" (Sandholtz & Ringstaff, 1996, p. 286). Their use of technological resources was simple and limited.

In the adoption stage, teachers began to develop more fluency with technology. They become more focused on the functions of technology. "Their concerns shifted from connecting the computers to using them" (Sandholtz & Ringstaff, 1996, p. 286). When they moved into the adaptation stage, "teachers increasingly incorporated technology in their instruction" (p. 286). They began to observe improved efficiency of the instructional process and notice changes in student learning and engagement.

The last two stages, appropriation and invention, saw more creative uses of technology to accomplish real tasks. Teachers at these stages should have reached the generative level in terms of technology knowledge. "They came to understand technology and used it effortlessly to accomplish real work—their roles began to shift noticeably and new instructional patterns emerged . . . teachers began to reflect on teaching, to question old patterns, to speculate about causes behind the changes they were seeing in their students" (Sandholtz & Ringstaff, 1996, p. 287). This indicates freedom from technology. Teachers are no longer constrained by the prescribed mechanical functions of technology. They invent and reinvent the uses of technology in their own teaching. In these last stages, technology has become part of teacher knowledge and pedagogy.

EFFECTIVE PROFESSIONAL DEVELOPMENT FOR TEACHING WITH TECHNOLOGY: TEACHERS' RESPONSES

Thus far we have discussed the essential elements of the capacity for teaching with technology as well as its developmental trajectory. Effective professional development experiences should provide opportunities and support for teachers to develop such capacities. What kind of professional development programs can provide such experiences? In this section, we describe a set of qualities that characterize effective professional development programs.

We began our study with an extensive search of the literature, looking for examples of effective professional development programs from which we might identify important dimensions and practices. We searched journals using the key words *technology* and *professional development*, and we identified well-known volumes on the topic (e.g., N. Davis, 1997). Much of the literature described general principles for technology professional development, or described the professional development but did not attend to the effect of professional development on use of technology. Ultimately, we identified four large-scale efforts that were shown to be effective in affecting teachers' use of technology.

- *The Project-Based Learning Multimedia Model (PBLMM)*. This project was funded through a Challenge 2000 grant and carried out in nine districts in the Silicon Valley area. PBLMM offered teachers five project-wide workdays when all participants convened at central locations. The project's goal was to help teachers develop student-centered projects and teaching practices using technology (Means & Golan, 1998).
- *The Galileo Education Network Association (GENA)*. This project was carried out by provincial education experts from Alberta, Canada. Experts were assigned to work intensively with teachers at schools in the province for a total of 80 days. During that time, teachers learned how to use technology, how to design interdisciplinary technology projects, and how to negotiate the teaching of technology skills to children (Jacobsen, 2001).
- *Project Information Technology (PIT)*. This project was conducted in the Netherlands during the mid-1990s. Two thousand teachers in 196 schools in the Netherlands were invited to join groups related to their areas of expertise. The thematic groups met six times a year to work on common projects (Collis & Moonen, 1995; Hogenbirk, 1997).
- *Generation Y model*. In this project, a unique on-site mentorship was developed. Students attended training sessions to become technology mentors and then worked individually with teachers to help them develop technology-focus projects. The training sessions were developed into a specific curriculum that was often taught as an elective in middle and high school and as an extracurricular unit for elementary students (Coe & Yap, 2000).

From these studies and other literature we identified key dimensions along which technology professional development could differ:

Organization: duration, location, costs, etc.
Origination: teachers, board, etc.

Goals: introduce technology, apply technology to the curriculum, etc.
Motivation of participants: rewards and incentives, innovativeness
Type of evaluation: descriptive, comprehensive, longitudinal, etc.

Drawing on these dimensions, we surveyed technology coordinators and teachers in multiple districts. Our goal was to characterize existing technology professional development and explore its relationship to changes in teachers' implementation of computer use.

The portion of the study we report on here was conducted during the 2001–02 school year. It is based on two administrations of the teacher survey instrument at the ends of successive school years. Our sample included all teaching staff from all elementary schools in four school districts. A total of more than 400 teachers participated in this study. In order to obtain an accurate representation of teachers' uses of technology, we attempted to ensure a response rate of 90% or greater (in fact, the actual response rate was approximately 93%).

Dependent Variable: Teachers' Uses of Computers

Our primary dependent variable was based on teachers' uses of computers. The variable was constructed from teachers' responses to the following questions:
How frequently do you or your students use computers for:

- Classroom management and/or incentives for students?
- Student-to-student communication?
- Student inquiry?
- Student expression?
- Core curriculum?
- Remediation?
- Development of basic computer skills?

Responses were assigned the following values: *never* = 0, *yearly* = 1, *monthly* = 2, *weekly* = 3, *daily* = 4 (alpha = .76). Thus these items tap teachers' use of computers for core tasks as opposed to mere percentages of general use.

From our data, we found that several key factors positively influenced teachers' use of computers. Many of these factors addressed the qualities we have previously mentioned as being crucial to a teacher's ability to learn to use technology:

1. Knowledge of technology as a solution to teachers' problems
2. Beliefs about and attitudes toward technology and its compatibility with existing practices and potential for improving student learning
3. The teacher's knowledge about and perception of enabling conditions
4. The teacher's social capital—his or her access to assistance from others

Finding. Use of computers was positively correlated (.3) with the extent to which a teacher was able to experiment with district-supported software.

Why? Experimenting or "playing" with technology, especially technology that is or will become available in their classrooms, is a remarkably effective professional development experience for teachers. By playing with technology in nonorganized professional development sessions, teachers can make mistakes without embarrassment, take the time that is often necessary to figure out what a technology can do, and practice their skills at their own pace. More importantly, they can try to interpret the value of technology in their own context. Free experimentation with technology also helps teachers to become comfortable with it. Furthermore, it is through continuous experimentation with technology that teachers move from a mechanical understanding to a more generative understanding of technology. Providing experimentation time after an organized form of technology professional development allows teachers to practice what they have learned, see what problems might crop up with a technology, and then go back and learn more (N. Davis, 1997). In this way, experimentation can lead teachers to develop knowledge of the ways computers can be teaching solutions for them.

Teachers will undoubtedly run into technical problems or have questions during their experimentation. Just-in-time assistance is most beneficial for learning. Thus school districts should make available technical assistance to teachers during the school day. On-site help allows teachers to build social relationships with "helpers" (Jacobsen, 2001). Having a trusted colleague help a teacher through a risk-taking process can help ease the teacher's worries about failing (N. Davis, 1997). Support staff who are located in a teacher's school will also have knowledge of the school's context and be able to help teachers find ways to use technology that address their teaching needs (N. Davis, 1997). On-site tech support also ensures that technical problems can be resolved quickly—which is important because teachers are less likely to use technology if they feel that problems they encounter are likely to take a long period of time to be fixed (Means & Golan, 1998).

How? Schools can support teachers' experimentation with technology by providing convenient access to hardware, software, and other technology-related resources. Teachers should be able to check out and take home, if possible, these items to play with. Technology "playrooms" that teachers can easily use when they have time during the school day are also a good idea. Additionally, schools should have clear policies and procedures about how teachers can check out technology items and/or purchase them.

Experimentation takes time. Therefore, schools should make the effort to build in play time for teachers during the school day. Even organized professional development sessions should build in free time for teachers to play with technology on their own. Professional development experiences should not be limited only to instructional sessions or organized events. They should also include activities in which teachers engage all the time. Thus schools should develop a culture instead of a program of professional development. Such a culture should provide teachers with adequate resources and time to experience and experiment with district-supported technologies.

Ideally, on-site technology mentors, people who are also on the teaching staff at a given school, should provide technology support. By having technical support personnel located at schools, support staff work with teachers to co-teach classes (N. Davis, 1997; Jacobsen, 2001). When classroom teachers are able to team up with technology experts in this way, teachers can see firsthand how they can use technology in their classrooms and how to negotiate its use with students. When support staff are located at the school, they can help ensure that technology professional development is always tailored to the educational needs of the school (McDougall & Betts, 1997).

Such on-site mentorship occurred in three of the successful technology professional development models that we identified in the literature. PBLMM provided project-wide workdays. During these times teachers were able to experiment with new technologies. Further, each PBLMM school had a technology learning coordinator who was a teacher on special assignment (Means & Golan, 1998). In the GENA model, teachers' close contact with technology experts who co-taught with them doubtless gave the teachers opportunities to experiment with new technologies. In the Generation Y model, teachers had multiple opportunities to explore the use of technology with their student technology guides, who in turn could support teachers in solving any problems they encountered.

Connecting Technology with Teachers' Work

Finding. Teachers' use of computers was positively correlated (.4) with the extent to which the content of professional development was focused on student learning ("What percentage of your technology professional development: helped you improve students? helped you improve the content you taught? helped you improve student achievement? helped you improve your teaching style? involved content directly linked to your curriculum? helped you learn integrate technology into the curriculum? engaged you in the planning stages?" alpha = .81).

Why? Technology professional development that is directly tied to student learning allows teachers to learn not just how to use computers but to develop new beliefs about their value for teaching.

How? Organized professional development sessions should have a strong focus on teaching technology as a solution to the problems teachers face; technology professional development should stem from the school's goals and curricula (Means & Golan, 1998). (For a discussion of the importance of linking technology use to the curriculum teachers are using, see chapter 4 by Nancy Songer in this volume.) Helping teachers see technology as a solution to their problems not only enhances the probability of teachers actually using what they learn but also makes it easier for teachers to see the benefits of technology (N. Davis, 1997; Sheingold & Tucker, 1990). A successful technology development program helps teachers integrate technology into their curriculum (Potter & Mellar, 2000). By aligning technology professional development with curricular and institutional goals, the process of learning about technology becomes a natural part of the process of teachers exploring how to teach (Jacobsen, 2001).

First, the content of professional development programs should focus on using technology to improve student learning, since teachers are foremost concerned about student achievement. Professional development programs should demonstrate to teachers how technology can be used to teach subject matter content, improve classroom management, and enhance assessment. Second, it should help teachers learn how to use technology to perform their professional responsibilities more effectively and efficiently, such as communicating with parents, publishing newsletters, planning lessons, managing grades, and correcting homework. Finally, the content of professional development programs should teach teachers how to troubleshoot technology problems, access resources for teaching, and use technology for further development.

All four of the major technology professional development projects (GENA, PIT, Generation Y, and PBLMM) that we identified in the literature included a strong focus on linking technology directly to teachers' curricula and teaching needs (Coe & Yap, 2000; Hogenbirk, 1997; Jacobsen, 2001; Means & Golan, 1998). PBLMM and PIT worked to address these needs on a larger scale, with such tie-ins occurring at periodic large meetings. Generation Y and GENA addressed technology/curriculum integration by working with individual teachers one on one.

Building Social Connections and Learning Communities

Finding. Computer use was positively correlated (.2) with the extent to which teachers accessed other teachers' expertise (based on prior use of computers for teachers' and students' purposes and the extent to which another teacher provided help to others).

Why? Help and support from colleagues have been found to be extremely important in the long process whereby teachers develop their capacity for teaching with technology (Sandholtz & Ringstaff, 1996; Zhao & Frank, 2003). The perception that there is help available helps offset teachers' concern about "costs"—that they may have to spend lots of time troubleshooting technology problems or get stuck. When a larger portion of the teaching staff buys into the use of technology, a critical mass of technology users develops in a school that in turn facilitates the further spread of technology use through the school. This finding is a measure of the health of the school's social capital system and how well it can help spread an innovation.

How? Effective professional development efforts should aim at building learning communities among teachers and establishing social connections among teachers and support staff so that they can offer help and support to one another.

Schools should create ample opportunities for informal interactions around technology issues among teachers, technical staff, and administrators so that they know one another's intentions, needs, work habits, and expertise in order to become comfortable enough with one another to seek and offer assistance. Schools should also create opportunities for and encourage collaboration on technology issues among teachers, technical staff, and administrators. As mentioned above, it is good practice to identify and develop experts purposefully among teachers in a school so that they can become leaders or centers of assistance. Incentives should also be offered to encourage teachers to provide assistance to their colleagues. Developing local expertise and making it available help tremendously in starting communities of practices around technology integration.

PIT and PBLMM worked to create networks of teachers using technology. Both addressed this goal by having focus groups meet periodically to work on common concerns (Coe & Yap, 2000; Hogenbirk, 1997). Generation Y taps a different network, the relationships between students and parents, to accomplish the same goals.

Localizing Professional Development

Finding. Computer use was positively correlated (.2 for each) with the extent to which professional development was provided locally, either in the classroom or school lab. ("Approximately what percentage of your technology professional development during this school year took place in your classroom/in your school computer lab?")

Why? Teachers need to be able to see immediate benefits of using technology without having to wait for a long period of time. Additionally, teachers need to develop a good sense of what they have access to in their immediate environment and familiarity with policies and procedures for obtaining technology and technical assistance in their schools. Further, as discussed earlier in this chapter, (1) teachers need to make the connection between technology and their own teaching practices and curricula and (2) technology professional development needs to draw on and stem from the social context of the school. Locating technology professional development in schools works to achieve all of these goals.

How? Organized professional development programs should be conducted in settings that are similar to the teaching contexts of teachers. First, sessions should take place where teachers are most likely to use the technology or in settings that have similar technology configurations. Second, sessions should focus on teaching about technology that is already available so that teachers can start using the technology when they return to their teaching. Third, the sessions should expose teachers to the technology infrastructure, configurations, and access protocols of their schools/districts.

Of the four models that we identified in the literature, two models clearly engaged in this type of professional development. GENA's intensive one-on-one mentorship—the main aspect of their technology professional development—provided the most professional development at the school, much of it in the teacher's own classroom (Jacobsen, 2001). Generation Y also achieved this level of localization through its use of student technology mentors who worked with teachers to create individualized projects.

SUMMARY

We started with a discussion of what constitutes the capacity for teaching with technology. We then discussed the process by which teachers develop the capacity for teaching with technology, followed by a set of suggestions for creating effective professional development experiences for teachers. We conclude with a summary of these suggestions and recommend a set of actions for school and district leaders.

1. Our finding that the extent to which a teacher was able to experiment with district-supported software was positively correlated with use of computers suggests the following: Professional development is not limited to organized sessions or events. Instead it should be considered a process that includes both organized sessions and opportunities for self-exploration.
2. Our finding that the extent to which professional development was provided locally, either in the classroom or school lab, was positively correlated with computer use suggests the following: Professional development should take place in contexts similar to teachers' current teaching settings.
3. Our finding that the extent to which the content of professional development was focused on student learning was positively correlated with teachers' use of computers suggests the following: Professional development should not teach isolated technology skills, but rather solutions to teachers' problems.
4. Our finding that the extent to which teachers accessed other teachers' expertise was positively correlated with computer use suggests the following: Professional development should cultivate social capital and develop communities.

As a synthesis, effective technology professional development should draw on teachers' own creativity (i.e., experimentation), draw on school resources (expertise of other teachers), and be delivered in the local context (in the classroom or school lab).

RECOMMENDED ACTIONS:
WHAT SCHOOL DISTRICTS CAN DO TO PROMOTE
PROFESSIONAL DEVELOPMENT FOR TEACHING
FOR MEANINGFUL LEARNING WITH TECHNOLOGY

In accordance with these suggested principles, we recommend two sets of actions for school/district leaders:

Organize Teachers into Problem-Based Design Teams

1. Create groups of teachers who face similar challenges. Teachers teaching the same subject matter or grade are likely to have similar challenges. Therefore a district or school, if it is large enough, can organize teachers facing similar problems into design teams. Focus design teams on the task of identifying significant, authentic problems they face in teaching their curricula. Have design teams work together to identify ways in which technology might be used in service of their curricula.

2. Center all activities on common problems instead of technological capacities. A design team should include technology experts. However, the role of technology experts should be to provide information about the capacity of technology in relation to the problems teachers need to solve. In other words, the technology experts serve as assistants to rather than leaders of teachers. Aim for practicable solutions with available technology. The design team should focus on identifying or developing technology uses that can be implemented immediately by the teachers using resources that are at hand.

3. Develop ways of teaching others how to implement the technology solutions they have devised.

Build a Support Infrastructure

1. Cultivate a network of school-based technology experts. Recruit early adopters from each building and give them additional training in technology leadership and district network protocols. Schedule times for the technology experts to work with their colleagues before, during, and after the school day.

2. Set up an equipment/software checkout service for teachers. Teachers should be able to check out equipment and software as easily as they can from a library.

3. Arrange some common free time for teachers who teach the same subject matter or grades.

4. Place new equipment/software in the teachers' lounge.

5. Establish an e-mail account, Web forums, chat rooms, or a phone line to provide instant support to teachers.

6. Use students who are interested in and have expertise in technology as technical assistants for teachers.

CHAPTER 9

Professional Development for Meaningful Learning Using Technology

ROBERT E. FLODEN & JOHN E. BELL

Scholars, policymakers, and practitioners alike now recognize that teachers are central to successfully improving student learning. Whatever curricula and materials are available, whatever policies are in place, whatever support the parents and community members offer, teachers are ultimately the ones who engage with students. It is what teachers are capable of doing, as they plan instruction, select materials, and respond to the myriad events that transpire in the classroom, that most powerfully affects what students learn.

At least since the publication of *A Nation at Risk* (National Commission on Excellence in Education, 1983), the goals for student learning have extended beyond mastery of basic skills to include a deep understanding of academic subjects. As content standards have been written in the various subject areas, teachers have been encouraged to push their students to master a range of challenging content.

At the same time, many scholars and policymakers have expressed high hopes for educational technologies, especially computers and the Internet, while others have noted that past hopes for an educational technology revolution have usually been disappointed. In this atmosphere that mixes hope and skepticism, local, state, and federal agencies have invested heavily in educational technology, counting on teachers to make productive use of these resources to promote student learning.

The recognition that teaching is central, that student learning should include conceptual understanding, and that educational technology's potential has seldom been tapped effectively to support teaching for understanding leads to the conclusion that offering professional development to assist teachers in teaching for meaningful learning using technology should be an important educational goal.

This has been a goal often stated, but seldom articulated, however, with clarity and detail. Much has been written about the goal of meaningful learning—how meaningful learning differs from rote learning. And many authors have described examples to illustrate the instructional practices, some involving technology, that promise to lead to meaningful learning.

But the discussion seldom progresses to consider what knowledge and skills teachers would need to teach for meaningful learning, much less to teach for meaningful learning using technology. Even more rare is consideration of how teachers might acquire such knowledge and skills. Unless teachers are expected to acquire such knowledge and skills in college or on their own, school systems must begin to offer such professional development in order for their investments in technology to enhance pupils' understanding of key academic subjects.

The questions used as organizers for this volume are thus critically important. Beginning to answer these questions will give school districts greater clarity about what the district's professional development goals should be and how they might be reached. Those organizing questions are:

- The Teacher Learning Content question: What do teachers need to know, believe, and be able to do to teach for meaningful learning using technology (MLT)?
- The Teacher Learning Context question: What do district leaders need to know, believe, and do to support teaching for MLT?

One additional question must be answered to move from an understanding of what teachers need to know to a description of what district leaders should do to help teachers learn:

- The Learning Process Question: How can teachers learn what they need to know, believe, and be able to do?

A description of what district leaders need to know should be grounded in ideas about the professional development experiences that will move teachers in the intended direction. To make concrete, workable plans for professional development, district leaders must also know what programs of professional development and ongoing technical support are feasible and sustainable, given the fiscal, organizational, and political dimensions of their districts. For example, if district leaders want to plan a series of workshops, they should focus on using reliable technologies (e.g., Web browsers or spreadsheet programs) with applications tied to particular parts of the district's curriculum. They should not be providing training in the use of a "glitzy" program that only specialized consultants know how to support and that has uncertain connections to teachers' instructional goals.

THEMES IN ANSWERS TO THE ESSENTIAL QUESTIONS

The chapters in this volume each address these questions, with some chapters focusing more on one question than the other. Reading across the chapters, several recurrent themes can be seen in the responses given. Each theme can be seen as cutting across the questions, with a claim about needed teacher knowledge leading to ideas about the professional development directed at that knowledge, leading in turn to associated ideas about district leadership. To help pull these ideas together, we elaborate each theme, across all three questions, and in some instances go beyond what the essays treat explicitly. The six themes we address are:

- Deep, flexible subject matter knowledge
- Organizing group inquiries
- Assessment of meaningful learning
- Skill with a small set of technological tools
- Collaboration
- Working beyond school walls

Deep, Flexible Subject Matter Knowledge

In both social studies and science, the subject areas highlighted in this volume, the authors emphasize the ways in which meaningful learning involves working from big ideas and learning methods of inquiry that are central to the subject matter. In social studies, for example, teachers may be teaching big ideas about culture as a human creation or about the ways in which people claim physical spaces and give them meaning, turning them into "places." In science, teachers may be helping students to learn about weather as the movement of energy, or about the geographical distribution of plant and animal species. Methods of inquiry in both social studies and science include both gathering information—often using the Internet or wirelessly connected small computers—and evaluating that information, determining its trustworthiness and its fit with the big ideas.

The authors illustrate the differences between superficial, rote knowledge and deep understanding of a subject with examples of instructional activities that help build understanding. As Wiske notes, teachers' deep, flexible understanding of the subject matter is needed for them to have clear learning goals for students that address understanding, be able to judge whether those goals are being met, and make instructional decisions that promote this kind of learning. For example, teachers of history, as Bain points out, must understand key historical concepts such as cause and effect, evidence, motivation, migration, and revolution. Because students may come up with unexpected comments, questions, and examples, teachers need a depth of understanding that will help them judge whether a novel suggestion is promising, misleading, or in error. The recent shift toward having students search the Internet to gather information adds to the need for flexibility as students locate information of initially unknown validity, which may be completely unfamiliar to the teacher. When students got their "facts" mostly from standard references and the school library, the range of "facts" was limited, with all the students drawing on the same sources. Now teachers may have 30 students locating 50 different Web sites, likely to include a wider range of "facts" to be considered.

Adding a technology like Internet access extends the range of material that may enter the classroom discussion, increasing the frequency with which students and teachers confront questions and claims that go beyond the standard text. As students read and discuss accounts of contemporary and historical events, teachers must have sufficient depth of subject matter knowledge to make sense of these accounts, including how to use them to help students grasp the big ideas and develop standards for judging the quality of arguments.

Teachers vary, obviously, in the depth and flexibility of their subject matter knowledge, especially across grade levels. Although some may have quite sophisticated understandings, teachers often have a mechanical, rote grasp of subject matter concepts in their major field. Thus professional development to support meaningful learning with technology must address teachers' subject matter knowledge. As a starting point, professional development must include activities likely to strengthen subject matter knowledge—something seldom found in the menu of district offerings. The most familiar examples of professional development focused on teachers' subject matter knowledge are summer programs, such as NSF (National Science Foundation) summer workshops and foundation-sponsored summer workshops in history or literature. Professional development that engages teachers deeply with a topic or with intellectually challenging materials seems more likely to develop depth and flexibility than workshops designed as surveys or oriented around a teaching method. Some authors in this volume recommend engaging teachers in professional development that resembles the learning tasks they will use with students, building teachers' meaningful understanding of subject topics and methods through engagement in technology-supported inquiries. The relative effectiveness of different approaches to deepening teachers' subject matter knowledge remains, however, a topic in need of research.

For school district leaders, the key may be a recognition that deepening teachers' subject matter knowledge should be a part of the overall plan for professional development. Although teachers' subject matter knowledge is widely cited as critical to teacher quality, discussions of teacher quality too often assume that the need for subject area study is completely satisfied by the coursework required for a teaching certificate. Because understanding of the subject is so central to teacher quality, it may seem risky or demeaning to design professional development aimed at building deep understanding. Or it might seem that the amount of time available for professional development is too small to add significantly to subject matter depth, or that the wide range of content areas needed by different teachers makes the professional development task overwhelming. For teachers' success with meaningful learning with technology, however, the importance of deep, flexible understanding of the subject makes it imperative that school district leaders see that their system of professional development gives it attention, perhaps by organizing subject-specific teacher study groups or adding higher-education faculty from the disciplines to the teacher curriculum planning teams. A district wishing to improve student understanding of immigration patterns might, for example, organize opportunities for groups of teachers to meet with a demographer, examining the detailed census data available online, looking for patterns of change in different geographic areas. In-depth study of these data could increase teachers' understanding of central concepts in geography, economics, and history; it could also be a rich source of ideas for having students work with these primary sources.

Organizing Group Inquiries with Technology

Meaningful learning entails having students engaged in active inquiry, working with one another as they construct arguments, solve problems, and make connections among concepts. Thus teachers need skill in managing group inquiries, which have features quite different from the teacher-centered, highly structured lessons that are still prevalent in U.S. schools. Because these inquiries require students to work together and have discussions with one another, rather than simply responding to the teacher, classroom management takes on new dimensions. Furthermore, technology adds to the openness of inquiry, as well as the complexity of management. Teachers need skill in supporting interactions among students, while still maintaining engagement with the learning tasks. Because the course of student inquiry is inherently unpredictable, teachers also need skill in responding to students' unexpected questions, comments, and interests and in helping students keep their inquiries focused and on schedule, while still allowing enough freedom to give the inquiry some authenticity.

The authors in this volume, like other experts in teacher professional development, suggest that teachers learn the skills needed to guide student inquiry through a combination of conducting their own inquiries, practicing the use of inquiry with some outside guidance, and reflecting on their own experiences with student inquiry projects. Like most skills, practice with feedback is a critical component of learning. To help teachers acquire these skills, district leaders need to understand the importance of giving teachers opportunities for guided practice. Trying to adopt inquiry approaches without the assistance of a coach, mentor, or collegial team may lead to confusion and frustration, where the potential for promoting meaningful learning does not seem worth the struggle to learn new instructional practices. As teachers develop skill in managing student inquiry projects, they can see the benefits in student learning, but support will often be needed in the early stages, support that the school and district should offer. It will likely take a year, or longer for some teachers, before teachers develop the skills needed and consequently lose some of their initial skeptical worries about the payoff from making use of technology-based group inquiries. The study reported by Linn describes the way in which teachers, over the course of 2 years' work, shift from seeing technology-based group inquiry as just another version of science laboratory work to seeing new opportunities for teaching and learning.

Assessment of Meaningful Learning

As Wiske notes in her chapter, the standard modes of classroom assessment are not well aligned with the pursuit of meaningful learning. For promoting meaningful learning, teachers need to learn how to judge whether student work indicates understanding. They also need to learn how to help students share in the task of assessment, beginning to take some of the responsibility for monitoring their intellectual progress.

Technology can support and help manage assessment, such as by creating public records of student accomplishments linked to evaluations of the work and of explicit criteria used for evaluation. Initial teacher preparation may have given teachers some initial foundation for learning to use new approaches to assessment, such as public presentations of solutions to mathematics problems as a venue for evaluating student understandings of mathematics, reviews of student laboratory notes to check their understanding of scientific concepts, or writing portfolios as a basis for judging student mastery of various genres. Building on this foundation, professional development will be crucial for helping teachers make assessment of student understanding an ongoing part of their practice.

Materials and modules have been developed that focus on helping teachers learn to assess student work, looking for evidence of meaningful learning in various subject areas (e.g., Stiggins, 1997; Wiggins & McTighe, 1998). District leaders need to understand the importance of this area of teacher learning, recognizing also that the current context of education creates strong pressures to focus on mandated state assessments, which will not always emphasize meaningful learning. Districts can support teachers by building evaluation of meaningful learning into district systems for student assessment, making explicit both the links to state assessments and the ways in which district assessments go beyond those required by the state. Visible statements about the priority that meaningful learning has as a district learning goal, and about the importance of documenting progress toward that goal, can help teachers maintain attention to meaningful learning, even when that requires going beyond preparation for state tests.

Skill with a Small Set of Technological Tools

It is easy to construct a long list of the technological tools that teachers might try to master. Those writing in this volume, however, avoid the "more is better" approach, arguing instead that teachers should develop skill with a small set of tools. McCrory writes of the importance of having a portfolio of tools that fit with their approach to teaching. Zhao, Frank, and Ellefson argue that teachers' use of technology should start with their classroom practices, looking for ways technology can support them, rather than by starting with learning to master some set of technologies. Likewise, Songer emphasizes that teachers must see the technology as a tool for meeting their teaching goals, not a separate area in which they must work. And Ashburn makes the argument that technologies must support learning that is meaningful.

To learn how technological tools can be integrated into their practice, teachers need sustained work, tied to their curriculum, preferably involving the assistance of coaches who can model how the technology can be used to promote meaningful learning and who can offer specific feedback on the teachers' own attempts. For the teachers Linn studied, the mentor was able to shape attitudes toward the use of technology throughout the school, in addition to giving examples and suggestions to the individual teachers. By working with the mentor, for example, teachers learned how to try different approaches to working groups of students, such as engaging students in working out a problem they were having, rather than simply telling the students what to do. The mentor's inquiry stance was an important model to teachers as they worked to use data in their own practice to develop effective ways to work with new instructional technologies.

School district leaders can help expand this focus by supporting professional development that concentrates on using technologies selected to achieve learning goals, rather than giving the impression that teachers must master technical details or try out every new innovation that hits the press. Allocating professional development resources for employing coaches who have mastered the set of technology tools, tied to curriculum in use, will help teachers see what is possible and support teachers' learning.

Collaboration

The importance of working together to learn is a theme that comes through in several chapters. For students, working together to evaluate historical evidence or conduct a scientific inquiry is a key component of meaningful learning. Technology can support development of these norms by supporting extended small and large group discussions and by making thinking visible. Technology is also a conduit for bringing in information beyond the classroom, which must be collaboratively judged for its credibility and its relevance to the task.

Collaborative learning communities are also important for supporting teachers in learning how to teach for MLT. Teachers need to learn how to change the patterns of classroom discussion so that students address comments and questions to fellow students as well as to the teacher. They need to know how to help student groups learn to learn from one another in solving problems that come up in trying to understand a text or use a computer application, so that the groups can sustain attention to their learning tasks, rather than waiting for the teacher's assistance. As students gain experience in working together, teachers must become skilled in helping the groups deepen their discussions and evaluate evidence and reasoning as a regular feature of their classroom work.

Districts can provide leadership for the creation of learning communities both by helping teachers gain such skills and by supporting creation of classroom environments that encourage collaboration. Classrooms arranged so that groups of students can talk to one another, for example, rather than always face the teacher, change the physical cues that suggest patterns of conversation; similarly, flexible computer setups allow reconfiguration of groups to fit their learning tasks. In moving toward teaching for MLT in such contexts, teachers should inform and be informed by the efforts of colleagues.

Collaboration is as important in professional development as it is in classroom learning. Teachers need to break deeply engrained habits of isolated work and perceptions of professional development as a source of tips and resources for individual use. To enable the creation of professional learning communities, districts must address schedules of instruction so that time is built in for extended, recurring discussions of practice, particularly in regard to learning to teach for MLT.

Working Beyond Classroom Walls

We mention one more theme that, though not prominent in the chapters in this volume, came out in discussion with district leaders during meetings prior to the symposium. The theme focuses more on what districts can do to support teacher learning than on the specific knowledge and skills teachers need to learn.

As districts work to support teachers' learning to teach for meaningful learning using technology, they should foster activities that work beyond the walls of their classrooms. Project TIME, the technology innovation initiative that led to this volume, united four school districts, a set of private schools, and a research university in its efforts to design curriculum, establish systems of professional development, and move schools toward greater use of technology to support meaningful learning. The collaborative project brought experts in technology, curriculum, subject matter, and professional development together with education practitioners from public and private schools serving diverse student populations. The resources of the collective were available to the individual districts, helping them all to find ways to sustain the effort needed to shift their goals toward meaningful learning and to work through the difficulties of learning to use new tools and new approaches to teaching.

Teaching for meaningful learning using technology engages students with the world outside their classroom walls, allowing them to connect with people and resources that can enrich and inform their learning. Similarly, teachers can locate and take advantage of materials and expertise matched to the particular ideas and topics around which they organize their instruction. Classroom texts still may be central in their instruction, but questions that arise as students and teachers try to probe more deeply can often be answered by searching the Internet for data, information, documents, and experts. Inquiry becomes more authentic when significant topics of immediate interest to students are addressed, whether or not they are explicitly covered in classroom texts.

Teachers may find the expansion beyond the classroom walls both exciting and challenging. The possibilities for student projects that expand and deepen their responses to essential questions are exhilarating. Opening the range of material that can be brought to bear also means, however, reducing the predictability of classroom activities. Uncertainty is an endemic part of teaching (Floden & Buchmann, 1993), which teachers must accept and manage. The ways in which teaching for meaningful learning using technology takes instruction beyond the classroom walls increases that uncertainty, creating both potential and demands. Districts can enhance this potential by supporting the engagement with content-specific information and experts outside the building and district, but they must also guide teachers in working toward a productive balance of novelty and predictability.

Further Questions Emerge

The themes in these chapters give a start toward answering our essential questions about what teachers need to learn, and how they will learn, to make schools successful in teaching for meaningful learning with technology. But the answers are at best partial, and the themes described are, to an extent, extrapolations or inferences, rather than summaries of explicit statements.

Reading through the chapters with the essential questions in mind, one is likely to be struck by the emphasis in many papers on teaching for meaningful learning for *pupils*, rather than on what *teachers* need to know or how they might learn it. That drift toward description of the teaching, rather than the knowledge needed for teaching, is not unusual.

One reason for the drift may be that the authors feel that the idea of teaching for meaningful learning with technology is still new enough, or at least unfamiliar enough, to require explanation and justification. If those reading these chapters need to understand what meaningful learning is, or need to be persuaded that it represents a direction in education worth taking, even when accountability systems may appear to push in a different direction, then the authors have good reason to begin there.

But that does not explain why the discussion often stops with teaching, or does little more to address needed teacher knowledge than saying that teachers need to know how to teach in the ways described. Another explanation may that these essential questions are much more difficult to answer than their simple form suggests, or at least that it is difficult to offer well-supported answers. As Ball (1996) said in the context of teaching mathematics for understanding, the knowledge teachers need for that kind of teaching is more difficult to describe than the knowledge needed to teach basic skills. Interactions with students are less predictable, and teachers must be ready to take whatever comes and figure out how to move students from their current conceptions to a deeper understanding of established knowledge in the area. It seems as though the teacher must know more than can be learned through a few sessions of professional development, making it harder to say what teacher knowledge is most important to develop in the short term. The suggestions of McCrory and Zhao, Frank, and Ellefson that teachers should focus on a few technology tools sound all the more reasonable in this context.

Another topic that seems likely to come up, yet absent from most of the chapters, is what role technology should play in the system of professional development itself. Wiske points out that though computers and the Internet have obvious uses as repositories of texts, images, and tools for teachers, putting such resources in a technological environment does not directly address many of the perennial challenges facing professional development. Norms of isolation, the sense that each teacher's needs are unique, limitations of subject matter understanding, and challenges in mastering new approaches to teaching all limit professional development, whether or not it is supported by technology.

Moreover, some technologies that seemed to promise rapid changes in professional development have delivered less than anticipated. New means of communication—e-mail, instant messaging, even cell phones—have led to sustained changes in some people's lives, but they have not, by themselves, drawn all, or even many, teachers into productive professional communities. In some school districts, progress has been surprisingly slow, with e-mail yet to become a reliable method of distributing information, let alone an infrastructure supporting professional community.

Just as these chapters address questions about pupil learning more directly than questions about teacher learning, they give more attention to uses of technology in K–12 instruction than to uses in professional development. Teachers must, of course, interact (or play with) educational technologies as part of learning to teach with them. But with the exception of Wiske, these chapters propose person-to-person interactions with professional development instructors and other teachers as the method for learning to teach for MLT. Wiske describes how Web-based systems of communication can enable teachers to access experts, many of them also teachers, overcoming barriers of geographical and organizational distance. But even her chapter describes technology as a way of supplementing other structures for professional development, rather than arguing forcefully for the use of technologies as an essential component of professional development. This relative lack of attention to the uses of technology as part of professional development reflects the charge to the authors, not an explicit rejection of technology in professional development. The ways in which technology could enhance or transform professional development is a topic that still needs creative exploration and analysis.

These chapters also leave unanswered the question that teachers and administrators repeatedly raise about learning to teach for MLT: How will teachers find the time needed to learn everything described above? The need for time is a perennial issue in professional development. Teachers feel that their work lives are already heavily loaded, making it challenging to devote time to professional learning.

This question is always raised, and must be taken seriously. It should be taken as a reminder of the reality of teachers' dual commitments to their current students and to the learning needed to move their instruction in a new direction. The authors in this chapter have ideas about what might be done, and probably recognize that each idea would take time and effort to be moved to classroom practice. The authors were not explicitly asked to propose ways of finding the needed time, though perhaps the question about what district leaders need to learn is an invitation to talk about time. Given the constant press of time teachers experience, the changes needed for moving instruction toward MLT will only be made if districts decide that these changes are a sufficiently high priority to set schedules for instruction and professional development that reflect this priority. With MLT as a systemwide priority, teachers will have the time needed for change in the face of competing demands.

A Look to the Future

The topics addressed in these chapters are in some ways timeless, in other ways quickly outdated. The relative emphasis given to different educational goals varies over the decades, but an interest in making learning more meaningful can always be found in the writings of educators and citizens. Similarly, hopes that technology can increase teachers' efficiency and effectiveness have been a part of the discussions of education for many years.

The priority schools assign to meaningful learning, relative to other learning goals, may vary over time. Competing policy emphases could either heighten interest in meaningful learning or push it to one side. On the one hand, policy groups are calling for more challenging content, higher standards, and teachers with greater knowledge of the subjects they teach. On the other hand, the press for accountability, as measured by large-scale assessments, pulls teachers toward concentrating on content most likely to be tested. After a period of interest in performance assessments, the federal requirements for increased testing create pressure for lower-cost methods of testing, which have traditionally put more emphasis on memorization and skill mastery. The importance of moving toward credible measures of meaningful learning is repeatedly noted in these chapters. The current climate of assessment-based accountability adds one more argument in support of that direction.

The particular technologies that are at the forefront of discussions change, however, so that papers from the 1960s about the ways in which television will transform schools now seem quaint and naïve. The chapters in this book hold out hopes for Internet access and multimedia packages. Those technologies, too, will probably seem quaint someday.

What will replace them? The increasing ubiquity of wireless connectivity, combined with a trajectory toward miniaturization, creates opportunities for all those in classrooms to be connected to sources of information, to classmates, and to students and teachers outside their school and community. Songer's chapter gives one example of how such technologies can support a particular curriculum. If more teachers, administrators, and curriculum developers gain experience with these technologies and develop an understanding of and commitment to meaningful learning, undreamed-of educational applications may appear. If school districts can learn to support professional development needed to teach for MLT, those applications may become so widespread that it will be difficult to imagine schools without them.

APPENDIX A

Site Map: MLToolbox.org

Map from "Work as Teacher" Mode

You will reach the login page by entering www.mltoolbox.org. You must have a user name and password to enter the site. You may enter "About MLToolbox" without logging in.

After logging in, you will select a class to work with. Teachers create these classes as described in the Tutorial. You may access the Tutorials via "Help" on this page.

After selecting a class, you will be at the **Front page**.

A. Unit
   1. Inquiry: A Way of Knowing Differently
      a. Unit Home
         i. Lesson 1: Asking Questions & Gathering Information (Learning Tasks with Links)
- Teacher Mode
- Teacher Plan (For each Learning Task)
- Lesson Checklist
- Read Me First (Assessing lesson outcomes, background information, lesson technology, connection to standards)

        ii. Lesson 2: Forming a Community of Inquiry (Each lesson follows the same format as Lesson 1)
       iii. Lesson 3: Identifying Investigative Questions
       iv. Lesson 4: Analyzing & Interpreting Information: Making Valid Generalizations
        v. Lesson 5: Analyzing & Interpreting Information: Photographs
       vi. Lesson 6: Gathering & Evaluating Information
      vii. Lesson 7: Analyzing an Interpretive Account

2. Mexico & Migration
   a. Unit Home
      i. Part 1: Developing Understanding of Mexico & Migration
         - Lesson 1: Probing Students' Experiences with Moving (Each lesson follows the same format as Lesson 1 in Inquiry Unit)
         - Lesson 2: Using a Case Study to Further Explore Mexico & Migration
         - Lesson 3: Comparing Mexican Migration Trends with Personal & Family Migration Experiences
         - Lesson 4: Reflecting on the Process of Fitting In
         - Lesson 5: Inquiring into Borders & Classroom Spaces
         - Lesson 6: Exploring Water Issues on the Border
         - Lesson 7: Exploring the Culture of the Borderlands
      ii. Part 2: Investigating Mexico & Migration & Communicating Findings
         - Lesson 8: Reading Historical Narratives as Interpretive Accounts About the Past
         - Lesson 9: Generating Investigative Questions & Choosing a Special Audience
         - Lesson 10: Organizing Group Investigations & Performing Initial Investigations
         - Lesson 11: Analyzing, Interpreting & Using Information
         - Lesson 12: Using Information to Write Historical Narratives
         - Lesson 13: Submitting Tentative Claims for Feedback & Making Revisions
         - Lesson 14: Revising & Preparing to Share Historical Narratives
         - Lesson 15: Presenting the Historical Narratives & Debriefing the Experience
   b. Overview (Same as Inquiry Unit)
   c. Inquiry Process Chart (Same as Inquiry Unit)
   d. Core Learning Tools (Same as Inquiry Unit)
3. Unit Creator (Create MLT units and lessons)
   a. New Unit
      - Title
      - Authors
      - Content Area
      - Grade Level
      - Time Required
      - Big Idea(s)
      - Standards

- Enduring Understandings
- Essential Questions
- Indicators
- Inquiry Process
- Performance Assessment
- Unit Wide Resources
- Revision Log
  b. New Lesson
    - Lesson Number and Title
    - Time Required
    - Benchmarks
    - Lesson Outcomes
    - Formative Assessment
    - Focus Question
    - Key Vocabulary
    - Lesson Launch
    - Learning Tasks
    - Closure
  c. Edit Lesson
    - Preview
  d. Print

B. iMail
  1. New (Create new mail)
  2. Search (Inbox)
  3. Mail Preferences (& creating, editing and deleting Folders & Groups)
  4. Search Class (Work as Teacher mode only)
  5. Class (Lists)
  6. My Tutor—How do I . . . ? (Page-specific tutorials)

C. iJournal
  1. New (Create new entry)
  2. Search
  3. First Text (iJournals in chronological order)
  4. View Class
  5. All Text (Teacher mode)
  6. View Projects
  7. My Tutor— How do I . . . ? (Page-specific tutorials)

D. IS (Inquiry Station)
  1. Questions
  2. Gather/Evaluate

      3. Analyze/Interpret

      4. Communicate

      5. My Site

      6. Investigative Question

      7. My Tutor— How do I . . . ? (Page-specific tutorials)

      8. My Clips

E. SE (Source Explorer)

      1. New

      2. Search

      3. View Class

      4. Class Plug-ins

      5. Current Explorations

      6. My Tutor—How do I . . . ? (Page-specific tutorials)

F. Today in the Toolbox (Announcements)

G. My Projects (Inquiry Station Sites)

H. Preferences

      1. People in This Class

      2. Block Student Access

      3. Class Groups

      4. Change Your Password

      5. Select a Different Class

      6. Download Student Work

      7. Class Preferences

      8. Surveys

      9. Edit/Add Announcements

I. My Tutor

      1. View Help Topics

          a. Tutorials (35, on various aspects of processing information within the toolbox)

APPENDIX B

MLToolbox Description

MEANINGFUL LEARNING TOOLBOX

www.mltoolbox.org is a password protected Web-based application
designed to:

- Promote *inquiry*
- Strengthen *collaboration* for *intentional learning*
- Make *thinking visible*
- Structure *collaborative unit/lesson-building*
- Support *careful assessment and valid use of Web-based resources*

This database of tools and model curriculum units is the result of 5 years'
work to develop technology that fully supports meaningful learning in the
classroom. We define *meaningful learning* as *the achievement of deep understanding of complex ideas that are relevant to students' lives*. www.mltoolbox.org*
is innovative in its integration of technology into a larger instructional
environment that creates a workflow from conceptualizing units and lesson plans through implementation in the classroom.

www.mltoolbox.org houses *two curriculum units* designed to *model* how these
tools can fully integrate technology into meaningful learning experiences.
It also enables teachers to co-author Web-based curriculum units with
lessons to be used by students. This tool—the *unitCreator/lessonBuilder*—
scaffolds teachers' thinking to align standards, learning outcomes, assessments, and learning tasks. The resulting lessons allow students to make full
use of the integrated MLToolbox tools through links on their Lesson Launch
sites.

---

*www.mltoolbox.org was developed by Project TIME, a U.S. Department of Education
Technology Innovation Challenge Grant (Award No. R303A990109) to Battle Creek–area
school districts in partnership with Michigan State University.

The Web-Based Complement of Meaningful Learning Tools Includes:

iMail. An internal mail system allowing students within a class or between classes to send and receive messages with their colleagues and teacher. While mirroring standard e-mail system features, this system eliminates inherent dangers found on public systems.

iJournal. A student journaling system designed to support inquiry and make students' thinking visible. The tool allows teachers to post questions for students to respond individually or in small groups. Fully searchable responses can be projected with or without student names to generate whole-class discussions. Teachers can provide feedback via iMail.

Inquiry Station. Guides students through a recursive inquiry process resulting in the creation of student Web sites constructed in response to student-generated investigative questions. Working individually or in small groups, students create data/information clips from a variety of sources, organize them into coherent interpretive accounts, and publish their sites online.

Source Explorer. Allows students to evaluate information and record their findings in response to primary sources, maps, charts, images, literary pieces, Web sites, and short video clips. A series of teacher-created prompts guides students in simultaneously viewing a source and entering their responses. Teachers have immediate access to the fully searchable database of student responses and can project them for whole-class discussion, respond to them via iMail, and use them for assessment of student work.

APPENDIX C

Historical Narrative Rubric

Following are nine dimensions suggested for assessing student learning on the historical narratives constructed as the final performance task in the Mexico and Migration Unit. Each dimension has descriptions for four levels, with 4 being the highest score. Choose the dimensions most relevant and useful to you and your students.

Score	Quality of Question	Sources of Information	Quality of Claims and Evidence
4	Clear guiding question with possible related sub-questions for each section. Guiding question supports a good historical narrative by addressing a significant problem that can be developed chronologically.	Use of relevant and credible sources that relate clearly to the question and support the historical narrative.	Thorough and focused claims in each section of the historical narrative that address relevant issues raised by the guiding question. Each section has claims supported by evidence.
3	Clearly stated, but may not adequately support historical investigation. The question has sufficient depth and breadth to support a historical narrative about Mexico and Migration.	Sources are relevant and support the historical narrative, but credibility of a number of sources is in question.	Claims in the historical narrative address appropriate issues, but in limited depth. Claims are made but are supported by limited evidence.
2	Question is about Mexico and Migration, but is relatively simplistic and does not support a quality historical narrative.	Some information from sources is not related to the guiding questions, and credibility of sources is not considered or demonstrated.	Claims do not address obvious and important issues for each section raised by the investigative question. Claims are not clearly stated and have little or no supporting evidence.
1	Is not about Mexico and Migration and doesn't support the development of a historical narrative.	Much of the reported information is unrelated to the question. The sources are not documented and credibility is not considered.	No clear claims are made in the historical narrative.

Score	Mexico and Migration Content	Big Idea: Culture as Human Creation	Big Idea: Space Becomes Place
4	Demonstrates an understanding of the migration of Mexican people and causes of migration. Addresses a significant problem, develops the problem chronologically, provides tentative conclusions, and reflects upon how the group worked on the narrative.	Shows thorough understanding of culture, the differences among cultures, and the process of cultural change. Shows that the culture of a place changes as a result of migration.	Shows clear understanding of area enclosed by a boundary, the uses of the space, and attaching meaning to the space. Describes how a space becomes a place.
3	Provides some demonstration of understanding of migration, but is overly simplified. Adequately addresses at least 2 or 3 of the 4 requirements of historical narrative (significance, chronology, conclusions, reflections).	Shows some understanding of culture, cultural change, and cultural relativism.	Provides examples of spaces within a boundary and uses of the space, but does not show understanding of attaching meaning to the space.
2	Presents oversimplified discussion that reflects superficial understanding about migration. It fails to adequately address the 3 requirements of historical narrative (significance, chronology, conclusions).	Some evidence is provided for understanding the concept of culture, but there is no depth of understanding.	Ideas about boundaries are clearly presented, but concept of use and attaching meaning are not included.
1	Nothing about migration in the historical narrative.	Little or no information about culture is presented.	Little or no information about space or place is presented.

Score	Big Idea: Knowledge Is Subject to Change/Interpretation	Structure of Narrative	Mechanics
4	Actively compares two or more perspectives on a topic. Awareness of perspectives and tentative nature of claims pervades historical narrative.	Well-structured, with clear purpose. Well-developed ideas that support the purposes. Addresses a significant problem, develops the problem chronologically, provides tentative conclusions, and provides a description and reflection of the group's work in developing the narrative.	Materials meet the conventions of standard written English with only a few minor typos. All sources are well-documented.
3	Shows understanding of history as interpretive and subject to change and includes at least two perspectives on some topic.	Has a clear purpose, but ideas are disjointed and connections to the investigative question are not clear. Adequately addresses at least 3 of the 4 requirements of historical narrative (significance, chronology, conclusions, reflections).	Some significant mechanical errors, but they do not interfere with the communication of ideas. Some sources are not documented.
2	Shows awareness of author's perspective, but multiple perspectives are not considered.	No clearly stated main theme, but some individual ideas are well developed. Fails to adequately address the 4 requirements of historical narrative (significance, chronology, conclusions, reflections).	Some areas are hard to understand because of problems with mechanics. Little documentation of sources.
1	No awareness of author of information. Information accepted as universal truth.	No main theme is evident and none of the ideas or sections of the narrative are sufficiently developed.	Text of narrative is difficult to understand because of problems with mechanics. No documentation of sources.

References

Agron, J. (1998). The urban challenge. *American School and University, 70*(11), 18–20.

Alberts, B. (2001, April 30). *Expanding the institutions of science.* Retrieved on March 4, 2005, from the National Academy of Sciences Web site: http://www.nationalacademies.org/nas/nashome.nsf

American Meteorological Society. (2004). *DataStream atmosphere.* Retrieved March 7, 2005, from http://www.ametsoc.org/dstreme/

Aronson, E. (1978). *The jigsaw classroom.* Beverly Hills, CA: Sage.

Atwater, M., & Wiggins, J. (1995). A study of urban middle school students with high and low attitudes towards science. *Journal of Research in Science Teaching, 32*(6), 665–677.

Bain, R. B. (1997). Building an essential world history tool: Teaching comparative history. In H. Roup (Ed.), *Teaching world history* (pp. 29–33). New York: Sharpe.

Bain, R. B. (1999). *Web-supported world history course presentation index.* Retrieved March 4, 2005, from University of Michigan Web site: http://www.personal.umich.edu/~bbain/display/talkingpoints.htm

Bain, R. B. (2000a). Into the breach: Using research and theory to shape history instruction. In P. Seixas, P. Stearns, & S. Wineburg (Eds.), *Knowing, teaching & learning history: National and international perspectives* (pp. 331–353). New York: New York University Press.

Bain, R. B. (2000b, June). *The tabula rasa problem in world history: Toward an instructional logic in world history.* Paper presented at the annual meeting of the World History Association, Boston, MA.

Bain, R. B. (n.d.). Web-supported World History Course Presentation Index. Retrieved on June 24, 2005, from http://www.personal.umich.edu/~bbain/display/talkingpoints.htm

Bain, R. B., & Ellenbogen, K. M. (2001). Placing objects within disciplinary perspectives: Examples from history and science. In S. Paris (Ed.), *Perspectives on object-centered learning in museums* (pp. 153–170). Mahwah, NJ: Erlbaum.

Ball, D. L. (1992). Magical hopes: Manipulatives and the reform of mathematics education. *American Educator, 16*(2), 14–18, 46–47.

Ball, D. L. (1996). Teacher learning and the mathematics reforms: What do we think we know and what do we need to learn? *Phi Delta Kappan, 77*(7), 500–508.

Ball, D. L., & Cohen, D. K. (1996). Reform by the book: What is—or might be—the role of curriculum materials in teacher learning and instructional reform? *Educational Researcher, 25*(9), 6–14.

Ballard, R. (2005). *Real science and math. Real time. Real learning.* Needham Heights, MA: Jason Foundation for Education. Retrieved March 7, 2005, from http://www.jason.org/jason_science/expeditions/learnMore.htm

Barton, A. C. (1998). Reframing "Science for All" through the politics of poverty. *Educational Policy, 5*(12), 525–541.

Battle Creek Area Educators' Task Force. (2002). *Project TIME.* Retrieved March 4, 2005 from http://www.projecttime.org/about/meaningfullearning.html

Baumgartner, E. (2004). Synergy research and knowledge integration: Customizing activities around stream ecology. In M. C. Linn, P. Bell, & E. A. Davis (Eds.), *Internet environments for science education* (pp. 261–288). Mahwah, NJ: Erlbaum.

Becker, H. J. (1999). *Internet use by teachers.* Retrieved on March 4, 2005, from the Web site of the Center for Research on Information Technology and Organizations, University of California, Irvine, and University of Minnesota: http://www.crito.uci.edu/TLC/FINDINGS/internet-use/

Becker, H. J. (2000). Who's wired and who's not: Children's access to and use of computer technology. *Children and Computer Technology, 10*(2), 43–75.

Becker, H. J. (2001, April). *How are teachers using computers in instruction?* Paper presented at the Annual Meeting of the American Educational Research Association, Seattle, WA.

Becker, H. J., & Anderson, R. E. (1999). *Internet use by teachers: Conditions of professional use and teacher-directed student use* (Report #1). Irvine: Center for Research on Information Technology and Organizations (CRITO), University of California, Irvine.

Becker, H. J., Ravitz, J. L., & Wong, Y. (1999). *Teacher and teacher-directed student use of computers and software* (Report #3). Irvine, CA: Center for Research on Information Technology and Organizations (CRITO), University of California, Irvine.

Bell, P. (1998). *Designing for students' conceptual change in science using argumentation and classroom debate.* Unpublished doctoral dissertation, University of California, Berkeley, CA.

Bell, P., & Linn, M. C. (2002). Beliefs about science: How does science instruction contribute? In B. K. Hofer & P. R. Pintrich (Eds.), *Personal epistemology: The psychology of beliefs about knowledge and knowing* (pp. 321–346). Mahwah, NJ: Erlbaum.

Bereiter, C. (1985). Toward a solution of the learning paradox. *Review of Educational Research, 55*(2), 201–226.

Blacker, D. (1993). Allowing educational technologies to reveal: A Deweyan perspective. *Educational Theory, 43*(2), 181–194.

Blumenfeld, P. C., Fishman, B. J., Krajcik, J. S., Marx, R. W., & Soloway, E. (2000). Creating useable innovations in systemic reforms: Scaling up technology embedded project-based science in urban schools. *Educational Psychologist, 35*(3), 149–164.

Blythe, T. (1998). *The teaching for understanding guide.* San Francisco: Jossey-Bass.

Boix-Mansilla, V., & Gardner, H. (1998). What are the qualities of understanding? In M. S. Wiske (Ed.), *Teaching for understanding: Linking research with practice* (pp. 161–196). San Francisco: Jossey-Bass.

Bolman, L. G., & Deal, T. E. (1991). *Reframing organizations: Artistry, choice, and leadership*. San Francisco: Jossey-Bass.

Borko, H., Wolf, S. A., Simone, G., & Uchiyama, K. P. (2003). Schools in transition: Reform efforts and school capacity in Washington state. *Educational Evaluation and Policy Analysis, 25*(2), 171–201.

Brandt, S. B. (2005). *Great Lake Environmental and Research Laboratory*. Ann Arbor, MI: National Oceanic and Atmospheric Administration. Retrieved March 7, 2005, from http://www.glerl.noaa.gov/

Bransford, J. D., Brown, A. L., & Cocking, R. (2000). *How people learn: Brain, mind, experience, and school*. Washington, DC: National Academy Press.

Britt, M. A., Rouet, J. F., Georgi, M. C., & Perfetti, C. A. (1994). Learning from history texts: From causal analysis to argument models. In G. Leinhardt, I. L. Beck, & C. Stainton (Eds.), *Teaching and learning in history* (pp. 47–84). Mahwah, NJ: Erlbaum.

Bromley, H. (1998). Introduction: Data-driven democracy? Social assessment of educational computing. In H. Bromley & M. Apple (Eds.), *Education, technology, power* (pp. 1–28). Albany, NY: State University of New York Press.

Brophy, J., & Alleman, J. (1998). Classroom management in a social studies learning community. *Social Education, 62*(1), 56.

Brown, A. L., & Campione, J. C. (1994). Guided discovery in a community of learners. In K. McGilly (Ed.), *Classroom lessons: Integrating cognitive theory and classroom practice*. Cambridge: MIT/Bradford.

Brown, A. L., & Campione, J. C. (1998). Designing a community of young learners: Theoretical and practical lessons. In N. M. Lambert & B. L. McCombs (Eds.), *How students learn: Reforming schools through learner-centered education* (pp. 153–186). Washington, DC: American Psychological Association.

Brown, R. H. (1996). Learning how to learn: The Amherst Project and history education in the schools. *The Social Studies, 87*(6), 267–273.

Bruce, B. C., & Hogan, M. P. (1998). The disappearance of technology: Toward an ecological model of literacy. In D. Reinking, M. C. McKenna, L. D. Labbo, & R. D. Kieffer (Eds.), *Handbook of literacy and technology: Transformations in a post-typographic world* (pp. 269–281). Mahwah, NJ: Erlbaum.

Bruer, J. T. (1993). *Schools for thought: A science of learning in the classroom*. Cambridge, MA: M.I.T. Press.

Burns, M. (2002). From compliance to commitment: Technology as a catalyst for communities of learning. *Phi Delta Kappan, 84*(4), 295–302.

Carretero, M., Jacott, L., Limon, M., Lopez-Manron, A., & Leon, J. A. (1994). Historical knowledge: Cognitive and instructional implications. In M. Carretero & J. F. Voss (Eds.), *Cognitive and instructional processes in history and the social sciences* (pp. 357–376). Mahwah, NJ: Erlbaum.

Carter, K., Cushing, K., Sabers, D., Pamela, S., & Berliner, D. (1988). Expert–novice differences in perceiving and processing visual classroom information. *Journal of Teacher Education, 1988* (May–June), 25–31.

Cattagni, A., & Farris, E. (2001). *Internet access in U.S. public schools and classrooms: 1994–2000*. Washington, DC: National Center for Educational Statistics.

Cavanaugh, S. (2002). *Can virtual dissections replace the real thing?* Paper presented at the National Association of Research in Science Teaching (NARST) Annual Meeting, New Orleans, LA.

Champagne, A. B., Klopfer, L. E., & Anderson, J. H. (1980). Factors influencing the learning of classical mechanics. *American Journal of Physics, 48*, 1074–1079.

Chi, M. T. H., deLeeuw, N., et al. (1994). Eliciting self-explanations improves understanding. *Cognitive Science, 18*, 439–477.

Clark, C. M., & Peterson, P. L. (1986). Teachers' thought processes. In M. C. Wittrock (Ed.), *Handbook of research on teaching* (pp. 255–293). New York: MacMillan.

Clark, D. (2000). *Scaffolding knowledge integration through curricular depth*. Unpublished doctoral dissertation. University of California, Berkeley, CA.

Clark, D., & Linn, M. C. (2003). Designing for knowledge integration: The impact of instructional time. *Journal of Learning Sciences, 12*(4), 451–494.

Clarke, J. (1994). Pieces of the puzzle: The jigsaw method. In S. Sharan (Ed.), *Handbook of cooperative learning methods* (pp. 34–50). Westport, CT: Greenwood Press.

Coe, M. T., & Yap, K. (2000). *Generation YES: Youth and Educators Succeeding, 4th Annual Performance Report May, 2000*. Portland, OR: Northwest Regional Educational Laboratory. Retrieved March 4, 2005, at http://www.genyes.org/media/annual4th.pdf

Cognition and Technology Group at Vanderbilt (CTGV). (1997). *The Jasper project: Lessons in curriculum, instruction, assessment, and professional development*. Mahwah, NJ: Erlbaum.

Cohen, D., & Ball, D. (2002). Resources, instruction and research. In F. Mosteller & R. Boruch (Eds.), *Evidence matters: Randomized trials in educational research* (pp. 80–119). Washington, DC: Brookings Institution Press.

Cole, M. (1996). *Cultural psychology: A once and future discipline*. Cambridge, MA: Belknap Press of Harvard University Press.

Collis, B., & Moonen, B. (1995). Teacher networking: A nation-wide approach to supporting instructional use of computers in the Netherlands. *Australian Educational Computing*, September, 4–9.

Corr, D. (2001). *Teaching for understanding using new technologies*. Slides for the Project Zero Summer Institute, July 2001. Retrieved March 4, 2005, from http://learnweb.harvard.edu/ent/library/TfUwithNewTechnologies/frame.htm

Crismore, A. (1984). The rhetoric of textbooks: Metadiscourse. *Journal of Curriculum Studies, 16*, 279–293.

Cuban, L. (1986). *Teachers and machines: The classroom use of technology since 1920*. New York: Teachers College Press.

Cuban, L. (2001). *Oversold and underused: Computers in the classroom*. Cambridge, MA: Harvard University Press.

Cuban, L., Kirkpatrick, H., & Peck, C. (2001). High access and low use of technologies in high school classrooms: Explaining an apparent paradox. *American Education Research Journal, 38*(4), 813–834.

David, J. L. (1996). Developing and spreading accomplished teaching: Policy lessons from a unique partnership. In C. Fisher, D. C. Dwyer, & K. Yokam (Eds.), *Education and technology: Reflections on computing classrooms* (pp. 237–250). San Francisco: Jossey-Bass.

Davis, E. A. (1998). *Scaffolding students' reflection for science learning.* Unpublished doctoral dissertation, University of California, Berkeley, CA.

Davis, E. A. (2004). Creating critique projects. In M. Linn, E. Davis, & P. Bell (Eds.), *Internet environments for science education* (pp. 89–114). Mahwah, NJ: Erlbaum.

Davis, N. (1997). Strategies for staff and institutional development for IT in education: An integrated approach. In B. Somekh & N. Davis (Eds.), *Using information technology effectively in teaching and learning: Studies in pre-service and in-service teacher education* (pp. 225–268). London: Routledge.

diSessa, A. (2000). *Changing minds: Computers, learning, and literacy.* Cambridge, MA: MIT Press.

Driver, R. (1985). Changing perspectives on science lessons. In N. Bennett & C. Desforges (Eds.), *Recent advances in classroom research. British Journal of Psychology Monograph Series, 2,* 58–74. Edinburgh, Scotland: Scottish Academy Press.

Dweck, C. (1986). Motivation processes affecting learning. *American Psychologist, 41*(10), 1040–1048.

Epstein, A., Wahba, R., & Tau, R. (2004). *StarLogo on the web* (Version 2.1) [Computer Software]. Cambridge, MA: Media Laboratory, Teacher Education Program, & MIT. Retrieved March 7, 2005, at http://www.media.mit.edu/starlogo/

Epstein, T. L. (1997). Sociocultural approaches to young people's historical understanding. *Social Education, 61*(1), 28–31.

Equiano, O. (1791). *The interesting narrative of the life of Olaudah Equiano or Gustavus Vassa, The African* (1st. American ed.). New York: Printed and sold by W. Durell.

Erlwanger, S. H. (1973). Benny's conception of rules and answers in IPI mathematics. *Journal of Children's Mathematical Behavior, 1*(2), 7–26.

Fisher, C., Dwyer, D. C., & Yocam, K. (Eds.). (1996). *Education and technology: Reflections on computing in classrooms.* San Francisco: Jossey-Bass.

Floden, R. E., & Buchmann, M. (1993). Between routines and anarchy: Preparing teachers for uncertainty. In M. Buchmann & R. E. Floden (Eds.), *Detachment and concern: Conversations in the philosophy of teaching and teacher education* (pp. 211–221). New York: Teachers College Press.

Fullan, M. (1991). *The new meaning of educational change.* New York: Teachers College Press.

Gabella, M. S. (1994). Beyond the looking glass: Bringing students into the conversations of historical inquiry. *Theory and Research in Social Education, 23,* 340–363.

Gaddis, J. L. (2002). *The landscape of history: How historians map the past.* New York: Oxford University Press.

Gardner, H. (1991). *The unschooled mind: How children think in schools and how schools should teach*. New York: Basic Books.

Gibson, J. J. (1977). The theory of affordances. In R. E. Shaw & J. D. Bransford (Eds.), *Perceiving, acting, and knowing: Toward an ecological psychology* (pp. 67–82). Mahwah, NJ: Erlbaum.

Glaser, R. (1976). Cognitive psychology and instructional design. In D. Klahr (Ed.), *Cognition and instruction* (pp. 303–316). Mahwah, NJ: Erlbaum.

Globe Program. (2005). Boulder, CO: University Corporation for Atmospheric Research. Retrieved March 7, 2005, from http://www.globe.gov

Hall, G. S. (Ed.). (1886). *Methods of teaching history* (Second ed.). Boston: Heath.

Hallden, O. (1994a). Constructing the learning task in history instruction. In M. Carretero & J. F. Voss (Eds.), *Cognitive and instructional processes in history and the social sciences* (pp. 187–200). Mahwah, NJ: Erlbaum.

Hallden, O. (1994b). On the paradox of understanding history in an educational setting. In G. Leinhardt, I. L. Beck, & C. Stainton (Eds.), *Teaching and learning in history* (pp. 27–46). Mahwah, NJ: Erlbaum.

Harvard Graduate School of Education. (1998). *ALPS: Active learning practices for schools*. Retrieved March 2, 2005, from http://learnweb.harvard.edu/alps

Harvard Graduate School of Education. (n.d.). *Education with new technologies (ENT)*. Retrieved March 4, 2005, from http://learnweb.harvard.edu/ent

Hexter, J. H. (1971). *The history primer*. New York: Basic Books.

HI-CE. (2003–2005). University of Michigan's Center for Highly Interactive Computing in Education. *ModelIt* [Computer Software]. Ann Arbor, MI: GoKnow, Inc. Retrieved March 7, 2005, from http://www.hice.org/soft_modelit.html

Hickman, L. A. (1990). *John Dewey's pragmatic technology*. Bloomington: Indiana University Press.

Hill, R., & Hughes, D. (2001–2004). *Froguts subscription service* [Computer Software]. Seattle, WA: Froguts, Inc. Retrieved March 7, 2005 at http://www.froguts.com

Hipscham, R., Webmaster. (1993). *The Science Learning Network cow's eye dissection* [Computer Software]. San Francisco, CA: Exploratorium/Science Learning Network. Retrieved March 7, 2005, from http://www.exploratorium.edu/learning_studio/cow_eye/

Hirst, P. H. (1965). Liberal education and the nature of knowledge. In P. H. Hirst (Ed.), *Knowledge and the curriculum: A collection of philosophic papers* (pp. 30–54). London: Routledge.

Hogenbirk, P. (1997). The PIT-project: A teaching network approach for broad-scale use of ICT. In D. Passey & B. Samaways (Eds.), *Information technology: Supporting change through teacher education* (pp. 202–208). London: Chapman and Hall.

Human Space Flight. (2005). Washington, DC: National Aeronautics and Space Administration. Retrieved March 7, 2005, from http://spaceflight.nasa.gov/

Internet Movie Database. (1990–2005). *Memorable quotes from* Ferris Bueller's Day Off. Retrieved March 4, 2005, from http://us.imdb.com/Quotes?0091042

Jacobsen, D. M. (2001). *Building different bridges: Technology integration, engaged student learning, and new approaches to professional development*. Paper presented at the Annual Meeting of the American Educational Research Association, Seattle, WA.

Johnson, D., & Johnson, R. (1998). Effective staff development in cooperative learning: Training, transfer, and long-term use. In Brody, C. M., & Davidson, N., *Professional development for cooperative learning: Issues and approaches* (pp. 223–242). Albany, NY: State University of New York Press.

Jonassen, D. H., Peck, K. L., & Wilson, B. G. (1999). *Learning with technology: A constructivist perspective.* Upper Saddle River, NJ: Prentice Hall.

Journey North. (2004). *A global study of wildlife migration and seasonal change.* Washington, DC: Annenberg/CPB Learner.org. Retrieved March 7, 2005, from http://www.learner.org/cgi-bin/jnorth/jn-sightings

Kali, Y., Bos, N., Linn, M., Underwood, J., & Hewitt, J. (2002). Design principles for educational software. *Computer supported collaborative learning proceedings.* Boulder, CO. A PDF file is available at: http://www.cs.colorado.edu/~l3d/cscl2002/proceedings.html

Kay, A. (1998, April). *Key note address.* Paper presented at the Association for Computing Machinery Conference on Human Factors in Computing Systems, Los Angeles, CA.

Kintsch, W. (1998). *Comprehension: A paradigm for cognition.* Cambridge, MA: Cambridge University Press.

Kozulin, A. (1998). *Psychological tools: A sociocultural approach to education.* Cambridge, MA: Harvard University Press.

Lampert, M. (1995). Managing the tensions in connecting students' inquiry with learning mathematics in school. In D. N. Perkins, J. L. Schwartz, M. M. West, & M. S. Wiske (Eds.), *Software goes to school* (pp. 213–232). New York: Oxford University Press.

Lederer, R. (2003). *World according to student bloopers.* Retrieved on March 4, 2005, from http://www.blarg.net/~jsl/humor/student-bloopers-world

Lee, H., & Songer, N. B. (2003). Making authentic science accessible to students. *International Journal of Science Education, 25*(1), 1–26.

Lee, P. J. (2005). Learning history: Principles into practice: Understanding history. In J. Bransford & S. Donovan (Eds.), *How people learn: Teacher edition* (pp. 31–77). Washington, DC: National Academy of Sciences.

Lee, P. J., & Ashby, R. (2000). Progression in historical understanding among students ages 7–14. In P. Seixas, P. Stearns, & S. Wineburg (Eds.), *Knowing, teaching & learning history: National and international perspectives* (pp. 199–222). New York: New York University Press.

Levstik, L., & Barton, K. (2001). *Doing history: Investigating with children in elementary and middle schools.* Mahwah, NJ: Erlbaum.

Lewis, E. L. (1996). Conceptual change among middle school students studying elementary thermodynamics. *Journal of Science Education and Technology, 5*(1), 3–31.

Liebenberg, L. (n.d.). *CyberTracker software (pty) ltd reg. no. 97/01908/07* (Version 2.77) [Computer software]. Retrieved March 4, 2005, from http://www.cybertracker.co.za/

Linn, M. C. (2005). WISE design for lifelong learning–Pivotal Cases. In P. Gärdenfors & P. Johannsson (Eds.), *Cognition, education and communication technology* (pp. 223–256). Mahwah, NJ: Erlbaum.

Linn, M. C. (in press). Knowledge integration perspective on learning and instruction. In R. K. Sawyer (Ed.), *Cambridge handbook for the learning sciences*. Cambridge, MA: Cambridge University Press.

Linn, M. C., Clark, D. B., & Slotta, J. D. (2003). WISE design for knowledge integration. In S. Barab (Ed.), *Building sustainable science curriculum: Acknowledging and accommodating local adaptation* [special issue]. *Science Education, 87,* 517–538.

Linn, M. C., Davis, E. A., & Bell, P. (2004). *Internet environments for science education*. Mahwah, NJ: Erlbaum.

Linn, M. C., & Eylon, B. S. (in press). Science education: Integrating views of Learning and Instruction. In P. A. Alexander & P. H. Winne (Eds.), *Handbook of educational psychology* (2nd ed.). Mahwah, NJ: Erlbaum.

Linn, M. C., Eylon, B. S., & Davis, E. A. (2004). The knowledge integration perspective on learning. In M. C. Linn, E. A. Davis, & P. Bell (Eds.), *Internet environments for science education*. Mahwah, NJ: Erlbaum.

Linn, M. C., & Hsi, S. (2000). *Computers, teachers, peers: Science learning partners*. Mahwah, NJ: Erlbaum.

Linn, M. C., Layman, J., & Nachmias, Y. (1987). The cognitive consequences of microcomputer-based laboratories: Graphing skills development. *Journal of Contemporary Educational Psychology, 12*(3), 244–253.

Linn, M. C., & Slotta, J. D. (2000). WISE science. *Educational Leadership, 28*(2), 29–32.

Little, J. W. (2001). Professional development in pursuit of school reform. In A. Lieberman & L. Miller (Eds.), *Teachers caught in the action* (pp. 23–44). New York: Teachers College Press.

Maryknoll World Productions (Producer). (2000). *Children of the earth series, Mexico close-up study guide* [Video]. (Available from Maryknoll World Productions, P.O. Box 308, Maryknoll, NY, 10545–0308. Call 1–800–227–8523 or order online at http://www.maryknollmall.org/index2.cfm?cat=videos.)

McDougall, A., & Betts, J. (1997). Teacher professional development in a technology immersion school. In D. Passey & B. Samaways (Eds.), *Information technology: Supporting change through teacher education* (pp. 222–227). London: Chapman and Hall.

McTighe, J., Seif, E., & Wiggins, G. (2004). You *can* teach for meaning. *Educational Leadership, 62*(1), 26–30.

Means, B. (1994). Using technology to advance educational goals. In B. Means (Ed.), *Technology and education reform: The reality behind the promise* (pp. 1–21). San Francisco: Jossey-Bass.

Means, B., & Golan, S. (1998). *Transforming teaching and learning with multimedia technology*. Stanford Research Institute. Retrieved on March 4, 2005, from http://pblmm.k12.ca.us/News/Challenge2K.pdf

Means, B., Penuel, W. R., & Padilla, C. (2001). *The connected school: Technology and learning in high school*. San Francisco: Jossey-Bass.

Michigan Department of Education. (1996). *Michigan Curriculum Framework*. Retrieved March 4, 2005, from http://www.michigan.gov/documents/MichiganCurriculumFramework_8172_7.pdf

Mislevy, B., Chudowsky, N., Fried, R., Haertel, G., Hamel, L., Kennedy, C., Long, K., Morrison, M., Pena, P., Rosenquist, A., Songer, N. B., & Wenk, A. (2002). *Design patterns for assessing science inquiry* (Technical Report). Menlo Park, CA: RI International.

Mistler-Jackson, M., & Songer, N. B. (2000). Student motivation and Internet technology: Are students empowered to learn science? *Journal of Research in Science Teaching, 37*(5), 459–479.

National Center for Education Statistics. (2000). *Teacher use of computers and the Internet in public schools* (Stats in brief No. NCES 2000–090). Washington, DC: U.S. Department of Education.

National Commission on Excellence in Education. (1983). *A nation at risk.* Washington, DC: U.S. Government Printing Office.

National Council for Accreditation of Teacher Education. (1997). *Technology and the new professional teacher: Preparing for the 21st century classroom.* Washington, DC: Author.

National Council for the Social Studies. (1994). *Expectations of excellence: Curriculum standards for social studies.* Washington, DC: Author.

National Research Council. (1996). *National science education standards.* Washington, DC: National Academy Press.

National Research Council. (2000). *Inquiry and the national science education standards.* Washington, DC: National Academy Press.

One Sky Many Voices. (2001). *Kids as global scientists* [Computer Software]. Ann Arbor, MI. Retrieved March 7, 2005, from http://www.onesky.umich.edu/kgs01.html

Perkins, D. N. (1998). What is understanding? In M. S. Wiske (Ed.), *Teaching for understanding: Linking research with practice* (pp. 39–58). San Francisco: Jossey-Bass.

Perkins, D. (2003). *King Arthur's round table: How collaborative conversations create smart organizations.* New York: Wiley.

Perkins, D. N., Schwartz, J. L., et al. (Eds.). (1995). *Software goes to school: Teaching for understanding with new technologies.* New York: Oxford University Press.

Potter, J., & Mellar, H. (2000). Identifying teachers' Internet training needs. *Journal of Information Technology for Teacher Education, 9*(1), 23–36.

President and Fellows of Harvard College. (2005). WIDE world. Retrieved March 4, 2005, from http://wideworld.pz.harvard.edu/professional/#online

Putnam, R. T., & Borko, H. (2000). What do new views of knowledge and thinking have to say about research on teacher learning? *Educational Researcher, 29*(1), 4–15.

Ravitch, D., & Finn, C. E. (1987). *What do our 17-year-olds know?: A report on the first national assessment of history and literature* (1st ed.). New York: Harper & Row.

Renzulli, J., Gentry, M., & Reis, S. M. (2004). A time and a place for authentic learning. *Educational Leadership, 62*(1), 73–77.

Resnick, L. B., & Klopfer, L. E. (1989). *Toward the thinking curriculum: Current cognitive research.* Alexandria, VA: Association for Supervision and Curriculum Development.

Richmond, B. (1985–2005). *STELLA* (Version 8.0) [Computer Software]. Lebanon, NH: ISEE Systems. Retrieved March 7, 2005, at http://www.iseesystems.com/

Roschelle, J., Kaput, J. J., & Stroup, W. (2000). SIMCALC: Accelerating students' engagement with the mathematics of change. In M. J. Jacobson & R. B. Kozma (Eds.), *Innovations in science and mathematics education: Advanced designs for technologies of learning* (pp. 47–75). Mahwah, NJ: Erlbaum.

Rosenzweig, R., & Thelen, D. P. (1998). *The presence of the past: Popular uses of history in American life*. New York: Columbia University Press.

Salomon, G. (1984). Television is "easy" and print is "tough": The differential investment of mental effort in learning as a function of perceptions and attributions. *Journal of Educational Psychology, 76*(4), 647–658.

Sandholtz, J. H., & Ringstaff, C. (1996). Teacher change in technology-rich classrooms. In C. Fisher, D. C. Dwyer, & K. Yocam (Eds.), *Education and technology: Reflections on computing in classrooms* (pp. 281–299). San Francisco: Jossey-Bass.

Sandholtz, J. H., Ringstaff, C., & Dwyer, D. C. (1997). *Teaching with technology: Creating student-centered classrooms*. New York: Teachers College Press.

Scardamalia, M., & Bereiter, C. (1992). Text-based and knowledge-based questioning by children. *Cognition and Instruction, 9,* 177–199.

Schlechty, P. C. (2002). *Working on the work: An action plan for teachers, principals, and superintendents*. San Francisco, CA: Jossey-Bass.

Schniedewind, N., & Davidson, E. (2000). Differentiating cooperative learning. *Educational Leadership, 58*(1), 24.

Schofield, J. W., Davidson, A., Stocks, J. E., & Futoran, G. (1997). The Internet in school: A case study of educator demand and its precursors. In S. Kiesler (Ed.), *Culture of the Internet* (pp. 361–384). Mahwah, NJ: Erlbaum.

Schwab, J. J. (1978a). The practical: Translation into curriculum. In I. Westbury & N. J. Wilkof (Eds.), *Science, curriculum, and liberal education: Selected essays* (pp. 365–383). Chicago: University of Chicago Press.

Schwab, J. J. (1978b). Education and the structure of the disciplines. In I. Westbury & N. Wilkof (Eds.), *Science, curriculum, and liberal education* (pp. 229–272). Chicago: University of Chicago Press.

Seixas, P. (1994). Students' understanding of historical significance. *Theory and Research in Social Education, 22,* 281–304.

Senge, P., Cambron-McCabe, N., Lucas, T., Smith, B., Dutton, J., & Kleiner, A. (2000). *Schools that learn: A fifth discipline resource*. New York: Doubleday.

Sheingold, K., & Tucker, M. S. (Eds.). (1990). *Restructuring for learning with technology*. New York: Bank Street College of Education, Center for Technology in Education; and Rochester, NY: National Center on Education and the Economy.

Shemilt, D. (1983). The devil's locomotive. *History and Theory, 224,* 1–18.

Shulman, L. (1987). Knowledge and teaching: Foundations of the new reform. *Harvard Educational Review, 57,* 1–22.

Simon, H. (1957). *Models of man*. New York: Wiley.

Singer, J., Marx, R. W., & Krajcik, J. (2000). Constructing extended inquiry projects: Curriculum materials for science education reform. *Educational Psychologist, 35*(3), 165–178.

Sisk-Hilton, S. (2002, October). *We'll take the parts that make sense: The evolution of an inquiry-oriented professional development model.* Paper presented at the Fifth International Conference of the Learning Sciences, Seattle, WA.

Slotta, J. D. (2004). The Web-based Science Inquiry Environment (WISE): Scaffolding knowledge integration in the classroom. In M. C. Linn, E. Davis, & P. Bell (Eds.), *Internet environments for science education* (pp. 203–232). Mahwah, NJ: Erlbaum.

Slotta, J., & Linn, M. C. (2000). The knowledge integration environment: Helping students use the Internet effectively. In M. J. Jacobson & R. Kozma (Eds.), *Innovations in science and mathematics education: Advanced designs for technologies of learning* (pp. 193–226). Mahwah, NJ: Erlbaum.

Songer, N. B. (2001). *BioKIDS: Kids' inquiry of diverse species.* Retrieved March 4, 2005, from http://www.biokids.umich.edu/critters/index.html

Songer, N. B. (in press). BioKIDS: An animated conversation on the development of curricular activity structures for inquiry science. In R. Keith Sawyer (Ed.), *Cambridge Handbook of the Learning Sciences.*

Songer, N. B., & Gotwals, A. (2005, April). *A systematic scheme for measuring science inquiry reasoning across curricular units.* Paper presented at the annual meeting of the American Educational Research Association.

Songer, N. B., Huber, A. E., Adams, K., Chang, H. Y., Lee, H. S., & Jones, T. (2002). *BioKIDS: Kids' inquiry of diverse species, an eight-week inquiry curriculum.* Ann Arbor, MI: The University of Michigan.

Songer, N. B., Lee, H., & Kam, R. (2002). Technology-rich inquiry science in urban classrooms: What are the barriers to inquiry pedagogy? *Journal of Research in Science Teaching, 39*(2), 128–150.

Songer, N. B., Lee, H., & McDonald, S. (2003). Research towards an expanded understanding of inquiry science beyond one idealized standard. *Science Education, 87*(4), 490–516.

Songer, N. B., & Wenk, A. (2003, April). *Measuring complex reasoning in science.* Paper presented at the annual meeting of the American Educational Research Association.

SPEC Associates. (2003). *Case studies of social studies instruction for meaningful learning using technology: Year 4 evaluation report.* Unpublished document.

Stearns, P. (1999). *Memory in the world history classroom.* Paper presented at the American Educational Research Association, Montreal, Canada.

Stiggins, R. J. (1997). *Student-centered classroom assessment.* Upper Saddle River, NJ: Merrill.

Tharp, R. G., & Gallimore, R. (1988). *Rousing minds to life: Teaching, learning, and schooling in social context.* Cambridge, MA: Cambridge University Press.

Thompson, C. L., & Zeuli, J. S. (1999). The frame and the tapestry: Standards-based reform and professional development. In L. Darling-Hammond & G. Sykes (Eds.), *Teaching as the learning profession: Handbook of policy and practice* (pp. 341–375). San Francisco: Jossey-Bass.

Tinker, R. (Ed.). (1996). *Microcomputer-based labs: Educational research and standards.* Berlin and New York: Springer-Verlag.

Unger, C., & Wilson, D. G. (with Jaramillo, R., & Dempsey, R.). (1998). What do students think about understanding? In M. S. Wiske (Ed.), *Teaching for understanding: Linking research with practice* (pp. 266–292). San Francisco: Jossey-Bass.

University of California, Berkeley. (n.d.). *WISE: Web-based inquiry science environment.* Retrieved on March 7, 2005, from http://wise.berkeley.edu/

U.S. Congressional Office of Technology Assessment. (1995). *Teachers and technology: Making the connection* (OTA-EHR-616). Washington, DC: Office of Technology Assessement.

VanSledright, B. (2002). Confronting history's interpretive paradox while teaching fifth graders to investigate the past. *American Educational Research Journal, 39*(4), 1089–1115.

Vinovskis, M. (1997). An analysis of the concept and uses of systemic educational reform. *American Educational Research Journal, 33*(1), 55–85.

Vygotsky, L. S. (1978). *Mind in society.* Cambridge, MA: Harvard University Press.

Wallace, R. M. (2002). *Teaching with the Internet: Curriculum making in a new medium.* Manuscript submitted for publication.

Wallace, R. M., Kupperman, J., Krajcik, J., & Soloway, E. (2000). Science on the Web: Students on-line in a sixth grade classroom. *Journal of the Learning Sciences, 9*(1), 75–104.

White, B. Y., & Fredricksen, J. R. (1998). Inquiry, modeling, and metacognition: Making science accessible to students. *Cognition and Instruction, 16,* 3–118.

White, R. T. (1988). *Learning science.* Oxford: Basil Blackwell.

Wiggins, G., & McTighe, J. (1998). *Understanding by design.* Alexandria, VA: Association for Supervision and Curriculum Development.

Williams, M., & Linn, M. C. (2002). WISE inquiry in fifth grade biology. *Research in Science Education, 32*(4), 415–436.

Wilson, S. M., & Berne, J. (1999). Teacher learning and the acquisition of professional knowledge: An examination of research on contemporary professional development. In A. Iran-Nejad & P. D. Pearson (Eds.), *Review of Research in Education* (Vol. 24, pp. 173–209). Washington, DC: American Educational Research Association.

Windschitl, M. (2002). Framing constructivism in practice as the negotiation of dilemmas: An analysis of the conceptual, pedagogical, cultural, and political challenges facing teachers. *Review of Educational Research, 72*(2), 131–175.

Wineburg, S. (1991a). Historical problem-solving: A study of the cognitive processes used in the evaluation of documentary and pictorial evidence. *Journal of Educational Psychology, 83*(1), 73–87.

Wineburg, S. (1991b). On the reading of historical texts: Notes on the breach between school and academy. *American Educational Research Journal, 28*(3), 495–519.

Wineburg, S. (1994). The cognitive representation of historical texts. In G. Leinhardt, I. L. Beck, & C. Stainton (Eds.), *Teaching and learning in history* (pp. 85–136). Mahwah, NJ: Erlbaum.

Wineburg, S. (1999). Historical thinking and other unnatural acts. *Phi Delta Kappan*, March, 488–499.

Wineburg, S. (2001). *Historical thinking and other unnatural acts: Charting the future of teaching the past*. Philadelphia, PA: Temple University Press.

Wiske, M. S. (1994). How teaching for understanding changes the rules in the classroom. *Educational Leadership, 51*(5), 19–21.

Wiske, M. S. (Ed.). (1998). *Teaching for understanding: Linking research with practice*. San Francisco: Jossey-Bass.

Yeager, E. A., & Davis, O. L. (1996). Classroom teachers' thinking about historical texts: An exploratory study. *Theory and Research in Social Education, 24*(2), 146–166.

Young, B. A. (2000). *Characteristics of the 100 largest public elementary and secondary school districts in the United States: 1998–1999*. Washington, DC: U.S. Department of Education, National Center for Educational Statistics.

Zhao, Y. (2003). *What should teachers know about technology: Perspectives and practices*. Greenwich, CT: Information Age Publishing.

Zhao, Y., Byers, J. L., Mishra, P., Topper, A., Cheng, H. J., Enfield, M., Pugh, K., Tan, S., & Ferdig, R. (2001). What do they know: A comprehensive portrait of exemplary technology using teachers. *Journal of Computing in Teacher Education, 17*(2), 24–36.

Zhao, Y., & Cziko, G. A. (2001). Teacher adoption of technology: A perceptual control theory perspective. *Journal of Technology and Teacher Education, 9*(1), 5–30.

Zhao, Y., & Frank, K. A. (2003). Technology uses in schools: An ecological perspective. *American Educational Research Journal, 40*(4), 807–840.

Zhao, Y., & Kendall, C. (2003). Educational technology standards for teachers: Issues of interpretation, incorporation and assessment. In Y. Zhao (Ed.), *What should teachers know about technology: Perspectives and practices* (pp. 31–44). Greenwich, CT: Information Age Publishing.

Zhao, Y., Pugh, K., Sheldon, S., & Byers, J. (2002). Conditions for classroom technology innovations. *Teachers College Record, 104*(3), 484–515.

Zull, J. E. (2002). *The art of the changing brain: Enriching the practice of teaching by exploring the biology of learning*. Sterling, VA: Stylus.

Zull, J. E. (2004). The art of changing the brain. *Educational Leadership, 62*(1), 68–72.

About the Contributors

Elizabeth A. Ashburn is the director of Project TIME and the Battle Creek Teaching American History Project, both funded by grants from the U.S. Department of Education to the Battle Creek–area school districts. She also is the director of the Battle Creek Community Literacy Collaborative. She holds a Ph.D. and M.Ed. in educational psychology from the State University of New York at Buffalo. As a senior research associate in the Office of Research, U.S. Department of Education, she was the project officer for the National Center for Research on Teacher Learning at Michigan State University. She also served as director of research and of the ERIC Clearinghouse on Teacher Education at the American Association of Colleges for Teacher Education. A former high school English teacher, she has also taught in teacher education and professional development programs.

Mark Baildon teaches humanities and Asian studies at the Taipei American School in Taiwan. He served as the Project TIME social studies team leader as an outreach specialist at the College of Education at Michigan State University. Baildon taught secondary social studies for 16 years in international schools in Israel, Singapore, and Saudi Arabia. He received his Ph.D. in teacher education at MSU; his research interests include teacher thinking and learning, inquiry-based social studies education, and curriculum theory.

Robert B. Bain is associate professor of history and social studies education at the School of Education at the University of Michigan (UM). He is also a Pew Fellow and Carnegie Scholar at the Carnegie Academy for the Scholarship of Teaching and Learning and a research scholar with the Center for Highly Interactive Computing Education (HI-CE). He earned his Ph.D. in history at Case Western Reserve University with a special concentration in the history of policy toward youth. Before joining UM, Bain taught high school history and social studies for 26 years in the Cleveland, Ohio, area. Bain's research investigates the relationships between history as a way of knowing, student thinking, and instruction. His current research projects include: a study of teaching and learning history in museums and with museum resources; an investigation of preservice teachers' pedagogical reasoning; professional development in history; and the design and use of history-specific technology for students engaging in historical inquiry.

John E. Bell is an associate professor in the Department of Counseling, Educational Psychology, and Special Education at Michigan State University. He earned his bachelor's in computer science from MSU and his M.S. and Ph.D. in computer science from the University of California, Berkeley. His current area of research and teaching is in the use of the Internet and video as environments for teaching and learning, particularly in teacher professional development (http://edutech.msu.edu and http://projecttime.org). Bell is also president of Effective Schools Productivity Systems, Inc., which is involved in the development of innovative Web-based communities and tools for school leaders (http://esleague.com).

James Damico is an assistant professor in Language Education at Indiana University, Bloomington. A former elementary and middle school teacher, he completed his Ph.D. in curriculum, teaching, and educational policy at Michigan State University and worked on the Project TIME social studies team. He has also worked with the Center for Improvement of Early Reading Achievement, creating Web-based video cases of exemplary literacy teachers in Pre-K–5 classrooms. His interests include: children's response to literature; critical literacies; dialogic discussions; and reading strategies with Internet texts and technologies.

Nicole C. Ellefson received her M.A. in curriculum and teaching from Michigan State University. During her 5 years as a teacher, she worked with a team of colleagues to develop innovative teaching uses for computers. Along with her colleagues, she wrote and was awarded two major grants from the State of Michigan Department of Education to do teacher technology professional development with teachers at her school. As part of their work, the team started an after-school technology club so that students would have skills to help their homeroom teachers during lab time. Her interests include finding ways to integrate technology into classroom teaching that transcends mere use of prepackaged software. She is particularly interested in the digital divide and the way in which districts use their technology funds.

Robert E. Floden is a professor of Teacher Education, Educational Psychology, and Measurement & Quantitative Methods at Michigan State University, where he also directs the Institute for Research on Teaching and Learning. Floden has an A.B. in philosophy (with honors) from Princeton University and an M.S. in mathematical statistics and Ph.D. in education from Stanford University. Floden is one of the leaders of Michigan State University's *Teachers for a New Era* project, funded in part by a grant from the Carnegie Corporation of New York, the Annenberg Foundation, and the Ford Foundation. He has written on a range of topics, including chapters in both the *Handbook of Research on Teaching* and the *Handbook of Research on Teacher Education*. Floden recently completed (with Suzanne Wilson and Joan Ferrini-Mundy) a synthesis of research on teacher education. Other current projects include studies of the development of leaders in mathematics and science education and of the preparation of mathematics teachers.

Kenneth A. Frank is an associate professor in the Department of Counseling, Educational Psychology and Special Education in the College of Education and in the Department of Fisheries and Wildlife in the College of Agriculture and Natural Resources at Michigan State University. He holds a Ph.D. in measurement, evaluation, and statistical analysis from the School of Education at the University of Chicago. His substantive interests include the study of schools as organizations, social structures of students and teachers and school decision-making, and social capital. His substantive areas are linked to several methodological interests: social network analysis, causal inference, and multilevel models. His publications include quantitative methods for representing relations among actors in a social network, robustness indices for inferences, and the effects of social capital in schools and other social contexts. He teaches general introductory courses in research methods and quantitative methods as well as advanced courses in multivariate analysis and seminars in social network analysis and causal inference.

Marcia C. Linn is a professor of development and cognition specializing in education in mathematics, science, and technology in the Graduate School of Education at the University of California, Berkeley. She holds a B.A. and Ph.D. from Stanford University. A fellow of the American Association for the Advancement of Science, she investigates science teaching and learning, gender equity, and design of learning environments. In 1998, the Council of Scientific Society Presidents selected her for its first award in educational research. In 1995–96 and 2001–02 she was a fellow at the Center for Advanced Study in the Behavioral Sciences. Her publications include *Computers, Teachers, Peers—Science Learning Partners*, with S. Hsi; "WISE Science" with J. D. Slotta in *Educational Leadership*; "The Tyranny of the Mean: Gender and Expectations," in *Notice of the American Mathematical Society*

(1994); *Designing Pascal Solutions*, with M. C. Clancy; and *Internet Environments for Science Education*, with Elizabeth Davis and Philip Bell.

Raven S. McCrory is an assistant professor of learning, technology, and culture at Michigan State University. She holds a Ph.D. in education from the University of Michigan and an M.S. in mathematics from the University of Massachusetts. Her research and writing focus on teacher knowledge and teacher learning in mathematics, science, and technology. McCrory has taught in elementary and high school as well as in teacher preparation and professional development programs.

Shannan McNair is an associate professor of education at Oakland University in Rochester, Michigan. She holds an Ed.D. in early childhood education. Her work experience includes teaching and administering programs for students from birth through adult, educational research, and program evaluation. McNair's research and writing focus on assessment, teaching and learning, gender and technology, science and children, and program evaluation.

Nancy Butler Songer is an associate professor of science education and learning technologies in the School of Education at the University of Michigan and director of BioKids (www.biokids.umich.edu), a research project focusing on urban students' development of complex reasoning in science. Songer's scholarly interests include the longitudinal development of scientific thinking; science education among inner-city students; assessment and science education; and the design of learning technologies. She is the author of numerous articles on science education and learning technologies. In her work in urban schools, Songer works with communities of committed teachers toward demonstrations of complex reasoning that challenge "the pedagogy of poverty."

Martha Stone Wiske is a lecturer in the Technology Education program at the Harvard Graduate School of Education. Her focus is the mutual improvement of public education and educational theory through connecting educational research with practice. Her special interests include the integration of new technology to support teaching for understanding and the use of networked technologies for professional development and school improvement. Wiske's projects include the Education with New Technologies Web site (http://learnweb.harvard.edu/ent) and WIDE World (www.wideworld.pz.harvard.edu), which provides online professional development for educators. Wiske is co-editor and co-founder of *ECi* (Education, Communication, and Information at http://www.open.ac.uk/eci), an international journal for dialogue about new developments in educational theory, practice, and technology, and editor of *Teaching for Understanding: Linking Research with Practice* (Jossey-Bass).

Yong Zhao is university distinguished professor of technology in education in the Department of Counseling, Educational Psychology and Special Education at the College of Education at Michigan State University, where he also directs the Center for Teaching and Technology. He holds a Ph.D. in education from the College of Education at the University of Illinois at Urbana-Champaign. His research interests include teacher adoption of technology; technology diffusion in schools; technology and education in international settings; informal learning environments; and network-based learning environments. He has directed a number of large-scale international, federal, and state-level educational technology projects. He is editor of *What Should Teachers Know about Technology: Perspectives and Practices* and co-editor of *Hanging Out: Community-Based After-School Programs for Children.*

Index

223